UNIVERSAL ACCESS **Interactive Reading**

- **Word Analysis, Fluency, and Systematic Vocabulary Development**
- **Reading Comprehension**
- **Literary Response and Analysis**

HOLT, RINEHART AND WINSTON

A Harcourt Classroom Education Company

Austin · New York · Orlando · Atlanta · San Francisco · Boston · Dallas · Toronto · London

Credits

Editorial

Project Director: Kathleen Daniel
Editor: Amy Fleming
Managing Editor: Mike Topp
Manager of Editorial Services: Abigail Winograd
Senior Product Manager: Don Wulbrecht
Editorial Staff: Susan Kent Cakars, Steven Fechter,
 Rob Giannetto, Kerry Johnson, Brenda Sanabria, Dan Unger
Project Administration: Elizabeth LaManna
Editorial Support: Renée Benitez, Louise Fernandez, Soojung Christine Han,
 Bret Isaacs, Laurie Muir
Editorial Permissions: David Smith, Carrie Jones
Conceptual Framework and Writing: e2 Publishing Services, Inc.

Art, Design, and Production

Director: Athena Blackorby
Senior Design Director: Betty Mintz
Series Design: Proof Positive/Farrowlyne Associates, Inc.
Design and Electronic Files: Proof Positive/Farrowlyne Associates, Inc.
Photo Research: Proof Positive/Farrowlyne Associates, Inc.
Production Manager: Catherine Gessner

Printed in the United States of America
ISBN 0-03-065028-3

3 4 5 6 32 05 04 03 02

Contents

Mastering the California Standards in Reading*

Chapter 1 Structures: Clarifying Meaning
Standards Focus

Vocabulary Development 1.3 Clarify word meanings through the use of definition, example, restatement, or contrast.

Reading Comprehension (Focus on Informational Materials) 2.1 Understand and analyze the differences in structure and purpose between various categories of informational materials (for example, textbooks, newspapers, instructional manuals, signs).

Literary Response and Analysis 3.2 Identify events that advance the plot, and determine how each event explains past or present action(s) or foreshadows future action(s).

Chapter 2 Characters: Living Many Lives
Standards Focus

Vocabulary Development 1.2 Use knowledge of Greek, Latin, and Anglo-Saxon roots and affixes to understand content-area vocabulary.

Reading Comprehension (Focus on Informational Materials) 2.2 (Grade 6 Review) Analyze text that uses the compare-and-contrast organizational pattern.

Literary Response and Analysis 3.3 Analyze characterization as delineated through a character's thoughts, words, speech patterns, and actions; the narrator's description; and the thoughts, words, and actions of other characters.

Chapter 3 Themes Across Time
Standards Focus

Vocabulary Development 1.1 Identify idioms, analogies, metaphors, and similes in prose and poetry.

Reading Comprehension (Focus on Informational Materials) 2.3 Analyze text that uses the cause-and-effect organizational pattern.

Literary Response and Analysis 3.4 Identify and analyze recurring themes across works (for example, the value of bravery, loyalty, and friendship; the effects of loneliness).

Chapter 4 Point of View: Who's Talking?
Standards Focus

Vocabulary Development 1.3 Clarify word meanings through the use of definition, example, restatement, or contrast.

---

* Unless otherwise noted, the standards listed are grade-level standards.

Reading Comprehension (Focus on Informational Materials) 2.4 Identify and trace the development of an author's argument, point of view, or perspective in text.

Literary Response and Analysis 3.5 Contrast points of view (for example, first and third person, limited and omniscient, subjective and objective) in narrative text, and explain how they affect the overall theme of the work.

Chapter 5   Worlds of Words: Prose and Poetry
Standards Focus

Vocabulary Development 1.1 Identify idioms, analogies, metaphors, and similes in prose and poetry.

Reading Comprehension (Focus on Informational Materials) 2.2 (Grade 6 Review) Analyze text that uses the compare-and-contrast organizational pattern.

Reading Comprehension (Focus on Informational Materials) 2.4 (Grade 6 Review) Clarify an understanding of texts by creating outlines, logical notes, summaries, or reports.

Literary Response and Analysis 3.1 Articulate the expressed purposes and characteristics of different forms of prose (for example, short story, novel, novella, essay).

Chapter 6   Where I Stand: Literary Criticism
Standards Focus

Vocabulary Development 1.2 Use knowledge of Greek, Latin, and Anglo-Saxon roots and affixes to understand content-area vocabulary.

Reading Comprehension (Focus on Informational Materials) 2.6 Assess the adequacy, accuracy, and appropriateness of the author's evidence to support claims and assertions, noting instances of bias and stereotyping.

Literary Response and Analysis 3.6 Analyze a range of responses to a literary work, and determine the extent to which the literary elements in the work shaped those responses.

Chapter 7   Reading for Life
Standards Focus

Reading Comprehension (Focus on Informational Materials) 2.2 Locate information by using a variety of consumer, workplace, and public documents.

Reading Comprehension (Focus on Informational Materials) 2.5 Understand and explain the use of a simple mechanical device by following technical directions.

To the Student

A Book for You

A book is like a garden carried in the pocket.
—Chinese Proverb

Picture this: a book chock full of intriguing stories that you want to read and informational articles that are really interesting. Make it a book that actually tells you to write in it, circling, underlining, adding your own questions, jotting down responses. Fill it with graphic organizers that encourage you to think in a different way. Make it a size that's easy to carry around. That's *Interactive Reading*—a book created especially for you.

A Book Designed for Success

Reading is a creative activity. You have to visualize the characters,
you have to hear what their voices sound like.
—Madeleine L'Engle

Interactive Reading is designed to accompany *Holt Literature and Language Arts.* Like *Holt Literature and Language Arts,* it's designed to help you interact with the literature and master the California language arts content standards.

Each chapter has three parts:
- Getting Ready
- Graphic Organizers for use with the selections in *Holt Literature and Language Arts*
- Interactive Readings for Independence

Getting Ready
Actors, athletes, dancers, and musicians all prepare before they perform. Getting Ready helps you prepare to read each chapter in *Holt Literature and Language Arts.*

To help you prepare, Getting Ready provides—
- an overview of what to expect in the chapter
- a strategy that will help you read the selections successfully and master the standards

- a Practice Read that is easy and fun to read
- questions and comments to help you interact with the Practice Read and apply the strategy
- a graphic organizer or chart for applying the strategy

Graphic Organizers for *Holt Literature and Language Arts*

Reading effectively involves interacting with the text. Graphic organizers give you a visual and fun way to organize, interpret, and understand the selections in *Holt Literature and Language Arts.*

To help you organize, interpret, and understand the selections, the graphic organizers provide—
- support for reading each literary and informational selection
- support for mastering the standards
- a creative way for you to think about and interact with the selections

Interactive Readings for Independence

Each chapter ends with new selections for you to read as you build toward independence. These selections provide new opportunities for you to apply your skills and strategies and interact with the text.

In this section, you will find—
- new literary and informational selections
- information for author study
- questions and comments to guide your reading and help you interact with the text
- projects that help you explore ideas and extend your knowledge

A Book for Your Thoughts and Ideas

....

Reading helps you think about things, it helps you imagine what it feels like to be somebody else . . . even somebody you don't like!
—Paula Fox

....

Reading is about you. It is about your own thoughts and feelings. It is about making connections between what you read and your own life and experience. The more you give of yourself to your reading, the more you get out of it.

A Walk Through the Book

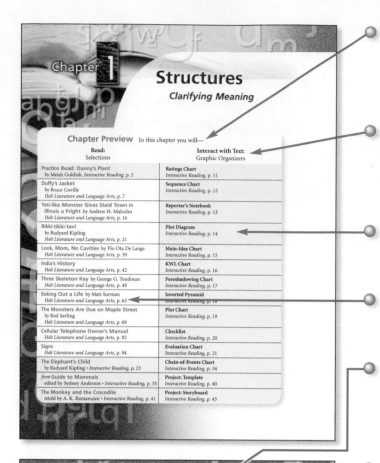

Chapter Preview
Knowing what to expect helps you be more successful. The Chapter Preview provides an overview of what's in each *Interactive Reading* chapter.

Read and Interact
In each chapter you will read both literary and informational texts and use graphic organizers as one way of interacting with the selections.

Highlighted Selections
The highlighted selections appear only in *Interactive Reading*.

Other Selections
The unhighlighted selections appear only in *Holt Literature and Language Arts.*

Strategy Launch
This page is designed to give you an advantage. Like strategies used in sports and business, reading strategies help you reach your goal—mastery of the standards.

Literary Focus
This feature introduces a literary focus for the chapter. The focus ties into a California reading standard.

A Strategy That Works
This feature introduces a reading strategy that will be used throughout the chapter. Each strategy helps you make sense of the text and understand the literary focus. It guides you in exploring and interpreting the text in a creative way while mastering the standard.

Pointers
See at a glance how to use the strategy. Pointers make each strategy easy to follow and use.

Reading Standards
Here are the California reading standards that are covered in this chapter. Each part of the chapter is designed to help you master these standards.

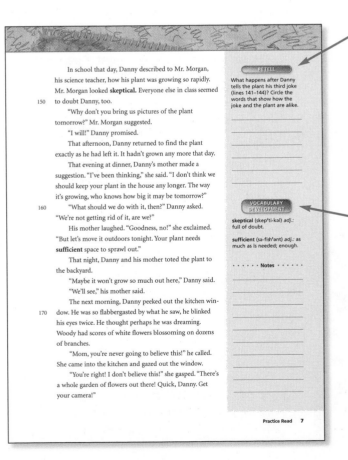

Practice Read

A Practice Read is an easy-to-read selection that gives you practice in applying the strategy and interacting with the text. Using the Practice Read helps you warm up before reading the selections in *Holt Literature and Language Arts.*

Before You Read

This feature tells you what the selection is about and gives you background information.

Side-Column Notes

Each selection is accompanied by notes in the side columns. They guide your interaction with the selection and show you how to apply the reading strategy. Many notes ask you to circle or underline in the text itself. Others provide lines on which you can write your responses to questions.

Types of Notes

The different types of notes throughout the selection help you—

- apply the reading strategy
- use reading skills to comprehend and interpret
- focus on a literary element
- build vocabulary
- develop word knowledge
- decode unfamiliar words

Vocabulary Development

Vocabulary words for you to learn and own are set in boldface in the selection, letting you see words in context. Vocabulary words are defined for you right there in the side column.

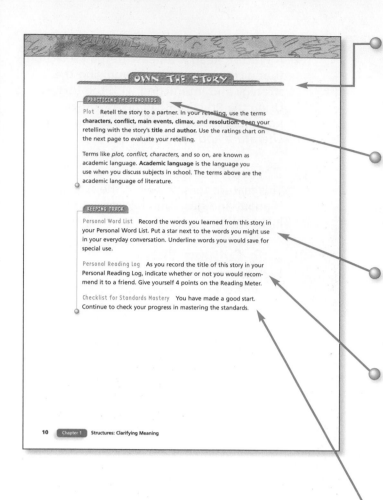

Own the Story, Text, or Poem

The meaning you take from a selection is based on the thought and reflection you put into it. Make each selection your own. Mark it up with your own comments and questions.

Practicing the Standards

You have a major goal in front of you: to master the California standards. This feature appears at the end of each selection to help you practice the skill in the standard.

Personal Word List

At the back of the book, you will find a Personal Word List for recording words you have learned and words you especially like.

Personal Reading Log

The more you read, the better you will read. Keep track of how much you read in your Personal Reading Log at the end of the book. By the year's end the Reading Meter will show the approximate number of words you have read in the book.

Checklist for Standards Mastery

With each selection you read and each standard you master, you come closer and closer to reaching your goal. Keep track of your progress with the Checklist for Standards Mastery at the end of the book.

Reading Strategy Graphic Organizer

At the end of every Practice Read is a graphic organizer that guides you in applying the reading strategy to the selection.

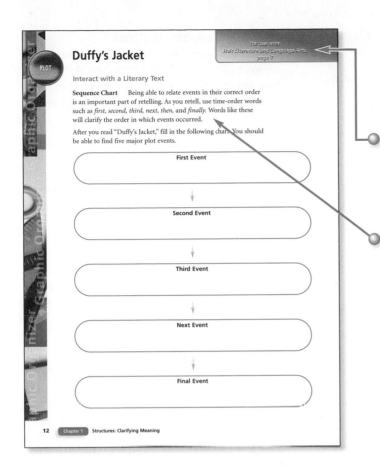

Interact with a Literary Text

For every literary selection in *Holt Literature and Language Arts,* there is a graphic organizer to help you read the text with increased understanding.

Reading Standard

Each graphic organizer reinforces the literary focus and moves you closer toward mastering a California reading standard.

Holt Literature and Language Arts

Now that you have prepared and practiced, it's time to turn to the selections in *Holt Literature and Language Arts.*

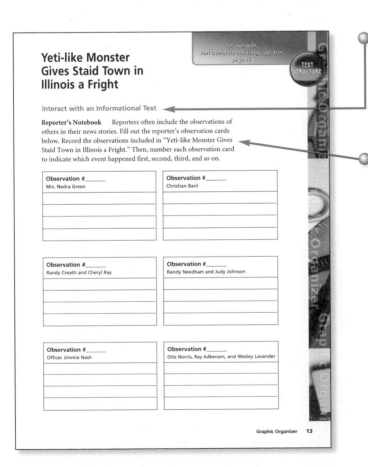

Interact with an Informational Text

For every informational selection in *Holt Literature and Language Arts,* there is a graphic organizer to help you read the text with increased understanding.

Reading Standard

Each graphic organizer reinforces the informational focus and moves you closer toward mastering a California reading standard.

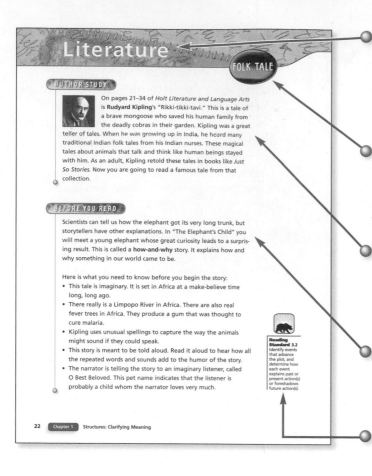

Interactive Selections

After you read the selections in a chapter of *Holt Literature and Language Arts,* build toward independence by reading the selections at the end of each *Interactive Reading* chapter.

Types of Literature

Effective readers are skilled at reading many different types of text. Each text type is identified so that you can keep track of your mastery.

Author Study

Some interactive selections give you an opportunity to read more by an author you have studied in *Holt Literature and Language Arts.*

Before You Read

This feature tells you what the selection is about and gives you background information.

Reading Standard

The California reading standard you will concentrate on with each interactive selection is identified here in the side column.

Side-Column Notes

Each selection is accompanied by notes in the side columns. They guide your interaction with the selection and show you how to apply the reading strategy. Many notes ask you to circle or underline in the text itself. The different types of notes are designed to help you—

- apply the reading strategy
- use reading skills to comprehend and interpret
- focus on a literary element
- build vocabulary
- develop word knowledge
- decode unfamiliar words
- understand text structures
- build fluency

Footnotes

Difficult or unusual terms are defined in footnotes.

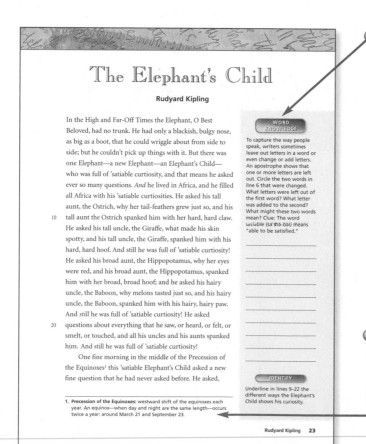

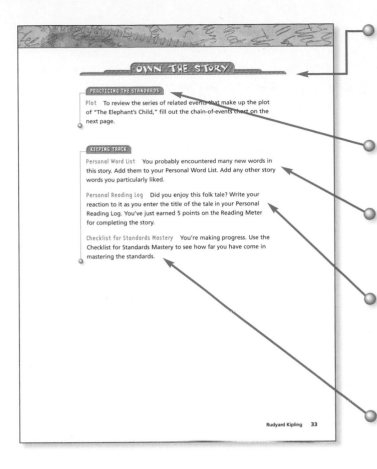

Own the Story, Text, or Poem

The meaning you take from a selection is based on the thought and reflection you put into it. Make each selection your own. Mark it up with your own comments and questions.

Practicing the Standards

This feature appears at the end of each selection to help you check your mastery.

Personal Word List

Record words you have learned and words you especially like in the Personal Word List at the end of the book.

Personal Reading Log

Keep track of how much you read in your Personal Reading Log at the end of the book. By the year's end the Reading Meter will show the approximate number of words you have read in the book.

Checklist for Standards Mastery

With each selection you read and each standard you master, you come closer and closer to reaching your goal. Keep track of your progress with the Checklist for Standards Mastery at the end of the book.

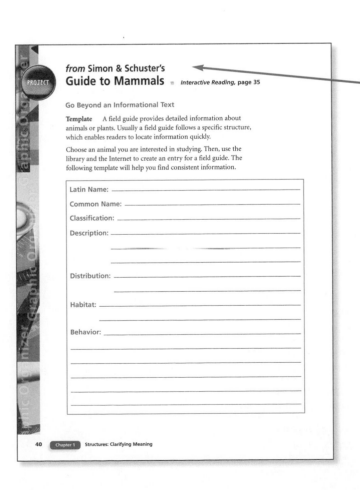

Project Graphic Organizer

Don't just stop after you read the selection. The project graphic organizer helps you go beyond the selection and extend your knowledge and understanding.

Chapter 1

Structures
Clarifying Meaning

Chapter Preview   In this chapter you will—

Strategy Launch: "Retelling"

LITERARY FOCUS: PLOT

Plot is the series of related events that make up a story. Most plots revolve around a **conflict,** or problem, that needs to be solved. The story's main **character** takes action to solve the problem, setting off a series of events that build to a high point of suspense. The plot reaches its **climax** as the reader finds out how the conflict is settled. In the story's **resolution** any lingering story problems are settled.

A STRATEGY THAT WORKS: "RETELLING"

One strategy to help you keep track of the plot is retelling. **Retelling** means putting what happens in the story into your own words. You can use this strategy to keep track of events while you are reading and to sum up events when you have finished reading.

POINTERS FOR RETELLING A STORY

))➡ Begin with the story's **title** and **author.** Tell where and when the story takes place, if it's important.

))➡ Give the **characters'** names and relationships. Tell what the main character wants.

))➡ Tell who is the **protagonist,** or hero, and who is the **antagonist,** or person working against the hero.

))➡ Describe the **conflict,** or problem. (What keeps the main character from getting what he or she wants?)

))➡ Cite the **main events** in the correct sequence.

))➡ Provide important **supporting details.**

))➡ Identify the **climax,** or most exciting point of the story.

))➡ Explain how the problem is finally **resolved.**

Reading Standard 1.3 Clarify word meanings through the use of definition, example, restatement, or contrast.

Reading Standard 2.1 Understand and analyze the differences in structure and purpose between various categories of informational materials.

Reading Standard 3.2 Identify events that advance the plot, and determine how each event explains past or present action(s) or foreshadows future action(s).

BEFORE YOU READ

If you like stories containing mystery, unusual happenings, and surprising events, you will certainly enjoy "Danny's Plant." If you like a good joke, this story is for you too.

Danny's Plant

Meish Goldish

IDENTIFY

Circle the names of the two characters introduced in the first paragraph.

RETELL

What does Danny's mother do that Danny finds unusual (lines 7–9)? Circle the words that tell you this.

_____

_____

_____

_____

_____

_____

VOCABULARY DEVELOPMENT

elates (ē·lāts′) *v.:* makes happy.

Danny sat on the sofa, watching his mother water the living room plants. He wouldn't have minded if she just poured water on the plants. But when she began talking to them, that's when he voiced his protest.

"Mom, what are you doing?" Danny asked.

His mother gave him a puzzled look. "Isn't it obvious?" she replied. "I'm talking to my plants, dear. It helps them to grow."

Danny sighed, "Mom, they're plants, not people.
10 I don't think they understand English . . . or any other language, for that matter."

"I disagree," his mother said, smiling. "Plants are living and loving things, just like we are. It helps them to know that someone cares enough to ask them how they're doing. It lifts their spirits. It **elates** them."

Danny's eyes rolled up in his head. He found her explanation less than convincing.

"Here, Danny," she offered, holding out the watering can. "Would you care to give Betsy some water? I know
20 she's awfully thirsty."

Danny shook his head. "No, thanks, Mom. You're the plant grower around here, not me. I'm not the least bit interested in plants. It's bad enough I have to study about them in school now. I don't need homework, too!"

His mother turned to the plant and cooed, "Ah, poor Betsy. I know you're thirsty. Here's your drink." She poured water on the potted soil. After tending to the rest of the plants, she sat down next to Danny and put her arm around him.

30 "You know, Danny," she began, "I'll bet you're better at horticulture than you think."

"Better at *what?*" Danny asked.

"Horticulture . . . growing plants," his mother explained. "In fact, if I gave you a plant, I'll bet you could get it to grow in no time."

"I doubt that," Danny replied. "I'd feel uncomfortable talking to a plant." Then he joked, "Besides, you taught me never to speak to strangers."

"That's funny," his mother chuckled. "Danny, you've 40 got a good sense of humor. I'll bet if you told your plant a joke while you watered it, it would grow like crazy for you."

"Or it might just drive me crazy," Danny replied.

"Another good joke!" his mother exclaimed.

The next morning, Danny's mother summoned him to the living room. Perched on the window ledge was a flowerpot with a seedling in it. Danny had never seen the tiny green plant before. It was only about three inches high.

"What's that?" Danny asked, curiously.

50 "That's your plant," his mother announced.

"*My* plant?" Danny exclaimed. "Mom, I told you yesterday, I don't want any plants."

WORD KNOWLEDGE

What context clue helps you figure out the meaning of *horticulture* in line 31? Circle the clue.

RETELL

Pause at line 35. What has happened so far? Retell the story up to this point.

_____

_____

_____

_____

_____

_____

RETELL

Pause at line 52, and identify the **conflict** in this story.

_____

_____

_____

_____

_____

_____

_____

_____

RETELL

Pause at line 62. Describe the deal Danny and his mother make.

_____

_____

_____

_____

_____

_____

_____

_____

_____

RETELL

Look at the passage containing lines 78–100. What happens after Danny tells the plant his first joke? Circle the words in the passage that show how the plant's behavior relates to Danny's joke.

_____

_____

_____

_____

_____

_____

His mother ignored the remark. "Let's make a deal, Danny," she offered. "I'll bet that if you tell this plant a joke a day as you water it, you'll make it grow like crazy. If I'm wrong, I'll buy you that new music tape you've been asking for."

Suddenly, Danny's face lit up. "Really?" he exclaimed. "And what if you're right?"

60 His mother paused and then laughed, "Well, then, I guess you'll have a plant that grows like crazy!"

Danny felt confident. With his lack of interest in gardening, he doubted the plant would grow at all. He knew it couldn't really understand jokes. And even if it did, he was positive it wouldn't grow "like crazy." So what was there to lose?

"When do we start?" Danny asked.

"There's no time like the present!" his mother boomed. She led Danny to the window ledge and handed him the 70 watering can.

"Now, remember," she instructed him, "Your job is to water the plant once a day. And to tell it a joke while doing so."

"Okay," Danny sighed, turning to the plant. "Let's see, plant, I suppose you'll need a name." He looked at the plant stem and became inspired. "I know!" Danny cried. "I'll call you Woody."

"Very good!" his mother laughed.

Danny poured water on the potted soil as he spoke.
80 "So, Woody, did you hear the one about the tree that started its own company? It was so successful, it had to branch out!"

"Excellent!" his mother cried.

Danny felt a little foolish but said no more about the matter. In fact, he forgot about the plant for the rest of the day.

The next morning, Danny raced downstairs for breakfast. He was shocked when he glanced at the windowsill. The stem of his plant had grown over a foot long! It
90 seemed to be climbing right up the windowsill!

"Mom, come here right away!" Danny cried. His mother quickly **emerged** from the kitchen.

"What is it?" she asked. Seeing the plant, she gasped, "My goodness, Danny! What did you do?"

Danny and his mother walked over to the plant and studied it carefully. Thin branches were shooting from the main stem, and each branch had small buds growing on it.

"Woody sure seems to have branched out," Danny said. "Just like in my joke." Then he added, "What kind of plant
100 is this, Mom?"

"I'm not sure," his mother said. "I found it at the neighborhood plant nursery. I bet you could make it grow like crazy, but I had no idea it could reach this height so rapidly."

"Should I water it again today?" Danny asked. "Maybe I gave it too much yesterday."

"You didn't give it too much," his mother said. "I watched you. Maybe it just had an unusual growing spurt. Give it another drink today. The usual amount."

110 Danny filled the watering can and walked to the window ledge.

"All right, Woody," he said, watering the plant. "I guess you were really thirsty yesterday. And you really seemed to like my joke. So I'll tell you another one. Hmmm, let's see." Danny brainstormed until he had an idea.

emerged (ē·murjd′) v.: came into view; became visible.

· · · · · · Notes · · · · · ·

PREDICT

Circle the important word in Danny's second joke (lines 116–117). What do you predict will happen to the plant?

_____

_____

_____

_____

_____

_____

_____

VOCABULARY DEVELOPMENT

extract (ek·strakt′) v.: remove with effort.

INTERPRET

Pause at line 140. How is Danny's attitude toward growing plants changing?

_____

_____

_____

_____

_____

_____

_____

"Got one!" he cried. "Hey, Woody, how can you tell when a plant is jealous? Give up? It turns green with envy!"

"I like that one," his mother said, applauding.

That afternoon, Danny returned from school and

120 eagerly checked on the plant. To his surprise, its appearance hadn't changed since the morning. "Woody, I guess you weren't so crazy about that last joke," he teased. "Looks like I may still win the bet after all."

When Danny came down for breakfast the next morning, he tripped at the bottom of the stairs. He looked down and saw his shoes were entangled in plant branches. Overnight, Woody had grown several feet long and was sprawled all over the carpet. Each branch had several large, green leaves on them. It almost made the white carpet seem

130 like a green one. Danny had never seen anything like it in his life.

"Mom, come quick!" he shouted, trying to untangle a branch from his shoes. His mother appeared from the kitchen.

"What in the world is this?" she gasped. She bent down and helped her son **extract** himself from the leaves.

"My plant grew even more last night!" Danny cried. "You were right, Mom. I *am* making it grow like crazy! Wait'll I tell my friends about this." Then Danny asked,

140 "Should I water Woody this morning?"

"I never heard of a green plant that didn't need water," she sighed. "Go ahead."

Danny fetched the watering can, filled it, and walked to the plant pot. He said, "I've got a great joke for you today, Woody. What did Mrs. Plant say to Mr. Plant? 'Hey, Bud, I like how you always bring me flowers.'"

In school that day, Danny described to Mr. Morgan, his science teacher, how his plant was growing so rapidly. Mr. Morgan looked **skeptical.** Everyone else in class seemed to doubt Danny, too.

150

"Why don't you bring us pictures of the plant tomorrow?" Mr. Morgan suggested.

"I will!" Danny promised.

That afternoon, Danny returned to find the plant exactly as he had left it. It hadn't grown any more that day.

That evening at dinner, Danny's mother made a suggestion. "I've been thinking," she said. "I don't think we should keep your plant in the house any longer. The way it's growing, who knows how big it may be tomorrow?"

160

"What should we do with it, then?" Danny asked. "We're not getting rid of it, are we?"

His mother laughed. "Goodness, no!" she exclaimed. "But let's move it outdoors tonight. Your plant needs **sufficient** space to sprawl out."

That night, Danny and his mother toted the plant to the backyard.

"Maybe it won't grow so much out here," Danny said.

"We'll see," his mother said.

The next morning, Danny peeked out the kitchen win-

170

dow. He was so flabbergasted by what he saw, he blinked his eyes twice. He thought perhaps he was dreaming. Woody had scores of white flowers blossoming on dozens of branches.

"Mom, you're never going to believe this!" he called. She came into the kitchen and gazed out the window.

"You're right! I don't believe this!" she gasped. "There's a whole garden of flowers out there! Quick, Danny. Get your camera!"

RETELL

What happens after Danny tells the plant his third joke (lines 141–144)? Circle the words that show how the joke and the plant are alike.

_____

_____

_____

_____

_____

VOCABULARY DEVELOPMENT

skeptical (skep′ti·kəl) *adj.:* full of doubt.

sufficient (sə·fish′ənt) *adj.:* as much as is needed; enough.

· · · · · · Notes · · · · · ·

_____

_____

_____

_____

_____

_____

_____

_____

180 Danny raced to his bedroom and grabbed the camera on the desk. He and his mother ran outside. Danny began shooting pictures of Woody from every angle. Each picture popped from the camera and developed in less than a minute.

"This will convince Mr. Morgan that I'm telling the truth!" Danny exclaimed, viewing the photos.

In science class that afternoon, Danny showed Mr. Morgan the pictures he had taken. Mr. Morgan looked pleased.

"Now do you believe me?" Danny asked.

190 "Why, certainly," Mr. Morgan replied. "These pictures show a plant that looks remarkably like one I've been experimenting with at our local nursery. In fact, it's outside in the schoolyard right now. Class, please follow me."

The students followed Mr. Morgan outside. Danny was surprised when he saw the plant. It was identical to Woody. But what he saw next surprised Danny even more. On the ground, next to the large flowery Woody, was another Woody—the one with the giant green leaves that Danny had tripped over. And next to that was the Woody that had 200 a tall stem growing up the windowsill. And next to that was the tiny plant Danny's mother had first given him.

"I d-d-don't understand," Danny stammered, hardly able to speak. "All these four plants look just like mine."

"That's because they *are* yours," Danny's mother said, suddenly emerging from behind a tall bush. Danny was startled.

"Mom, what are *you* doing here?" he asked.

"Mr. Morgan asked me to help him with a little class experiment," she explained. "Last week he told me how you

210 weren't very interested in studying about plants. But he bet me that he could develop your interest, with my help."

Suddenly, everything became clear to Danny. "You mean, Woody wasn't really just one plant growing bigger each day?" he guessed. "You were replacing the plant each night with a larger one?"

"That's correct," Mr. Morgan chuckled. "Woody was actually four different plants. Of course, I won my bet, because you're clearly more interested in growing plants now."

220 "Don't you mean horticulture, Mr. Morgan?" Danny joked.

"Yes," Mr. Morgan boomed. "Horticulture! And since I won the bet, I'm happy to give you that music tape you wanted." He handed Danny the tape.

"Thank you," Danny smiled. "With all my plant jokes, it looks like this joke's on me. But I'll still get the last laugh. Mom, please, make like a tree and *leave!*"

Now we reach the **climax**—the point where everything becomes clear. Describe the trick that Mr. Morgan and Danny's mother played on Danny.

_____

_____

_____

_____

_____

_____

_____

_____

_____

IDENTIFY

What is the **resolution,** or outcome, of this story?

_____

_____

_____

_____

_____

_____

_____

_____

PRACTICING THE STANDARDS

Plot Retell the story to a partner. In your retelling, use the terms **characters, conflict, main events, climax,** and **resolution.** Open your retelling with the story's **title** and **author.** Use the ratings chart on the next page to evaluate your retelling.

Terms like *plot, conflict, characters,* and so on, are known as academic language. **Academic language** is the language you use when you discuss subjects in school. The terms above are the academic language of literature.

KEEPING TRACK

Personal Word List Record the words you learned from this story in your Personal Word List. Put a star next to the words you might use in your everyday conversation. Underline words you would save for special use.

Personal Reading Log As you record the title of this story in your Personal Reading Log, indicate whether or not you would recommend it to a friend. Give yourself 4 points on the Reading Meter.

Checklist for Standards Mastery You have made a good start. Continue to check your progress in mastering the standards.

Danny's Plant

PLOT

Interact with a Literary Text

Ratings Chart   Work with a partner. Take turns retelling "Danny's Plant." When you take the turn of the listener, use the ratings chart below to evaluate the retelling. A **0** on the scale means that the reteller didn't include the item at all; a **4** means that the reteller answered the question completely.

Reteller _____   Listener _____

Does this retelling	NO!				YES!
1. have an introduction that includes the title and the author?	0	1	2	3	4
2. include the characters' names and tell how they are related to each other?	0	1	2	3	4
3. tell who the main character is and identify what he wants?	0	1	2	3	4
4. identify the conflict, or problem?	0	1	2	3	4
5. keep the main events in correct chronological order?	0	1	2	3	4
6. describe what happens at the climax?	0	1	2	3	4
7. explain how the conflict, or problem, is finally resolved?	0	1	2	3	4
8. make sense?	0	1	2	3	4
9. sound organized?	0	1	2	3	4
Total score _____					

Comments from the listener about the retelling:

_____

_____

Suggestions for the next retelling:

_____

_____

Duffy's Jacket

for use with
Holt Literature and Language Arts,
page 7

Interact with a Literary Text

Sequence Chart   Being able to relate events in their correct order is an important part of retelling. As you retell, use time-order words such as *first, second, third, next, then,* and *finally.* Words like these will clarify the order in which events occurred.

After you read "Duffy's Jacket," fill in the following chart. You should be able to find five major plot events.

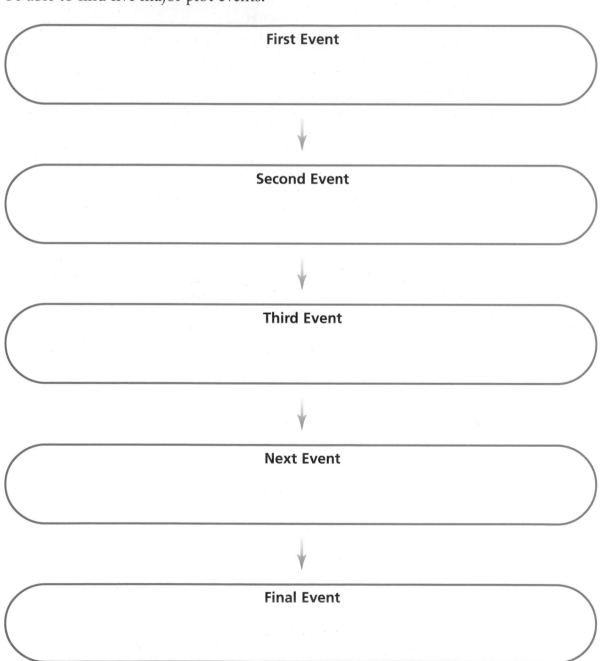

First Event

↓

Second Event

↓

Third Event

↓

Next Event

↓

Final Event

Yeti-like Monster Gives Staid Town in Illinois a Fright

for use with
Holt Literature and Language Arts,
page 16

TEXT
STRUCTURE

Interact with an Informational Text

Reporter's Notebook   Reporters often include the observations of others in their news stories. Fill out the reporter's observation cards below. Record the observations included in "Yeti-like Monster Gives Staid Town in Illinois a Fright." Then, number each observation card to indicate which event happened first, second, third, and so on.

Observation #_____
Mrs. Nedra Green

Observation #_____
Christian Baril

Observation #_____
Randy Creath and Cheryl Ray

Observation #_____
Randy Needham and Judy Johnson

Observation #_____
Officer Jimmie Nash

Observation #_____
Otis Norris, Ray Adkerson, and Wesley Lavander

Rikki-tikki-tavi

for use with
Holt Literature and Language Arts,
page 21

Interact with a Literary Text

Plot Diagram   Keeping track of the major elements of the plot will help you retell the story. Fill out the plot diagram below after you read "Rikki-tikki-tavi."

Basic Situation and Conflict:

Complications (problems, events):

Climax (crisis, big event):

Resolution:

Look, Mom, No Cavities

Interact with an Informational Text

Main-Idea Chart   The **main idea** of an informative article is the most important point the writer makes about the topic, or subject. In a well-written article the main idea is supported by details.

After you read "Look, Mom, No Cavities," fill out this chart. First, record the supporting details that the article provides about cobras. Then, think about these details, and write a statement that expresses the main idea.

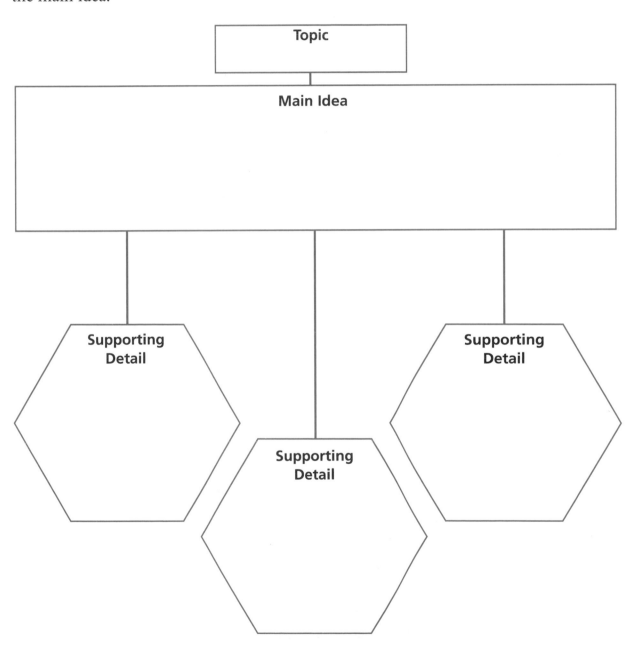

Topic

Main Idea

Supporting Detail

Supporting Detail

Supporting Detail

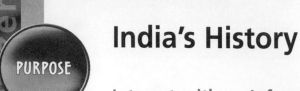

India's History

for use with
Holt Literature and Language Arts,
page 42

Interact with an Informational Text

KWL Chart   The setting of "Rikki-tikki-tavi" is India. What do you already know about India? What would you like to find out?

Before you start to read "India's History," fill out the first two columns of the KWL chart below. In the first column, jot down what you already know about India. In the second column, write what you would like to find out. Then, after you finish reading "India's History," fill out the third column, indicating what you learned from the selection.

K What I Know	W What I Want to Know	L What I Learned

Three Skeleton Key

Interact with a Literary Text

Foreshadowing Chart   When you read a suspenseful story, you notice clues that **foreshadow,** or hint at, later events. Sometimes, though, the author gives misleading clues to add suspense and surprise to a story. When you retell a story of suspense, make sure you include all of these clues.

Fill out the following foreshadowing chart after you read "Three Skeleton Key."

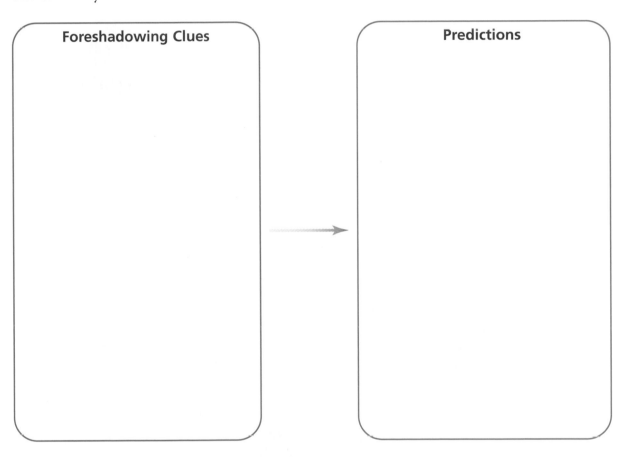

Foreshadowing Clues

Predictions

Climax Foreshadowed

Eeking Out a Life

for use with
Holt Literature and Language Arts,
page 63

Interact with an Informational Text

Inverted Pyramid   Many newspaper articles have a structure that follows that of an inverted pyramid. First the most important information is given, then important details, and then less important details.

As you read "Eeking Out a Life," fill out the inverted pyramid below with details from the article.

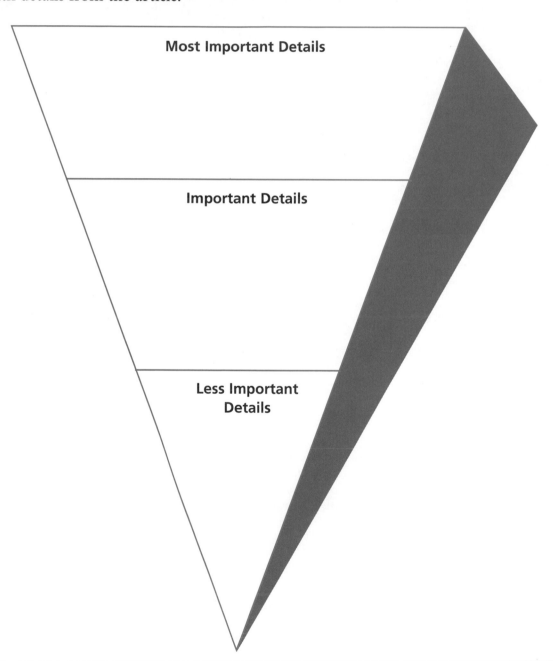

Most Important Details

Important Details

Less Important
Details

The Monsters Are Due on Maple Street

Interact with a Literary Text

Plot Chart   Complications keep a story interesting. **Complications** can be defined as plot events that deepen the story's conflict. Keeping track of the story's complications will help you with your retelling of the story.

Fill out the plot chart below as you read *The Monsters Are Due on Maple Street.*

```
┌─────────────────────────────────────────────────────────┐
│                    Initial Conflict                     │
│                                                         │
└─────────────────────────────────────────────────────────┘
                            ↓
┌─────────────────────────────────────────────────────────┐
│                   Complication 1:                       │
│                                                         │
│ - - - - - - - - - - - - - - - - - - - - - - - - - - - - │
│                   Complication 2:                       │
│                                                         │
│ - - - - - - - - - - - - - - - - - - - - - - - - - - - - │
│                   Complication 3:                       │
│                                                         │
└─────────────────────────────────────────────────────────┘
                            ↓
┌─────────────────────────────────────────────────────────┐
│                       Climax                            │
│                                                         │
└─────────────────────────────────────────────────────────┘
                            ↓
┌─────────────────────────────────────────────────────────┐
│                     Resolution                          │
│                                                         │
└─────────────────────────────────────────────────────────┘
```

Cellular Telephone Owner's Manual

Interact with an Informational Text

Checklist   To make sure you have followed directions in a manual completely, create a checklist for yourself. Turn each step in the manual into a question to ask yourself at each stage of the process. Complete each question starter with a step from the cell phone manual.

Standard Method

1. Did I _____

2. Did I _____

3. Did I _____

4. Did I _____

Quick-Change Method

1. Did I _____

2. Did I _____

3. Did I _____

4. Did I _____

Signs

Interact with an Informational Text

Evaluation Chart   A successful sign can be understood at a glance. As you read the signs, evaluate each one using the chart below. Rate each sign on a scale of 1–4, with 4 being the highest rating. If you think a sign could be made more effective, indicate how you would change it.

Evaluation Chart			
Sign	Purpose	Effectiveness	How I Would Change It
#1			
#2			
#3			
#4			
#5			
#6			
#7			
#8			
#9			
#10			
#11			

Literature

AUTHOR STUDY

On pages 21–34 of *Holt Literature and Language Arts* is **Rudyard Kipling**'s "Rikki-tikki-tavi." This is a tale of a brave mongoose who saved his human family from the deadly cobras in their garden. Kipling was a great teller of tales. When he was growing up in India, he heard many traditional Indian folk tales from his Indian nurses. These magical tales about animals that talk and think like human beings stayed with him. As an adult, Kipling retold these tales in books like *Just So Stories.* Now you are going to read a famous tale from that collection.

BEFORE YOU READ

Scientists can tell us how the elephant got its very long trunk, but storytellers have other explanations. In "The Elephant's Child" you will meet a young elephant whose great curiosity leads to a surprising result. This is called a **how-and-why** story. It explains how and why something in our world came to be.

Here is what you need to know before you begin the story:

- This tale is imaginary. It is set in Africa at a make-believe time long, long ago.
- There really is a Limpopo River in Africa. There are also real fever trees in Africa. They produce a gum that was thought to cure malaria.
- Kipling uses unusual spellings to capture the way the animals might sound if they could speak.
- This story is meant to be told aloud. Read it aloud to hear how all the repeated words and sounds add to the humor of the story.
- The narrator is telling the story to an imaginary listener, called O Best Beloved. This pet name indicates that the listener is probably a child whom the narrator loves very much.

Reading Standard 3.2 Identify events that advance the plot, and determine how each event explains past or present action(s) or foreshadows future action(s).

The Elephant's Child

Rudyard Kipling

In the High and Far-Off Times the Elephant, O Best
Beloved, had no trunk. He had only a blackish, bulgy nose,
as big as a boot, that he could wriggle about from side to
side; but he couldn't pick up things with it. But there was
one Elephant—a new Elephant—an Elephant's Child—
who was full of 'satiable curtiosity, and that means he asked
ever so many questions. *And* he lived in Africa, and he filled
all Africa with his 'satiable curtiosities. He asked his tall
aunt, the Ostrich, why her tail-feathers grew just so, and his
10 tall aunt the Ostrich spanked him with her hard, hard claw.
He asked his tall uncle, the Giraffe, what made his skin
spotty, and his tall uncle, the Giraffe, spanked him with his
hard, hard hoof. And still he was full of 'satiable curtiosity!
He asked his broad aunt, the Hippopotamus, why her eyes
were red, and his broad aunt, the Hippopotamus, spanked
him with her broad, broad hoof; and he asked his hairy
uncle, the Baboon, why melons tasted just so, and his hairy
uncle, the Baboon, spanked him with his hairy, hairy paw.
And *still* he was full of 'satiable curtiosity! He asked
20 questions about everything that he saw, or heard, or felt, or
smelt, or touched, and all his uncles and his aunts spanked
him. And still he was full of 'satiable curtiosity!

One fine morning in the middle of the Precession of
the Equinoxes[1] this 'satiable Elephant's Child asked a new
fine question that he had never asked before. He asked,

---

1. **Precession of the Equinoxes:** westward shift of the equinoxes each
   year. An equinox—when day and night are the same length—occurs
   twice a year: around March 21 and September 23.

WORD KNOWLEDGE

To capture the way people
speak, writers sometimes
leave out letters in a word or
even change or add letters.
An apostrophe shows that
one or more letters are left
out. Circle the two words in
line 6 that were changed.
What letters were left out of
the first word? What letter
was added to the second?
What might these two words
mean? Clue: The word
satiable (sā′shə·bəl) means
"able to be satisfied."

IDENTIFY

Underline in lines 9–22 the
different ways the Elephant's
Child shows his curiosity.

TEXT STRUCTURE

On the previous page, notice the raised number *1* by the term "Precession of the Equinoxes" (line 24). This raised number signals that this term is explained in a footnote at the bottom of the page.

DECODING TIP

Throughout this story, Kipling uses playful spellings. Circle the word in line 27 that is spelled in an unusual way. How is this word actually spelled? As you read, circle words you come across with unusual spellings.

_____

_____

_____

_____

_____

_____

_____

_____

_____

_____

VOCABULARY DEVELOPMENT

astonished (ə·stän′isht) *v.* used as *adj.*: filled with sudden wonder; surprised.

"What does the Crocodile have for dinner?" Then everybody said, "Hush!" in a loud and dretful tone, and they spanked him immediately and directly, without stopping, for a long time.

30 　By and by, when that was finished, he came upon Kolokolo Bird sitting in the middle of a wait-a-bit thorn-bush, and he said, "My father has spanked me, and my mother has spanked me; all my aunts and uncles have spanked me for my 'satiable curtiosity; and *still* I want to know what the Crocodile has for dinner!"

　Then Kolokolo Bird said, with a mournful cry, "Go to the banks of the great gray-green, greasy Limpopo River, all set about with fever-trees, and find out."

　That very next morning, when there was nothing left

40 of the Equinoxes, because the Precession had preceded according to precedent, this 'satiable Elephant's Child took a hundred pounds of bananas (the little short red kind), and a hundred pounds of sugar-cane (the long purple kind), and seventeen melons (the greeny-crackly kind), and said to all his dear families, "Good-bye. I am going to the great gray-green, greasy Limpopo River, all set about with fever-trees, to find out what the Crocodile has for dinner." And they all spanked him once more for luck, though he asked them most politely to stop.

50 　Then he went away, a little warm, but not at all **astonished,** eating melons, and throwing the rind about, because he could not pick it up.

　He went from Graham's Town to Kimberley, and from Kimberley to Khama's Country, and from Khama's Country he went east by north, eating melons all the time, till at last he came to the banks of the great gray-green, greasy Limpopo River, all set about with fever-trees, precisely as Kolokolo Bird had said.

Now you must know and understand, O Best Beloved,
60 that till that very week, and day, and hour, and minute, this 'satiable Elephant's Child had never seen a Crocodile, and did not know what one was like. It was all his 'satiable curtiosity.

The first thing that he found was a Bi-Colored-Python-Rock-Snake curled round a rock.

" 'Scuse me," said the Elephant's Child most politely, "but have you seen such a thing as a Crocodile in these promiscuous[2] parts?"

"Have I seen a Crocodile?" said the Bi-Colored-
70 Python-Rock-Snake, in a voice of dretful scorn. "What will you ask me next?"

" 'Scuse me," said the Elephant's Child, "but could you kindly tell me what he has for dinner?"

Then the Bi-Colored-Python-Rock-Snake uncoiled himself very quickly from the rock, and spanked the Elephant's Child with his scalesome, flailsome tail.

"That is odd," said the Elephant's Child, "because my father and my mother, and my uncle and my aunt, not to mention my other aunt, the Hippopotamus, and my other
80 uncle, the Baboon, have all spanked me for my 'satiable curtiosity—and I suppose this is the same thing."

So he said good-bye very politely to the Bi-Colored-Python-Rock-Snake, and helped to coil him up on the rock again, and went on, a little warm, but not at all astonished, eating melons, and throwing the rind about, because he could not pick it up, till he trod on what he thought was a

---

2. **promiscuous** (prə·mis′kyoo·əs): The Elephant's Child likes to use big words. *Promiscuous* means "diverse, different."

RETELL

What is the Elephant's Child's problem? Retell the story up to this point (line 63).

_____

_____

_____

_____

_____

_____

_____

_____

DECODING TIP

What is the meaning of the word *uncoiled* (line 74)? To figure this out, first find the word a few paragraphs back that tells you how the snake was positioned on the rock. Circle it. Now, notice the prefix *un-* in the word *uncoiled*. What does this prefix tell you? The word *uncoiled* describes how the snake changed its position on the rock. What do you think this word means?

_____

_____

_____

Rudyard Kipling 25

Retell what happens from
when the Elephant meets the
Python to this point in the
story (lines 64–90).

_____

_____

_____

_____

_____

_____

_____

_____

_____

_____

_____

_____

_____

_____

_____

_____

_____

_____

_____

_____

log of wood at the very edge of the great gray-green, greasy
Limpopo River, all set about with fever-trees.

But it was really the Crocodile, O Best Beloved, and the
90   Crocodile winked one eye—like this!

" 'Scuse me," said the Elephant's Child most politely,
"but do you happen to have seen a Crocodile in these
promiscuous parts?"

Then the Crocodile winked the other eye, and lifted
half his tail out of the mud; and the Elephant's Child
stepped back most politely, because he did not wish to be
spanked again.

"Come hither, Little One," said the Crocodile. "Why do
you ask such things?"

100   " 'Scuse me," said the Elephant's Child most politely,
"but my father has spanked me, my mother has spanked
me, not to mention my tall aunt, the Ostrich, and my tall
uncle, the Giraffe, who can kick ever so hard, as well as my
broad aunt, the Hippopotamus, and my hairy uncle, the
Baboon, _and_ including the Bi-Colored-Python-Rock-Snake,
with the scalesome, flailsome tail, just up the bank, who

spanks harder than any of them; and *so*, if it's quite all the same to you, I don't want to be spanked anymore."

"Come hither, Little One," said the Crocodile, "for I am the Crocodile," and he wept crocodile-tears to show it was quite true.

Then the Elephant's Child grew all breathless, and panted, and kneeled down on the bank and said, "You are the very person I have been looking for all these long days. Will you please tell me what you have for dinner?"

"Come hither, Little One," said the Crocodile, "and I'll whisper."

Then the Elephant's Child put his head down close to the Crocodile's musky, tusky mouth, and the Crocodile caught him by his little nose, which up to that very week, day, hour, and minute, had been no bigger than a boot, though much more useful.

"I think," said the Crocodile—and he said it between his teeth, like this—"I think today I will begin with Elephant's Child!"

At this, O Best Beloved, the Elephant's Child was much annoyed, and he said, speaking through his nose, like this, "Led go! You are hurtig be!"

Then the Bi-Colored-Python-Rock-Snake scuffled down from the bank and said, "My young friend, if you do not now, immediately and instantly, pull as hard as ever you can, it is my opinion that your acquaintance in the large-pattern leather ulster[3]" (and by this he meant the Crocodile) "will jerk you into yonder **limpid** stream before you can say Jack Robinson."

This is the way Bi-Colored-Python-Rock-Snake always talked.

---

3. **ulster:** overcoat.

Read aloud the boxed passage. Emphasize words like *musky* and *tusky*. Say the Crocodile's words, the Elephant's Child's words, and the Bi-Colored-Python-Rock-Snake's words as you think each character would say them.

IDENTIFY

Like many folk tales, this one is meant to be told aloud. What clue do you see in lines 126–127 that shows that this tale is meant to be told orally? Underline it.

VOCABULARY DEVELOPMENT

limpid (lim′pid) *adj.:* not cloudy; clear.

· · · · · · **Notes** · · · · · ·

RETELL

Kipling creates humor by putting big words in the mouths of characters, making the characters seem self-important. Retell the Bi-Colored-Python-Rock-Snake's words (lines 155–161) in simpler language.

_____

_____

_____

_____

_____

_____

_____

_____

_____

_____

_____

_____

_____

_____

_____

_____

_____

_____

140   Then the Elephant's Child sat back on his little **haunches,** and pulled, and pulled, and pulled, and his nose began to stretch. And the Crocodile floundered into the water, making it all creamy with great sweeps of his tail, and *he* pulled, and pulled, and pulled.

    And the Elephant's Child's nose kept on stretching; and the Elephant's Child spread all his little four legs and pulled, and pulled, and pulled, and his nose kept on stretching; and the Crocodile threshed his tail like an oar, and *he* pulled, and pulled, and pulled, and at each pull the Elephant's Child's nose grew longer and longer—and it hurt him . . . !

150   Then the Elephant's Child felt his legs slipping, and he said through his nose, which was now nearly five feet long, "This is too butch for be!"

    Then the Bi-Colored-Python-Rock-Snake came down from the bank, and knotted himself in a double-clove-hitch round the Elephant's Child's hind legs, and said, "Rash and inexperienced traveler, we will now seriously devote ourselves to a little high tension, because if we do not, it is my impression that yonder self-propelling man-of-war with the armor-plated upper deck" (and by this, O Best Beloved,

160 he meant the Crocodile), "will permanently vitiate[4] your future career."

    That is the way all Bi-Colored-Python-Rock Snakes always talked.

    So he pulled, and the Elephant's Child pulled, and the Crocodile pulled; but the Elephant's Child and the Bi-Colored-Python-Rock-Snake pulled hardest; and at last the Crocodile let go of the Elephant's Child's nose

---

4. **vitiate** (vish′ē·āt′): spoil.

with a plop that you could hear all up and down the Limpopo.

170   Then the Elephant's Child sat down most hard and sudden; but first he was careful to say "Thank you" to the Bi-Colored-Python-Rock-Snake; and next he was kind to his poor pulled nose, and wrapped it all up in cool banana leaves, and hung it in the great gray-green greasy Limpopo to cool.

    "What are you doing that for?" said the Bi-Colored-Python-Rock-Snake.

    " 'Scuse me," said the Elephant's Child, "but my nose is badly out of shape, and I am waiting for it to shrink."

180   "Then you will have to wait a long time," said the Bi-Colored-Python-Rock-Snake. "Some people do not know what is good for them."

    The Elephant's Child sat there for three days waiting for his nose to shrink. But it never grew any shorter, and, besides, it made him squint. For, O Best Beloved, you will see and understand that the Crocodile had pulled it out into a really truly trunk same as all Elephants have today.

    At the end of the third day a fly came and stung him on the shoulder, and before he knew what he was doing

190 he lifted up his trunk and hit that fly dead with the end of it.

    " 'Vantage number one!" said the Bi-Colored-Python-Rock-Snake. "You couldn't have done that with a mere-smear nose. Try and eat a little now."

    Before he thought what he was doing the Elephant's Child put out his trunk and plucked a large bundle of grass, dusted it clean against his fore-legs, and stuffed it into his mouth.

INTERPRET

Many tales that are read aloud contain words and phrases repeated over and over. Go back through the tale, and star every time the Elephant's Child mentions being spanked. What effect does the repeated phrase have?

_____

_____

_____

_____

_____

_____

_____

_____

_____

_____

_____

_____

_____

RETELL

Underline the three "'vantages" of the Elephant Child's new trunk. (See lines 190–209.)

_____

_____

_____

_____

_____

_____

_____

_____

_____

_____

_____

_____

_____

_____

_____

_____

200   " 'Vantage number two!" said the Bi-Colored-Python-Rock-Snake. "You couldn't have done that with a mere-smear nose. Don't you think the sun is very hot here?"

"It is," said the Elephant's Child, and before he thought what he was doing he schlooped up a schloop of mud from the banks of the great gray-green, greasy Limpopo, and slapped it on his head, where it made a cool schloopy-sloshy mud-cap all trickly behind his ears.

" 'Vantage number three!" said the Bi-Colored-Python-Rock-Snake. "You couldn't have done that with a mere-smear nose. Now how do you feel about being

210 spanked again?"

" 'Scuse me," said the Elephant's Child, "but I should not like it at all."

"How would you like to spank somebody?" said the Bi-Colored-Python-Rock-Snake.

"I should like it very much indeed," said the Elephant's Child.

"Well," said the Bi-Colored-Python-Rock-Snake, "you will find that new nose of yours very useful to spank people with."

220   "Thank you," said the Elephant's Child, "I'll remember that; and now I think I'll go home to all my dear families and try."

So the Elephant's Child went home across Africa frisking and whisking his trunk. When he wanted fruit to eat he pulled fruit down from a tree, instead of waiting for it to fall as he used to do. When he wanted grass he plucked grass up from the ground, instead of going on his knees as he used to do. When the flies bit him he broke off the branch of a tree and used it as a fly-whisk; and he made

230 himself a new, cool, slushy-squshy mud-cap whenever the

sun was hot. When he felt lonely walking through Africa he sang to himself down his trunk, and the noise was louder than several brass bands. He went especially out of his way to find a broad Hippopotamus (she was no relation of his), and he spanked her very hard, to make sure that the Bi-Colored-Python-Rock-Snake had spoken the truth about his new trunk. The rest of the time he picked up the melon rinds that he had dropped on his way to the Limpopo—for he was a Tidy Pachyderm.

240   One dark evening he came back to all his dear families, and he coiled up his trunk and said, "How do you do?" They were very glad to see him, and immediately said, "Come here and be spanked for your 'satiable curtiosity."

"Pooh," said the Elephant's Child. "I don't think you peoples know anything about spanking; but *I* do, and I'll show you."

The word *pachyderm* (pak′ə·dûrm′) (line 239) comes from two Greek words that mean "thick" and "skin." An elephant belongs to the group of mammals called pachyderms. What other animal in this paragraph might be a pachyderm? Circle it.

INTERPRET

The running joke about spanking is picked up again at the tale's end. What is the Elephant's Child about to do?

_____

_____

_____

_____

_____

_____

_____

_____

_____

_____

_____

_____

_____

_____

_____

INTERPRET

Why does the Elephant's Child spare the Kolokolo bird (line 267)?

_____

_____

_____

_____

VOCABULARY DEVELOPMENT

precisely (prē·sīs′lē) adv.: exactly.

IDENTIFY

What is the resolution, or outcome, of this story?

_____

_____

_____

_____

_____

_____

_____

YOU TRY IT

You can be a storyteller too. Think of an animal with a feature that you could write a how-and-why tale about. For example, "Why does the dog wag its tail?" or "Why is the crocodile so scaly?" Deliver your tale to an audience.

Then he uncurled his trunk and knocked two of his dear brothers head over heels.

"O Bananas!" said they, "Where did you learn that
250 trick, and what have you done to your nose?"

"I got a new one from the Crocodile on the banks of the gray-green, greasy Limpopo River," said the Elephant's Child. "I asked him what he had for dinner, and he gave me this to keep."

"It looks very ugly," said his hairy uncle, the Baboon.

"It does," said the Elephant's Child. "But it's very useful," and he picked up his hairy uncle, the Baboon, by one hairy leg, and hove[5] him into a hornets' nest.

Then the bad Elephant's Child spanked all his dear
260 families for a long time, till they were very warm and greatly astonished. He pulled out his tall Ostrich aunt's tail-feathers; and he caught his tall uncle, the Giraffe, by the hind-leg, and dragged him through a thorn-bush; and he shouted at his broad aunt, the Hippopotamus, and blew bubbles into her ear when she was sleeping in the water after meals; but he never let any one touch Kolokolo bird.

At last things grew so exciting that his dear families went off one by one in a hurry to the banks of the great
270 gray-green, greasy Limpopo River, all set about with fever-trees, to borrow new noses from the Crocodile. When they came back nobody spanked anybody any more; and ever since that day, O Best Beloved, all the Elephants you will ever see besides all those that you won't, have trunks **precisely** like the trunk of the 'satiable Elephant's Child.

---

5. **hove:** heaved.

OWN THE STORY

Plot   To review the series of related events that make up the plot of "The Elephant's Child," fill out the chain-of-events chart on the next page.

Personal Word List   You probably encountered many new words in this story. Add them to your Personal Word List. Add any other story words you particularly liked.

Personal Reading Log   Did you enjoy this folk tale? Write your reaction to it as you enter the title of the tale in your Personal Reading Log. You've just earned 5 points on the Reading Meter for completing the story.

Checklist for Standards Mastery   You're making progress. Use the Checklist for Standards Mastery to see how far you have come in mastering the standards.

The Elephant's Child ■ *Interactive Reading,* page 23

Interact with a Literary Text

Chain-of-Events Chart   The Elephant's Child in Kipling's story certainly has an adventure-filled life. Trace the series of plot events in "The Elephant's Child" by filling out this chain-of-events chart. You should be able to identify at least seven major events in the story.

Event 1:

Event 2:

Event 3:

Event 4:

Event 5:

Event 6:

Event 7:

Information

BEFORE YOU READ

Suppose you want to do research on elephants. You would use a source that provides factual information—information that you know is true. One source you could use is a field guide.

Here's what you need to know before you read this field guide:

- A field guide is an illustrated book that provides factual scientific information on plants or animals.
- Numbers help you identify the different entries in a field guide.
- Field guides often provide the Latin names for plants and animals. For guides to pronouncing these names, look for footnotes or a glossary.

Reading Standard 2.1
Understand and analyze the differences in structure and purpose between various categories of informational materials.

from Simon & Schuster's

Guide to Mammals

edited by Sydney Anderson

1   335   **Elephas maximus**[1] *(Indian elephant)*

Classification: Order Proboscidea,[2] Family Elephantidae.[3]

Description: They are usually gray and may have light blotches over the body. There are only a few long, stiff hairs present on the body; the tip of the tail, however, has a tuft of hairs. The forehead is flat. Its long trunk, formed of upper lip and nose, has a single process at the tip. Compared with the African elephant, the Indian elephant has much smaller ears,
10   4 nails on each hind foot instead of 3, and 19 pair of

---

1. **Elephas maximus** (el′ə·fəs maks′ə·məs): Latin for "largest elephant."
2. **Proboscidea** (prō′ bō·sə·dā′ ə): Latin for "long flexible snout" or "trunk."
3. **Elephantidae** (el′ ə·fən·tē′dī).

from Simon & Schuster's Guide to Mammals by Luigi Boitani and Stefania Bartoli. Published by Simon & Schuster, New York, 1983.

TEXT STRUCTURE

The entries in this field guide are numbered and begin with the Latin name of the mammal followed by its more common name. What five categories of information does each entry provide about this creature?

_____

_____

_____

_____

_____

habitat (hab′i·tat′) *n.:* region where a plant or an animal naturally grows or lives.

maturity (mə·choor′ə·tē) *n.:* state of being full grown; adulthood.

Read the sentence containing the word *gestation* (line 25). Underline the words that provide a clue to its meaning.

Three types of information are provided on this page. What are they? Circle the text that clued you in.

_____

_____

_____

_____

_____

_____

_____

_____

_____

_____

_____

Indian elephant.

ribs instead of 21; the tusks, present only in some males, are generally shorter. Length of head and body including trunk up to 6.5 m (21.3 ft), shoulder height 2.5–3.2 m (8.2–10.5 ft), weight up to 5400 kg (5.9 t); females somewhat smaller.

Distribution: India, the Indochinese peninsula, Sumatra, and Sri Lanka.

Habitat: Varied; from forests to plains.

Behavior: The Indian elephant lives in groups of 10–30,

20   although groups of this size are becoming increasingly rare. The group is made up of individuals which are closely related, and is led by an elderly female. It rests during the hottest hours of the day and frequently sprays dirt over itself to keep away insects. When the herd travels, it usually does so in single file. Gestation lasts for 18–22 months and a single young is born (although twins are not unknown), which weighs about 220 pounds at birth. Females reach **maturity** at

30 9–15 years of age, males at about 15 years. The life span is about 70–80 years.

336 Loxodonta africana[4] *(African elephant)*

Classification: Order Proboscidea, Family Elephantidae.

Description: This is the largest living terrestrial mammal. Its enormous ears serve to **dissipate** body heat and brush away insects from its eyes. The upper incisors form tusks, which average about 1.5 m (5 ft) long and weigh about 16 kg (35 lb). The trunk has two fingerlike processes at the tip. The forest subspecies of this elephant is smaller than the savanna race. Length of head and body including trunk up to 7.5 m (24.8 ft); shoulder height to 4 m (13 ft); weight may exceed 6000 kg (6.6 t).

Distribution: Sub-Saharan African except southern Africa.

40

African elephant.

4. **Loxodonta africana** (läks′ə·dän′tə af′ri·kan′ə). *Loxodonta* is a generic name for elephants. *Loxo* is from the Latin, meaning "lozenge," and *donta,* meaning "tooth." The name refers to the lozenge-shaped ridges on elephants' molars.

VOCABULARY DEVELOPMENT

matriarchal (mā′trē·ärk′əl) *adj.:* ruled by a mother or highly respected older woman.

· · · · · · Notes · · · · · ·

_____

_____

_____

_____

_____

_____

Habitat: From semidesert to forest at different altitudes.

Behavior: This elephant is a social creature living in family groups which have a **matriarchal** structure. The head of the group is an elderly female; she makes decisions about when and where to move, and keeps the peace. Groups of African elephants can number more than 100 individuals in periods of drought. The groups are constantly moving when the animals are feeding. The elephant must drink daily and enjoys bathing in waterholes. Breeding occurs all year, but a female will only give birth once every 4 years. Gestation lasts 22–24 months, at the end of which a single offspring is born, weighing about 220 pounds. It nurses for 2–3 years.

50

OWN THE TEXT

PRACTICING THE STANDARDS

Compare and Contrast   Fill in the Venn diagram below with details showing how the Indian elephant and African elephant are the same and how they are different. Review the completed diagram to see how much you've learned.

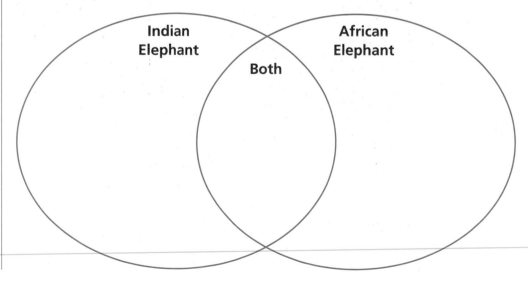

Indian Elephant

African Elephant

Both

Compare and Contrast Find another article or encyclopedia entry about elephants. Then, identify the ways in which the field guide and the other article present information. You may want to create a chart like this to fill in as you gather information:

	Purpose	Types of Details	Organization
Guide to Mammals			
Article 2			

KEEPING TRACK

Personal Word List This selection contains several special words used in science books about animals and their behavior. Record these words in your Personal Word List: *gestation, terrestrial, mammal, species* and *subspecies,* and *matriarchal.* Choose one word, and write a sentence using it.

Personal Reading Log As you add this selection to your Personal Reading Log, indicate when you would use a field guide like this one. What other field guides might be available? Give yourself 2 points on the Reading Meter.

Checklist for Standards Mastery See how much progress you have made by using the Checklist for Standards Mastery.

from Simon & Schuster's
Guide to Mammals ■ *Interactive Reading,* page 35

Go Beyond an Informational Text

Template   A field guide provides detailed information about animals or plants. Usually a field guide follows a specific structure, which enables readers to locate information quickly.

Choose an animal you are interested in studying. Then, use the library and the Internet to create an entry for a field guide. The following template will help you find consistent information.

Latin Name: _____

Common Name: _____

Classification: _____

Description: _____

_____

_____

Distribution: _____

_____

Habitat: _____

_____

Behavior: _____

_____

_____

_____

_____

_____

FOLK TALE

"The Elephant's Child" creates a picture of a sinister crocodile eager to eat the Elephant's Child. How is the crocodile presented in other folk tales? Read this traditional Indian folk tale to find out.

Here's what you need to know before you read this tale:

- The Ganges is a river in India.
- Crocodiles and monkeys are native to India.
- Crocodiles are carnivores (kär′nə·vôrz′), which means they eat meat (including monkeys).
- In folk tales, monkeys are often portrayed as being very clever. (Does this reflect a **fact** about monkeys?)

Reading Standard 3.2 Identify events that advance the plot, and determine how each event explains past or present action(s) or foreshadows future action(s).

The Monkey and the Crocodile

retold by **A. K. Ramanujan**

On the banks of the Ganges, a monkey lived in a rose-apple tree. The rose-apples were delicious and plentiful. While he was eating them with obvious **relish** one day, a crocodile came out of the river, and the monkey threw down a few rose-apples and said, "These are the best rose-apples in the world. They taste like nectar." The crocodile chomped on them and found them truly wonderful. The monkey and the crocodile became friends, and the crocodile took to visiting the monkey every day to eat the fruit of that
10 wonderful tree and to talk in its shade.

DECODING TIP

One way you can deal with unfamiliar words is by looking for familiar words within the new word. What two words do you find in the word *plentiful* (line 2)?

_____

_____

VOCABULARY DEVELOPMENT

relish (rel′ish) *n.:* enjoyment.

"The Monkey and the Crocodile" (Kannada/Tamil) from *Folktales from India: A Selection of Oral Tales from Twenty-two Languages*, selected and edited by A. K. Ramanujan. Copyright © 1991 by A. K. Ramanujan. Reprinted by permission of **Pantheon Books, a division of Random House, Inc.**

sulked (sulkt) *v.:* showed resentment or dissatisfaction by withdrawing.

Pause at line 32. Do you think the crocodile will end up killing the monkey? Why or why not?

_____

_____

_____

_____

_____

_____

_____

_____

_____

_____

Read the boxed passage aloud. Experiment with tone and volume to capture the ways the crocodile and the monkey would talk.

One day the crocodile went home and took some of the fruit to his wife. "These are wonderful. They taste like nectar. Where did you get them?" asked the wife.

He said, "From a tree on the banks of the Ganges."

"But you can't climb the tree. Did you pick them up from the sands?"

"No, I've a new friend who lives in the tree, a monkey. He throws them down for me and we talk."

20 "Oh, that's why you've been coming home late! A monkey that lives on such fruit must have such sweet flesh. His heart must taste like heaven. I'd love to eat it," said the crocodile wife.

The crocodile didn't like the turn the conversation was taking. "How can you talk like that? He's my friend! He's like a brother-in-law to you."

But the wife **sulked** and said, "I want his heart. Why are you so taken with this monkey? Is it a he or a she? Bring me his heart, or hers, which is even better. Or else I'll starve myself to death."

30 The crocodile tried his best to talk her out of her jealousy and ill-will, but he couldn't. He agreed to bring the monkey home on his back for a meal, as it were.

Next day, he invited the monkey to go home with him. "My wife has heard so much about you. She loved the rose-apples. She wants you to come home with me. If you come down from the tree and sit on my back, I'll take you there."

The monkey said, "You are a crocodile and live in the water. I can't even swim. I'll drown and die."

40 "Oh no, I'll take you carefully on my back. We don't live in the water. We live on a dry, sunny island in the middle of the river. Come with me. You'll enjoy it."

The monkey was persuaded and came down. He brought handfuls of rose-apples for the crocodile's wife. As the crocodile swam through the river, he felt terribly guilty. His **conscience** wouldn't allow him to take his friend home and let his wife make a meal of his heart, without at least telling him what he was doing. So he said, "I haven't been quite straight with you. My wife sent me today to bring you

50 home because she wants to eat your heart. That's what she wants, and I couldn't go against her wishes."

"Oh is that what she wants? My heart! Why didn't you tell me this before? I would have been happy to bring it down and give it to your wife," said the monkey.

"What do you mean?" asked the crocodile.

"I don't carry my heart around with me. I usually leave it in the tree when I come down. Let's go back and I'll give it to you."

The crocodile turned around and swam back to the

60 bank. The monkey quickly jumped off his back and **clambered** up the tree to safety.

OWN THE STORY

PRACTICING THE STANDARDS

Plot Check your understanding of the plot events in "The Monkey and the Crocodile" by filling in the chain-of-events chart below. You may add to this chain if you need to.

Chain of Events

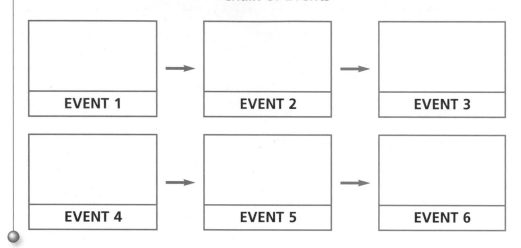

| EVENT 1 | → | EVENT 2 | → | EVENT 3 |

| EVENT 4 | → | EVENT 5 | → | EVENT 6 |

KEEPING TRACK

Personal Word List Record the new words you learned from this tale in your Personal Word List. Put a star next to the words that are especially descriptive.

Personal Reading Log As you add the title of this tale to your Personal Reading Log, indicate whether or not you found it easy to read. Give yourself 2 points on the Reading Meter for completing the tale.

Checklist for Standards Mastery The more you read, the more you learn. Use the Checklist for Standards Mastery to check your progress.

The Monkey and the Crocodile

Interactive Reading, page 41

Go Beyond a Literary Text

Storyboard   Directors often ask for storyboards of movies before filming begins. A storyboard is a map of the movie. It contains frames with drawings that show what is happening in each scene. Captions below the drawings briefly describe the scene. For example, the first frame of a storyboard for "The Monkey and the Crocodile" might show the monkey throwing rose apples to the crocodile. The caption under it might say, "The monkey and the crocodile become friends."

Create your own storyboard of "The Monkey and the Crocodile." In each frame, draw a scene. Write a description of each scene below your drawings.

Chapter 2

Characters
Living Many Lives

Strategy Launch: "It Says, I Say, And So"

LITERARY FOCUS: ANALYSIS OF CHARACTER

When you analyze a character in a story, you take the character apart to see what kind of person he or she is. Sometimes a writer directly describes a character. A writer might say, "Joe was a trusting soul." Usually, however, a writer reveals more indirectly what a character is like. The writer might describe the character's appearance, actions, speech, and thoughts and show us how other characters react to that person. Then we make up our own minds about the kind of person we are meeting.

A STRATEGY THAT WORKS: "IT SAYS, I SAY, AND SO"

To understand characters in literature—and in real life—we have to make inferences, or guesses based on evidence. A strategy that can help you make inferences about characters in stories is "It Says, I Say, And So."

POINTERS FOR USING "IT SAYS, I SAY, AND SO"

⟫➡ The "It Says" part of the strategy means that you identify what the text says about the character. Read the details that describe a character's looks, actions, and words. Look for how other people in the story feel about the character.

⟫➡ The "I Say" part of the strategy means that you say what *you* think. Give your opinion of the character's thoughts, words, or actions.

⟫➡ In the "And So" part of the strategy, combine the information in the text (It Says) with what you think about that information (I Say) to make an inference (And So).

Reading Standard 1.2 Use knowledge of Greek, Latin, and Anglo-Saxon roots and affixes to understand content-area vocabulary.

Reading Standard 2.2 (Grade 6 Review) Analyze text that uses the compare-and-contrast organizational pattern.

Reading Standard 3.3 Analyze characterization as delineated through a character's thoughts, words, speech patterns, and actions; the narrator's description; and the thoughts, words, and actions of other characters.

"The Musician" is a story about computers and music, but mostly it is about a relationship. You will meet two characters, a father and son. They have a lot in common, but they also have a few differences. That's what makes the story!

The Musician

Meish Goldish

INFER

Circle the names of the two characters introduced in the first two sentences. How do you think Tano knows what his father wants the moment he knocks on the door?

_____

_____

_____

_____

_____

_____

_____

IDENTIFY

Pause at line 16. Underline the words that show what Tano does. Then, circle the words that reveal what Tano thinks.

Tano knew what his dad would say the moment he knocked on Tano's open door.

"Why aren't you downstairs practicing the piano?" Dad asked, entering the bedroom.

Tano was sitting at his desk, surfing web sites on his computer.

"I'm doing some computer stuff now, Dad," Tano answered. "I'll practice a little later."

Dad began to peel the orange he was holding.

10 "There's no time like the present," Dad said, holding out a slice of orange to his son.

"No thanks, Dad. I don't really like oranges," said Tano.

"But they're good for you," Dad said. "Just like practicing the piano is good for you."

Tano rolled his eyes upward. Here we go again, he thought. The same old, tired speech I get week after week.

"Dad," said Tano, trying to sound respectful and not annoyed, "I eat plenty of healthy foods. All kinds of fruits and vegetables. I eat grapes, pears, plums, apples. I just

20   don't happen to like oranges."

After taking a deep breath, Tano added, "And I just don't happen to like playing the piano, either."

For a moment, Tano's father stared at his son with a distant look. Tano wasn't even sure his father was looking at him. It was more like he was daydreaming, Tano thought.

Suddenly, Dad shrugged his shoulders and said, "Sorry to bother you, son." He turned and left the room.

Tano turned back to his computer work but couldn't

30   **concentrate.** Guilt feelings began to creep inside him.

I know I shouldn't have said that to Dad, Tano thought. It's been so hard on him since Mom died. I should just do everything he asks me, without objecting. I should just be the perfect son.

Tano walked over to his bed and lay down. He thought about how much he missed his mother. It had been nearly a year since she died. Now just he and Dad were left in the house. Tano and his father were together at school as well, since his father was the music teacher there. About five

40   months ago, Dad had urged Tano to take up the piano. But much as he tried, Tano just didn't seem to enjoy it.

The sudden ringing of the telephone startled Tano.

"Hello?" he answered.

"Hey, Tano. It's Dave. Want to come over and spend some time on my computer?"

"I don't know, Dave. I really should be practicing the piano now."

"Oh, come on. You don't need the piano. And I just got some new computer games with awesome video

50   features. You could show me how to master them, like you always do."

INFER

Circle the words "guilt feelings" in line 30. Then draw an arrow from the words "guilt feelings" to two things that Tano has just told his father he doesn't like. Why do you think saying those things makes Tano feel guilty?

_____

_____

_____

_____

_____

_____

_____

_____

_____

VOCABULARY DEVELOPMENT

concentrate (kän′sən·trāt′) *v.:* direct or focus one's thoughts or actions.

Concentrate is built on the Latin word *centrum,* meaning "center," and the prefix *com-,* meaning "together."

IDENTIFY

Underline the words in lines 31–41 that help you understand why Tano and his dad are having a hard time.

_____

_____

_____

_____

_____

_____

_____

_____

_____

_____

_____

_____

_____

_____

_____

_____

INFER

Pause at line 80. Underline what Dave does that shows he is ready to listen to Tano. What kind of person does Dave seem to be?

_____

_____

_____

_____

_____

Tano thought for a moment. His best friend always knew how to get to him.

"Okay," Tano sighed. "I'll be there in about ten."

"Super."

Tano hung up and put on his jacket. He passed his father in the living room. Dad was reading the newspaper.

"I'm going over to Dave's house, Dad."

His father looked over the paper and raised an
60   eyebrow. "No piano?" he asked.

"I promise I'll practice twice as long tomorrow, Dad."

"Okay," his father replied. "Just don't stay out too late. Even on a weekend, you need to get your sleep."

"Right, Dad," Tano replied, closing the front door.

Dave was all smiles when Tano walked into his room. Music was playing loudly in the background.

"There's my man!" Dave called out. "Mister Computer Know-It-All. Just the guy I need right now!"

Tano looked around Dave's room. He couldn't believe
70   what a mess it was always in. Tano knew his own mother never would have let him be that sloppy.

"So where are these games you're too dense to figure out?" Tano asked sarcastically.

Dave took a large step backward. "Ouch!" he exclaimed. "What's with you and the attitude?"

Tano paused. "I'm sorry," he apologized. "You didn't deserve that. I guess I'm just kind of upset."

Dave turned down the music and sat in a chair. He pulled up another chair and motioned for Tano to sit.
80   "So tell me about it, my friend. What happened?"

Tano explained how his father had wanted him to practice the piano, and how he felt guilty telling him he didn't enjoy it. When Tano was finished, Dave stood up. He liked to pace around the room when speaking to someone.

Dave began, "Don't feel guilty about not wanting to play the piano. Your father loves to play the piano. And he's a great player, too. Everyone in school thinks he's a fantastic musician and a fantastic teacher. But that doesn't mean you have to follow in his footsteps. People shouldn't be forced
90 to take on other people's interests. You have your own interests. Why should you be a musician? Is your father a computer genius?"

Tano knew that, in a way, Dave's arguments made sense.

"No," Tano replied with a soft laugh. "Far from it." The idea of his father using a computer seemed funny to Tano. Dad wasn't very good with most simple machines, let alone a computer. He still didn't know how to program their VCR.
100 "Well, then, that's your answer," Dave offered. "If I were you, I'd tell your father, in a polite but firm way, that the piano lessons are over."

There was a moment of silence. Then Dave added, "And if I were your father, I'd get a little more interested in computers."

"Why's that?" Tano asked with a puzzled look. "I thought you just said people shouldn't be forced to take on other people's interests."

"That's true," Dave said. "But this is different."
110 "What do you mean?" asked Tano.

Dave sat down, leaned close to Tano, and lowered his voice.

"You didn't hear this from me," Dave confided, "but the other day, when I was waiting in the school office, I

IDENTIFY

Re-read lines 85–92. Circle things you learn about Tano's dad.

IDENTIFY

Re-read lines 109–112. Underline the text that tells that Dave is about to reveal a secret.

· · · · · · Notes · · · · · · ·

IDENTIFY

Underline Dave's words in lines 119–128 that introduce another problem into the story.

INFER

Pause at line 142. Underline the words that tell you Tano does not tell his father what the meeting is about. Does Tano seem to think it is important to keep promises? What does that reveal about Tano's character?

overheard Mr. Murray tell Ms. Vasquez that come September, the whole school is going to change big time. The entire office will become computerized. Every secretary will have to be trained to use the new system."

120   Tano looked puzzled. "So what's that got to do with my father?" he asked. "He's a music teacher, not a secretary."

Dave smiled and said, "Wait. There's more. Mr. Murray also said that other departments would be upgraded with computers, too. Your father is going to have to play some kind of digital keyboard, and teach it to students, too."

Tano laughed when he heard that.

"My father—a computerized keyboard? No way. He barely knows how to set his alarm clock."

"Hey," Dave responded, "I'm just telling you what I
130   heard. But you can't repeat it. Promise?"

"I promise."

For the next hour, Tano taught Dave how to play his new video games. There was no more talk about Tano's piano practicing or about the possible changes in school.

On Monday morning, Tano's father stopped his son in the school hallway.

"Son," his father said, "I'll be home a little late this evening. There's a big faculty meeting today after school. I have no idea what it's about."

140   Tano suspected why the meeting was called. He was tempted to tell his father, but remembered his promise to Dave.

When Dad returned home in the early evening, Tano was sitting at the piano, practicing. Dad sat down and listened as Tano finished his exercises.

"Very nice, son," Dad said with a smile. "Your mother would be quite proud of you."

Tano and his father went into the kitchen and began to make dinner together. Neither one of them knew how to prepare any fancy dishes. But they were great at making tuna casserole, which had become their favorite meal. When it was ready, the two sat down at the table to eat.

"So how did your meeting go?" Tano asked.

"Okay, I guess," Dad sighed.

"You don't sound so happy about that," Tano said.

For a while, the two ate in silence. Then Dad spoke up.

"Actually, the meeting was kind of upsetting," he confessed. "I guess the world is changing a little too fast for me. The principal announced that my music department would now have to **incorporate** digital equipment. He said that's what today's students want, and that's what the state board of education now wants. Only, it's not what I want. I can't play on a computer."

Tano asked, "Won't the school send you to take a course or something? They can't just expect you to learn it on your own, can they?"

"Well, they're planning to offer an in-service course," Dad explained. "They'll even pay me to take it. But I'm worried that I may not be able to master these new instruments. You know how I am with anything **electronic.**"

Tano sat quietly for a moment. He wasn't sure exactly what to say.

"My biggest problem," Dad continued, "is that I honestly don't understand why we need **computerized** keyboards. A piano is a piano. It was good enough for Bach, Beethoven, and Brahms. It should be good enough for kids today."

INFER

Re-read lines 148–152. Underline the things that Tano and his dad do together. What do their activities reveal about their relationship?

_____

_____

_____

_____

_____

VOCABULARY DEVELOPMENT

incorporate (in·kôr′pə·rāt′) v.: bring together into a single whole; merge.

Incorporate is built on the Latin word *corporare*, meaning "make into a body."

electronic (i·lek′trän′ik) adj.: operated or produced by the action of electrons.

Electronic is built on the word *electron,* which in turn is built on the word *electric.*

computerized (kəm·pyo͞ot′ər·īzd′) adj.: operated by means of a computer.

Computerized is built on the Latin word *putare,* meaning "count."

DECODING TIP

Divide the word *harpsichord* (line 181) into syllables. Draw a line between each syllable.

INFER

Pause at line 188. Underline what Tano has just said that explains why his dad hugs him.

INFER

Pause at line 205. How have Tano and his dad solved their problems?

_____

_____

_____

_____

_____

_____

_____

_____

_____

_____

VOCABULARY DEVELOPMENT

inspiration (in′spə·rā′shən) *n.:* creativity; brilliance.

Inspiration is built on the Latin *inspiratio,* meaning "breath in."

Tano let out a little laugh.

"What's so funny?" Dad asked.

180 "Well, Dad, I think you probably know that Bach actually played on a harpsichord not on a piano."

His father smiled. "My wise guy son," he laughed. "And when did you become such a music expert?"

"Well," Tano smiled, "I happen to be taking piano lessons, remember? And I've got a great teacher!"

Dad got up and gave Tano a big hug.

"Thanks. I needed that."

"So did I, Dad."

Dad said, "So what am I going to do about this whole 190 digital thing? The school expects me to start teaching with it in September."

A big smile crossed Tano's face.

"Say, Dad, I know a computer expert who could probably help you out. He knows something about the piano. He's even been taking lessons recently. Between his computer knowledge and your music knowledge, I'll bet you'd make a great team."

Tano's father smiled a big smile, too.

"So," he asked, "would this expert of yours be willing 200 to help me out?"

"Sure he would," Tano laughed.

"And would he keep taking his piano lessons?" Dad asked.

"He'd have to," Tano replied. "Just to be able to teach you how to play a digitized keyboard."

For a while, Tano and his father just sat at the table, laughing together. Tano laughed so hard that a tear rolled down his cheek. Finally, in a burst of **inspiration,** Dad spoke up.

210   "Hey, what do you say we have a bunch of grapes for dessert?" he suggested.

     "How about an orange?" Tano laughed.

INFER

Why do you think Tano suggests an orange for dessert?

_____

_____

_____

_____

_____

_____

_____

OWN THE STORY

PRACTICING THE STANDARDS

Characterization   Complete the "It Says, I Say, And So" chart on the following page. Share your completed chart with a classmate. Discuss ways in which your ideas about the story's characters are similar and/or different. You can use your chart to write an analysis of Tano or his dad.

KEEPING TRACK

Personal Word List   Enter the new words you learned from this story in your Personal Word List. As you listen to or watch news stories about technology, listen for some of the words you learned.

Personal Reading Log   As you record this title in your Personal Reading Log, note your general impressions of the story. Give yourself 4 points on the Reading Meter.

Checklist for Standards Mastery   Use the Checklist for Standards Mastery to check your progress in mastering the standards.

The Musician ▪ *Interactive Reading,* page 48

Interact with a Literary Text

"It Says, I Say, And So" Chart   Use this chart to make inferences about the characters in "The Musician." First, read the question. You may write several comments under the "It Says" and "I Say" columns. Write one response, or inference, that answers the numbered question in the "And So" column.

Question	It Says (What the text says)	I Say (My thoughts)	And So (My inference)
1. How does Tano feel about his dad at the beginning of the story?			
2. Do Tano and his dad respect each other?			
3. Have Tano and his dad changed in any ways by the end of the story?			

Mother and Daughter

Interact with a Literary Text

Character Comparison-and-Contrast Chart   When you **compare** characters, you tell how they are alike. When you **contrast** them, you tell how they are different. You can compare and contrast characters' words, looks, actions, and thoughts. You can also compare and contrast the way other people respond to them. Comparing and contrasting deepen your understanding of a character.

After you read "Mother and Daughter," fill out this chart. Find details in the story that show how Yollie and Mrs. Moreno are alike and different.

What is Yollie like?	What is Mrs. Moreno like?	How are Yollie and Mrs. Moreno similar?
Yollie . . .	Mrs. Moreno . . .	Both . . .

The Smallest Dragonboy

for use with
Holt Literature and Language Arts,
page 119

Interact with a Literary Text

Character-Traits Chart   A **character trait** is a quality in a person that can't be seen. Generosity, cruelty, kindness, jealousy, shyness—all are character traits. Sometimes a writer will tell you directly what a character's traits are, but more often traits are revealed through what a character says and does. When you read how a character faces a challenge or reacts to loss, you discover what kind of person he or she is.

The chart below lists key details from the story that reveal something about Keevan. Use the "It Says, I Say, And So" strategy to make inferences about what these details reveal about Keevan. Then, list Keevan's character traits below each event.

Character: Keevan			
What Keevan Does	**What Keevan Says**	**What the Writer Says**	**What Others Say**
Keevan drags himself to the Impression with a broken leg.	"You better make sure a dragon sees you this time, Beterli."	Keevan enjoys listening to the oldest dragonriders.	"You may be the smallest dragon-rider ever, young K'van," Flar said, "but you're one of the bravest."
Trait	**Trait**	**Trait**	**Trait**

Here Be Dragons

Interact with an Informational Text

Venn Diagram   "Here Be Dragons" compares and contrasts
Eastern and Western dragons using a structure called the block
method. In the block method, a writer first discusses all the features
of subject 1, then all the features of subject 2.

Use the organization of "Here Be Dragons" to sort out the
similarities and differences between Eastern and Western dragons.
Note the differences in each circle. In the center, where the circles
overlap, note the similarities.

Dragons

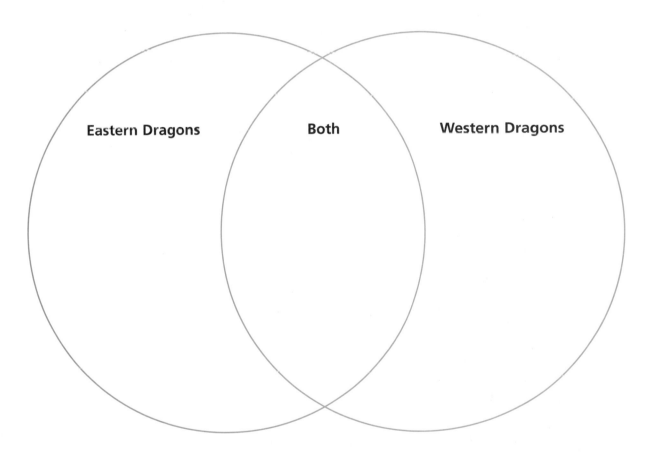

Eastern Dragons   Both   Western Dragons

A Rice Sandwich

CHARACTER

Interact with a Literary Text

Character-Analysis Questionnaire   You analyze a character by examining the character's actions, speech, appearance, thoughts, and effects on other people. When you analyze a character, you almost always also want to evaluate how realistic or believable the character is. You ask: Is this character like a person I might know in real life?

Answering the questions in this character-analysis questionnaire will help you analyze the character of Esperanza.

Character: Esperanza

1. What does Esperanza do in the story?

2. What are Esperanza's thoughts and feelings?

3. How do other characters respond to Esperanza?

4. Is Esperanza like people you know? Explain.

My Analysis of Esperanza

_____

_____

_____

_____

_____

The Tejano Soul of San Antonio

Interact with an Informational Text

Evidence Chart   Informational texts usually include facts. They may also include the writer's opinions. A **fact** is information that can be proved to be true. An **opinion** is a writer's belief and cannot be proved to be true or false. However, writers can offer **valid opinions:** opinions that are supported by evidence. An **invalid opinion** is based solely on emotions or feelings; there is no evidence to back it up.

The main idea of "The Tejano Soul of San Antonio" is that the city of San Antonio has a Tejano soul. Fill in this chart by listing four facts and four opinions that support the writer's main idea.

Topic: San Antonio Has a Tejano Soul	
Facts	Opinions

Literature

AUTHOR STUDY

Both of **Sandra Cisneros**'s parents are of Mexican ancestry. Her father was born in Mexico; her mother was born on Chicago's South Side, where Sandra grew up. The family traveled back and forth between Mexico and Chicago so often that it's not surprising that all her life Sandra longed for a nice little house of her own, like the ones she saw on television or read about in books. There is probably a lot of Sandra Cisneros in the character of Esperanza, the young girl who narrates the series of stories in *The House on Mango Street.* Cisneros eventually got her own home. It's in San Antonio, Texas, and it's painted purple, which she says is a Mexican color.

BEFORE YOU READ

Before you read, you should know the following facts:

- The first selection is a poem. *Abuelito* is Spanish for "grandfather."
- The stories are not traditional short stories. They are short, short stories, or **vignettes** (vin·yets') (and they all are linked in the book called *The House on Mango Street*).
- The stories are told by the little Latina girl Esperanza. (If you speak Spanish, you know what Esperanza's name means in English.)

Reading Standard 3.3 Analyze characterization as delineated through a character's thoughts, words, speech patterns, and actions; the narrator's description; and the thoughts, words, and actions of other characters.

Four Selections

Sandra Cisneros

Abuelito Who

Abuelito who throws coins like rain

and asks who loves him

who is dough and feathers

who is a watch and glass of water

5   whose hair is made of fur

is too sad to come downstairs today

who tells me in Spanish you are my diamond

who tells me in English you are my sky

whose little eyes are string

10   can't come out to play

sleeps in his little room all night and day

who used to laugh like the letter *k*

is sick

is a doorknob tied to a sour stick

15   is tired shut the door

doesn't live here anymore

is hiding underneath the bed

who talks to me inside my head

is blankets and spoons and big brown shoes

20   who snores up and down up and down up and down again

is the rain on the roof that falls like coins

asking who loves him

who loves him who?

INFER

Circle the words that describe how Abuelito throws coins. Underline the words that tell what he asks. What can you tell about Abuelito based on these actions?

_____

_____

_____

_____

_____

INFER

Circle the word in line 13 that tells why Abuelito can't come downstairs to play. Draw a line from that word to two words that tell how it makes him feel. What is happening to Abuelito?

_____

_____

INFER

How does the speaker feel about her *abuelito?*

_____

_____

_____

_____

_____

_____

VOCABULARY DEVELOPMENT

appreciate (ə·prē′shē·āt′) v.: think well of; enjoy.

ferocious (fə·rō′shəs) adj.: very great. *Ferocious* can also mean "fierce" or "savage."

despite (di·spīt′) prep.: in defiance of.

INFER

In the third paragraph, what do the trees teach the narrator?

_____

_____

_____

INFER

In the last paragraph, circle the three words that tell you how the narrator feels when she looks at the trees. How do the trees help her?

_____

_____

_____

_____

Four Skinny Trees

They are the only ones who understand me. I am the only one who understands them. Four skinny trees with skinny necks and pointy elbows like mine. Four who do not belong here but are here. Four raggedy excuses planted by the city. From our room we can hear them, but Nenny just sleeps and doesn't **appreciate** these things.

Their strength is secret. They send **ferocious** roots beneath the ground. They grow up and they grow down and grab the earth between their hairy toes and bite the sky 10 with violent teeth and never quit their anger. This is how they keep.

Let one forget his reason for being, they'd all droop like tulips in a glass, each with their arms around the other. Keep, keep, keep, trees say when I sleep. They teach.

When I am too sad and too skinny to keep keeping, when I am a tiny thing against so many bricks, then it is I look at trees. When there is nothing left to look at on this street. Four who grew **despite** concrete. Four who reach and do not forget to reach. Four whose only reason is to 20 be and be.

Bums in the Attic

I want a house on a hill like the ones with the gardens where Papa works. We go on Sundays, Papa's day off. I used to go. I don't anymore. You don't like to go out with us, Papa says. Getting too old? Getting too stuck-up, says Nenny. I don't tell them I am ashamed—all of us staring out the window like the hungry. I am tired of looking at what we can't have. When we win the lottery . . . Mama begins, and then I stop listening.

People who live on hills sleep so close to the stars they
10 forget those of us who live too much on earth. They don't look down at all except to be **content** to live on hills. They have nothing to do with last week's garbage or fear of rats. Night comes. Nothing wakes them but the wind.

One day I'll own my own house, but I won't forget who I am or where I came from. Passing bums will ask, Can I come in? I'll offer them the attic, ask them to stay, because I know how it is to be without a house.

Some days after dinner, guests and I will sit in front of a fire. Floorboards will squeak upstairs. The attic grumble.
20 Rats? they'll ask.
Bums, I'll say, and I'll be happy.

VOCABULARY DEVELOPMENT

content (kən·tent′) *adj.:* happy enough with what one has; satisfied.

Content is made up of the Latin prefix *con-,* meaning "with" or "together," and the Latin word *tener,* meaning "have" or "hold."

If you put the accent on the first syllable (kän′tent′), what does the word mean?

_____

_____

_____

INFER

Is the story's narrator generous? Explain. Box the text that helps you make your inference.

_____

_____

_____

_____

_____

_____

Sandra Cisneros   **65**

_____

_____

_____

A House of My Own

Not a flat. Not an apartment in back. Not a man's house. Not a daddy's. A house all my own. With my porch and my pillow, my pretty purple petunias. My books and my stories. My two shoes waiting beside the bed. Nobody to shake a stick at. Nobody's garbage to pick up after.

Only a house quiet as snow, a space for myself to go, clean as paper before the poem.

OWN THE SELECTIONS

PRACTICING THE STANDARDS

Characterization   A young girl speaks to you in a poem about her *abuelito* and in three stories. On a separate sheet of paper, write three sentences in which you describe the main character traits of this young girl. Then, cite three details from the poem and from the stories that support your analysis.

KEEPING TRACK

Personal Word List   There aren't many words at all in these selections, and very few of them are hard. Zero in on the ones that are new to you that you'd like to add to your Personal Word List.

Personal Reading Log   Which of the four selections did you like the best? Why? Which did you like the least? Why? Record your reactions to the selections in your Personal Reading Log. Then, give yourself 4 points on the Reading Meter.

Checklist for Standards Mastery   See how well you are mastering the standards, using the Checklist for Standards Mastery.

Four Selections ■ *Interactive Reading,* page 63

Go Beyond a Literary Text

Mexico Use the library and the Internet to gather information for a report on some aspect of Mexico, the country that Sandra Cisneros's family came from. To gather ideas for research, use the following chart. Choose a topic that you find interesting and for which there is lots of resource material. Be sure to keep track of where you find your information.

Subject Ideas	Internet Search	Library Search
Brief history of Mexico		
Mexican writers and artists		
Mexican tourism		
Great archaeological sites in Mexico		
The Aztec Empire		
Mexican-American War		

BEFORE YOU READ

This page from *The World Almanac for Kids* presents information about languages. Much of the information is given in the form of charts. The first chart shows the number of native speakers of the most commonly spoken languages in the world. The second chart shows the top twenty languages used at home in the United States. You can gain a lot of information from an almanac by comparing and contrasting the data presented.

When you read a chart, keep in mind these details about its structure:
• It may contain statistics and other scientific or mathematical data.
• A column reads from the top down; a row reads from left to right.
• Column and row headings identify the kind of information presented in each.

Reading Standard 2.2 (Grade 6 Review) Analyze text that uses the compare-and-contrast organizational pattern.

from **The World Almanac for Kids**

Top Ten Languages

VOCABULARY DEVELOPMENT

principal (prin′sə·pəl) *adj.:* first in rank or importance.

IDENTIFY

When were these two surveys of languages done? Underline the dates. Why are dates important to note in surveys like these?

_____

_____

_____

_____

10

Would you have guessed that Mandarin, the **principal** language of China, is the most common spoken language in the world? You may find more surprises in the chart on the following page, which lists languages spoken in 1999 by at least 100,000,000 native speakers (those for whom the language is their first language, or mother tongue) and some of the places where each one is spoken.

TOP TEN WORLD LANGUAGES 1999

Language	Where Spoken	Native Speakers
Mandarin	China, Taiwan	885,000,000
Hindi	India	375,000,000
Spanish	Spain, Latin America	358,000,000
English	U.S., Canada, Britain	347,000,000
Arabic	Arabian Peninsula	211,000,000
Bengali	India, Bangladesh	210,000,000
Portuguese	Portugal, Brazil	178,000,000
Russian	Russia	165,000,000
Japanese	Japan	125,000,000
German	Germany, Austria	100,000,000

20

Which Languages Are Spoken in the United States?

Since the beginning of American history, **immigrants** have come to the United States from all over the world and brought their native languages with them.

30 The table below lists the most frequently spoken languages in the United States, as of the 1990 **census,** starting with English. The number for English is the number of people who speak only English at home.

TOP TWENTY LANGUAGES IN THE U.S. 1990

Language Used at Home	Speakers over 5 Years Old
1. English only	198,601,000
2. Spanish	17,339,000
3. French	1,702,000
4. German	1,547,000
5. Italian	1,309,000
6. Chinese	1,249,000
7. Tagalog	843,000
8. Polish	723,000
9. Korean	626,000

40

Continued on next page.

Continued on next page.

TEXT STRUCTURE

What are the column headings of the chart at the top of the page? Circle them.

VOCABULARY DEVELOPMENT

immigrants (im′ə·grənts) *n.*: persons who settle in a new country or region.

Immigrants is made up of the prefix *im-*, meaning "in," the Latin word *migrare*, meaning "wander" or "move," and the suffix *-ant*, meaning "one who."

census (sen′səs) *n.*: official, periodic count of population and recording of economic status, age, gender, and so on.

Census comes from the Latin word *censere*, which means "assess."

COMPARE & CONTRAST

Using the chart on pages 69–70, how would you compare the number of Spanish speakers worldwide with the number of people over five years old who speak Spanish in the United States?

_____

_____

_____

_____

_____

_____

TOP TWENTY LANGUAGES IN THE U.S. 1990

(Continued from page 69.)

Language Used at Home	Speakers over 5 Years Old
10. Vietnamese	507,000
11. Portuguese	430,000
12. Japanese	428,000
13. Greek	388,000
14. Arabic	355,000
15. Hindi, Urdu, related languages	331,000
16. Russian	242,000
17. Yiddish	213,000
18. Thai	206,000
19. Persian	202,000
20. French Creole	188,000

50

OWN THE TEXT

PRACTICING THE STANDARDS

Analyze Text Team up with a partner. Take turns asking your partner questions based on information in the charts. For example: What is the second language most frequently used at home in the United States? The tenth most frequently used? Evaluate your partner's ability to locate information.

KEEPING TRACK

Personal Word List Record the new words you learned from this almanac in your Personal Word List.

Personal Reading Log Record this article in your Personal Reading Log. Give yourself 2 points on the Reading Meter.

Checklist for Standards Mastery Track your progress, using the Checklist for Standards Mastery.

Top Ten Languages  *Interactive Reading,* **page 68**

Go Beyond an Informational Text

Almanac An **almanac** is a reference book that contains facts and information. An almanac contains both written information and graphic organizers such as charts and tables. Many almanacs provide charts that show the differences between regions (in climate, geography, population, and so on).

Try it yourself! Make your own almanac page. Include a chart that shows how two regions differ in some way.

Your chart should include the following:
* a title that describes the information
* column headings that describe your topic
* row headings that identify the kind of information in that row
* statistical information

You may want to use the following chart as a starting point:

	Population	Rainfall/ Snowfall	Average Temperature
Region 1			
Region 2			

Literature

BEFORE YOU READ

How many languages do you know? Can you understand some words in another language? How does mastery of a language help you? This story is about a girl who learns the importance of speaking Spanish, her mother's native language, when she moves from Brooklyn, New York, to Panama.

Here are some details you should know before you read this story, which is part of a novel titled *Marisol and Magdalena.*

* Panama is a small country located in Central America. Spanish is the main language spoken there. *Abuela* means "grandmother" in Spanish.
* Marisol is a teenager from Brooklyn, New York. Her best friend there is Magdalena, or Magda. Marisol is sent by her mother to Panama to visit her grandmother (Abuela) for a year. Marisol's mother hopes that Marisol will learn more about Panama.

Reading Standard 3.3
Analyze characterization as delineated through a character's thoughts, words, speech patterns, and actions; the narrator's description; and the thoughts, words, and actions of other characters.

from Marisol and Magdalena

Learning to Float

Veronica Chambers

IDENTIFY

Who is telling you this story—who is the narrator?

_____

_____

_____

_____

_____

Abuela woke me up early. "We have to go to the market," she said, shaking me gently. "We don't have all day."

"*Abuela, please,*" I begged. "Five more minutes."

"Forget about it," she said, flipping on the lights and turning on the clock radio full blast. "I hope you like pancakes."

I sat up in the bed, groggy but hungry. "With blueberries?" I asked.

"You're in Panama," Abuela said, laughing. "Bananas or

10 coconut?"

Banana pancakes? Coconut pancakes? They both sounded pretty strange. "Can I get them mixed together?" I asked.

"Definitely," she said. "Now don't take all day in the shower."

I picked up the neatly folded pink towel that Abuela laid on my bed.

"You know, Mami was worried that you might be too poor to have an extra towel," I said.

20 "I can afford extra towels," Abuela said, waving her hand as if to dismiss the idea. "My retirement check isn't much, but I manage."

"Why don't you move to America?" I asked. "You could live with me and Mami."

"Why don't you move to Panama?" Abuela asked, placing her hand on her hip.

"I just *did*," I reminded her.

Abuela didn't say anything at first. She looked at me with a faraway look in her eye, then she nodded her head.

30 "I guess that's true," she said, smiling. "Now, don't be all day in the shower."

My banana-coconut pancakes were delicious, the best I'd ever had. And by eight o'clock Abuela and I were out the door. The market wasn't a grocery store as I had imagined it to be. It was more like a street fair, with people selling everything from spices to fruit and rice from stalls. Walking past the different *vendedores* selling their wares, I wondered if they could tell I was American. I was dressed in my favorite pair of jeans and my "Girls Rule" T-shirt. Most of

INFER

Re-read lines 7–10, and underline the names of fruits. What do you know about these fruits? How does Marisol's choice show that she has not been in Panama before?

_____

_____

_____

_____

_____

_____

_____

_____

FLUENCY

Take the role of Marisol or Abuela, and read and act out the boxed passage with another student. Underline the words that you will emphasize, or say in a louder voice.

_____

_____

_____

_____

Circle the word *vendors*.
Then find and circle the
word that looks almost like
vendors printed in italics in
the previous paragraph.
Read the words nearby that
help explain its meaning.
Vendors and *vendedores*
have the same meaning.
What does *vendors* mean?

_____

_____

_____

_____

DECODING TIP

Circle the word *practicando*.
Draw a line from this word
to another word in the
paragraph that resembles it.
What might *practicando*
mean?

_____

_____

_____

INFER

Look through the part of the
story you have read so far.
Box words and phrases that
reveal Marisol's problems
with speaking Spanish. How
would you feel in her place?

_____

_____

_____

40   the other girls I saw wore brightly colored sundresses, like
the one Ana had worn the day before.

When we stopped to buy rice or fruit, the vendors
always greeted me in Spanish and expected me to understand. I did, for the most part, but I was still nervous about
trying to use my Spanish. So when people spoke to me, I
nodded and smiled.

"You're going to have to speak Spanish at some point,"
Abuela said. I was surprised that she had noticed that I
wasn't talking.

50   "*La unica manera de mejorarse es practicando*," Abuela
said, taking my hand and leading me down another row of
vendedores. "The only way you'll get better is to practice."

"You don't understand," I said. "At home people make
fun of my Spanish."

"*People?*" Abuela asked, raising one eyebrow. "People
like who?"

"Like Roxana and my friend Magda's brothers
and sister."

"*No importa*," Abuela said. "It doesn't matter now.
60   You'll be speaking like a native in no time at all. That is,
if you speak. You've got to open your mouth and try."

We passed a stall where a woman was selling
homemade cookies. "Can I have some?" I asked Abuela.

She just looked at me. "I don't know," she said.
"Ask her."

I walked up to the woman's table and spoke slowly.
"*Buenos días, señora*."

The lady smiled and asked me what I wanted. "*Buenos
días, niña. Qué quieres?*"

70   "*Quiero dos galletes de chocolate*," I said. "I want two
chocolate cookies."

Just then, I felt a finger poke me in the back. "*No dices por favor?*" Abuela said.

"Please," I added.

The woman smiled again and handed me the cookies in a little plastic bag. I thanked her and we walked away.

"You spoke Spanish and no one laughed," Abuela said, raising her left eyebrow.

"No one laughed," I said, taking a bite of a cookie.

80   Two weeks later Abuela **registered** me for school. It was the first week of August and I couldn't help but feel that my summer vacation had been cut in half. At the school, Abuela and I met the guidance counselor, a woman named Mrs. Ortiz. She was beautiful—tall and dark skinned with wavy shoulder-length hair.

"All of your teachers speak English," Mrs. Ortiz explained. "They'll give you as much help as you need."

I looked at the printed schedule she had handed me. I was taking Spanish, English literature, and math in

90   the morning. Then science, history, gym, and art in the afternoon.

"Well, I think you're all set," Abuela said, standing up. "Make sure to meet Ana to walk home from school."

"Bye, Abuela," I said, smiling.

"This is really a terrific opportunity for you," Mrs. Ortiz said as we walked to my first class. "**Immersion** is the best way to learn a language. Maybe you could tutor one of the students in English, and the student could tutor you in Spanish. I'll talk to your homeroom teacher, Señora

100   Baptiste, about setting something up."

VOCABULARY DEVELOPMENT

registered (rej'is·tərd) *v.:* recorded or enrolled.

Registered comes from the Latin word *registrare,* which means "record."

immersion (i·mur'zhən) *n.:* act of being totally absorbed in studies or a culture.

Immersion comes from the Latin prefix *in-,* meaning "into" and the Latin word *mergere,* meaning "dip, plunge into, or sink." In this context, *immersion* means "be completely absorbed and surrounded by a new culture and language" as if being plunged into the "sea" of the new culture.

· · · · · · Notes · · · · · · ·

Look for familiar English word parts in the Spanish sentence *No te preocupes.* Underline the word or word parts you recognize. What does the Spanish sentence mean?

_____

_____

_____

_____

_____

_____

_____

Use context clues to figure out the meaning of the Spanish sentence *Estás de moda* in line 123. Circle those clues. What does the phrase mean?

_____

_____

_____

_____

_____

_____

_____

_____

_____

I started cracking my knuckles as soon as I walked into my homeroom class with Mrs. Ortiz. Standing in front of a classroom of total strangers was *not* my idea of a good time.

"Class, I want you to meet Marisol Mayaguéz," Señora Baptiste said.

It was strange hearing how Panamanian my name sounded, when I didn't feel Panamanian at all. I stared down at a square on the floor.

110   "You'll be fine," Mrs. Ortiz said. *"No te preocupes."*

At lunchtime I walked into the cafeteria. I just couldn't stop cracking my knuckles. It was the most knuckle cracking I'd ever done and my fingers were starting to hurt. Then I saw Ana, waving to me.

"Marisol, *ven aca,*" Ana said. "I saved you a place at my table."

I was relieved that I wouldn't have to sit alone, but afraid to sit at a table where all the kids spoke nothing but Spanish.

120   Ana was wearing a blue sundress with white flowers all over it, the same orange sandals, and the same orange-tinted sunglasses.

"*Estás de moda,* Ana," I said. "You look great."

"Thanks," she said, standing up and giving a little spin. "I guess I'm stylish enough for America."

I wasn't sure about that, but I didn't say anything. Ana was my only chance at a new friend so far. I wasn't going to hurt her feelings by telling her that the girls I knew in New York would never wear an outfit like hers.

130   After school I met Ana, and we walked home together.

"Tell me all about Nueva York," Ana said as we walked down the tiny winding street. "Do you know how lucky you are to come from New York, the Big Apple? *Wow!*"

"Well, nobody in New York calls it the Big Apple," I said, laughing.

"Do you go to clubs every night?" Ana asked, talking as fast in English as she did in Spanish. "Do you meet lots of rock stars and famous people?"

"As if," I said, jumping down a hopscotch drawn on the
140   sidewalk. At least some things were the same in Panama.

"*As if*," Ana repeated. "*Que significa* as if?"

"It means no way," I explained.

"So what do you do for fun?" Ana asked.

"Me and my best friend, Magda, we watch music videos and play punchball in the park," I said, shrugging. "Just regular stuff."

"Your regular stuff sounds *muy divertido* to me," Ana said.

"Do you have a best friend?" I asked as we crossed
150   the street. I knew where I was now. Abuela's apartment building was at the end of the block.

Ana scratched her arm and looked down. "I did have a best friend," she said quietly. "Her name was Digna. But she's not here anymore. She moved to Nicaragua to live with her father. I had to start the school year completely by myself."

I thought about Magda in New York. We were going to take Roberto Clemente Junior High School by storm this year—drill team, honor roll, everything. Now I was here
160   starting the school year completely by myself and Magda was there—in New York, without me.

DECODING TIP

What does *Nueva* in line 131 mean? Circle the context clue that states its meaning.

_____

DECODING TIP

Underline a familiar English word part in the Spanish phrase *Que significa* in line 141. Then circle a context clue that follows. What does the sentence mean?

_____

_____

_____

_____

INFER

Box the information about Ana's and Marisol's old friends. How are the girls' situations similar? How do you think they feel? Do you predict they will become friends? Why or why not?

_____

_____

_____

_____

_____

_____

INFER

In line 167, underline Marisol's allusion to a popular movie. What does she mean?

_____
_____
_____
_____
_____

WORD KNOWLEDGE

Underline the translation of *Como te fue hoy?* What does *cena* probably mean?

_____
_____

INFER

Pause at line 189. What might the narrator be feeling? How do you know?

_____
_____
_____
_____
_____
_____
_____

"I'm glad you came to Panama," Ana said, opening the door to her apartment.

"Thanks, Ana," I said. I stood on the porch for a second. Looking out onto Panama City, the palm trees blowing in the wind.

I thought about the scene in *The Wizard of Oz,* when Dorothy says, "We're not in Kansas anymore, Toto." That was exactly how I felt, and I didn't even have a dog to tell it
170 to. I was in this on my own.

"Como te fue hoy?" Abuela asked, wiping her hands on her apron. "How'd it go today?"

"Not bad," I said, trying to smile. "Not bad at all."

"OK, we'll talk over *cena,*" she said. "You go and relax."

I kept thinking about what Mrs. Ortiz had said, about how coming to Panama was an opportunity. She had said the best way to learn a language was through "immersion." It was a funny word—immersion. I kind of knew what it meant, but I had never heard anybody actually use the
180 word in regular conversation.

I went into the living room, to the shelf where Abuela kept all her books. I pulled out the *American Heritage Dictionary* that I had spotted a few days before. I opened it and was surprised to see my mother's maiden name, Inez Velásquez, written in her same perfect handwriting.

This dictionary must have belonged to Mami when she was in school, I thought, and even though it was just a book, I held it to my chest for a second.

I sat on Abuela's old red couch, the couch filled with
190 stuffing that had popped out on the side. I opened the dictionary and flipped to the I's. The word was listed under

its root word—*immerse.* The definition read: IMMERSE—
1. TO PLUNGE INTO A FLUID. 2. TO BAPTIZE BY
SUBMERGING IN WATER. 3. TO ABSORB, ENGROSS.

I thought about what I was doing last summer, at
exactly this time. I was in New York, and Tío Ricardo,
Magda's father, was teaching Magda and me how to swim
at the Y. He insisted that all we had to do was jump into the
cold water. Every day, he waited for us on the deep side of
200   the pool and held out his arms as we **plunged** in. He let us
struggle for a second, then pulled us up out of the water.
Eventually, we stopped struggling and started to float.

Holding Mami's dictionary open on my lap, I closed
my eyes and remembered how dark it had been underneath
the water, how the pool water burned going up my nose,
how the chlorine stung my eyes. Magda had been her usual
fearless self, but I was so scared.

Sitting in Abuela's living room, I remembered when
my arms and legs began to move in sync. It wasn't more
210   than a dog paddle, but it was the first time that I actually
didn't sink like a stone.

Panama—the language, the place, the people—was like
that pool, only deeper and wider.

There were oceans that now separated me from everything and everyone I'd ever known. But Tío Ricardo had
taught me that it was the body's natural **instinct** to float.

"Don't fight so hard to swim, *hija,*" he had said when I
splashed and splashed like my life depended on it.

"It'll come naturally," he said.

220   Now I was *immersed* again, plunged into this place that
everyone in my family called home.

"I've jumped in. Tío Ricardo always said that's the
hardest part," I whispered to myself as I put the dictionary
back on the shelf. "Now let's see if I can swim."

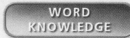

WORD
KNOWLEDGE

Tío is the Spanish word for
"uncle."

VOCABULARY
DEVELOPMENT

plunged (plunjd) *v.:* threw
oneself into a place or
situation.

instinct (in'stiŋkt') *n.:* inborn
tendency to behave in a
certain way.

INFER

What do you think Marisol
means in the last sentence of
the story? How does this
explain the title "Learning to
Float"?

_____

_____

_____

_____

_____

_____

_____

_____

_____

_____

_____

_____

OWN THE STORY

Analyzing Character   How well do you understand Marisol? Find three of Marisol's actions or statements that reveal her character to you. Then, write a paragraph analyzing Marisol's character—as it is revealed in this part of the novel. Open your paragraph with a sentence that names three character traits you noticed in Marisol. Then, describe Marisol's actions or quote her words that support your analysis.

_____

_____

_____

_____

_____

_____

_____

_____

_____

_____

_____

KEEPING TRACK

Personal Word List   Record the new words you learned from this story in your Personal Word List. Note also the Spanish words you learned, along with their meanings in English.

Personal Reading Log   Note your answer to this question: Would you like to read the novel that this story is taken from? Record the title of this story in your Personal Reading Log. Give yourself 4 points on the Reading Meter.

Checklist for Standards Mastery   Check your progress in mastering the standards. Review the standards you had trouble with, and work to improve your understanding.

Learning to Float *from* Marisol and Magdalena ■ *Interactive Reading,* page 72

Go Beyond a Literary Text

Prediction Chart   You have just read a chapter from the novel *Marisol and Magdalena.* In this selection from the novel, Marisol has left her home in Brooklyn to live in Panama for a year. Review what you know about the character of Marisol, and complete this prediction chart.

Question	Prediction	Story details supporting my prediction
Will Marisol and Ana become friends?		
Will Marisol learn to speak Spanish like a native speaker?		
What problems and conflicts might be ahead for Marisol?		

Chapter 3

Themes Across Time

Chapter Preview   In this chapter you will—

Strategy Launch: "Save the Last Word for Me"

LITERARY FOCUS: IDENTIFY AND ANALYZE THEME

A story's **theme** is what the story has to say about life. For example, the hero of a story faces impossible odds to rescue someone. After rescuing the person, the hero disappears and never takes credit for his good deed. That's what happens in the story, but what is the writer saying about human experience? You might decide that the theme of that story is "bravery is its own reward," or "truly brave people don't need recognition for their bravery."

A STRATEGY THAT WORKS: "SAVE THE LAST WORD FOR ME"

Writers don't usually directly come out and state the theme of a story. Instead, the writer invites you, the reader, to interpret the theme in your own way. To do this, think about what happened in the story, and relate it to your own knowledge and experience.

A strategy that can help you identify a theme is called "Save the Last Word for Me."

POINTERS FOR USING "SAVE THE LAST WORD FOR ME"

⟫➡ Read the story. Circle or underline passages that stand out.

⟫➡ Re-read the story. Locate the most significant passage.

⟫➡ Copy the passage; then write about why you chose it. Tell why you liked the passage or why you think it is important.

⟫➡ Read to your classmates the passage you copied from the text.

⟫➡ After listening to the passage you chose, your classmates should say what the passage means to them. Afterward, reveal your comments about the passage.

⟫➡ Discuss how your ideas were the same or different.

Reading Standard 1.1 Identify idioms, analogies, metaphors, and similes in prose and poetry.

Reading Standard 2.3 Analyze text that uses the cause-and-effect organizational pattern.

Reading Standard 3.4 Identify and analyze recurring themes across works (for example, the value of bravery, loyalty, and friendship; the effects of loneliness).

Practice Read

Get ready to sink your teeth into an adventure story with the rhyming rhythm of a poem! In this selection the legendary story of Robin Hood is retold as a narrative poem. "Robin Hood" has a hair-raising plot, fascinating characters, and a happy ending. Enjoy it!

Here's what you need to know before reading the poem:
- During the time of the story, King John ruled England. Under his rule the rich grew richer, and the poor grew poorer.
- Robin Hood and his merry band were highwaymen—men who robbed the rich and gave to the poor in olden times in England.

Robin Hood

retold by Meish Goldish

IDENTIFY

Pause at line 5. Underline the passage that tells you what Robin Hood's band does.

VOCABULARY DEVELOPMENT

foe (fō) *n.:* enemy.

· · · · · · Notes · · · · · ·

_____

_____

_____

_____

_____

Deep in the heart of Sherwood Forest, in Nottingham
    long ago,
There lived a band of merry men, and evil was their **foe.**
The merry band would help the poor, because their hearts
    were good.
The leader of that merry band was a man named Robin
    Hood,
5   A man named Robin Hood.

Robin was an outlaw, that's what rich folks said.
The sheriff of Nottingham hated him and meant to see
    him dead.
But the poor praised Robin as their hero, a good man
    brave and true.

He robbed the rich and gave to the poor, with his merry

    crew,

10   With his merry crew.

One of the crew was Friar Tuck, a fat and jolly priest.

He loved good Robin's worthy work and prayed it never

    ceased.

And even though all friars know that stealing is a sin,

Tuck said, "This stealing is allowed, so the **righteous** weak

    may win,

15   The righteous weak may win!"

Another member of the crew was a man called Little John.

His height was more than seven feet, a giant thereupon!

Skilled with bow and arrow, Little John could hit his mark,

A worthy aid to Robin Hood, in daylight or in dark,

20   In daylight or in dark.

In the olden days of England, King John ruled the land.

The King was a cruel **tyrant** whom the poor could not

    stand.

The poor had little property and worked hard, to the bone.

King John imposed high taxes on the meager land they

    owned,

25   The meager land they owned.

King John's soldiers and officers enforced his brutish laws.

They pounced on the powerless like a lion's angry claws.

They stole their money, they stole their grain,

They stole most everything, so nothing would remain,

30   So nothing would remain.

INTERPRET

Pause at line 15. Underline what Friar Tuck says. Why is his statement unusual?

_____

_____

_____

_____

_____

_____

_____

VOCABULARY DEVELOPMENT

righteous (rī'chəs) *adj.*: acting in a just, upright manner; doing what is right.

tyrant (tī'rənt) *n.*: cruel ruler.

INFER

Pause at line 30. Underline the actions of the king and his soldiers. What is the writer saying about how power affects people?

_____

_____

_____

_____

_____

Circle the name of the person who is compared to "a snake with a poisonous sting." This comparison is a **metaphor**, which compares two unlike things without using the word *like* or *as*. What does this metaphor tell you about the sheriff?

_____

_____

_____

_____

_____

Pause at line 40. What is Robin Hood threatening to do?

_____

_____

_____

_____

_____

_____

_____

justice (jus'tis) *n.:* fairness; the quality of being correct or right.

The evil sheriff of Nottingham cried, "Long live the King!"
The sheriff was, by all accounts, a snake with a poisonous
    sting.
Whenever the poor saw him, they'd shake like a leaf.
A visit from the sheriff brought a cry of stricken grief,
35   A cry of stricken grief.

Robin Hood heard their cries and said, "I know what I
    must do!
When a King's officer rides the road, I will be there, too."
Robin stopped the sheriff by surprise, and made a noose
    with rope.
He said, "Give me your money, or I'll leave you without
    hope,
40   I'll leave you without hope!"

That night, Robin and his men sneaked off to the grain
    house door.
Little John shot an arrow, and the lock fell to the floor.
The merry men broke inside, and put grain in every sack,
Then visited the poor at home, to give their stolen grain
    back,
45   To give the stolen grain back.

Word of Robin's daring deeds spread quickly near and far.
Justice was an outlaw; to the poor he was a star.
Robin and his merry men went robbing, day and night,
And gave their loot to the needy, an act of right against
    might,
50   An act of right against might.

And so did Robin's merry band of men then leave the
    woods.
Along the spacious countryside, they delivered precious
    goods.
The poor were very grateful for the help that Robin gave.
They hailed him a hero, so saintly and so brave,
55   So saintly and so brave.

Of course, King John would not describe Robin as a saint.
Of course, the sheriff of Nottingham had a similar
    complaint.
Now reader, you have learned the facts of Robin in his
    youth.
Was Robin Hood a hero or outlaw—what's the truth?
60   What's the honest truth?

INFER

Underline the poem's final question. What do you think the poet is hoping you will decide by answering this question?

_____

_____

_____

WORD KNOWLEDGE

An **idiom** is an expression used in a particular language. You cannot understand an idiom from the literal meaning of its words. Go back and underline the idiom "their hearts were good" in line 3. What does the idiom mean? What is the literal meaning of its words?

_____

_____

_____

_____

_____

Another idiom is in line 22. Underline "could not stand." What does "cannot stand" mean literally? What does the idiom mean?

_____

_____

_____

_____

_____

OWN THE POEM

Identifying Theme   Identify the theme of "Robin Hood." First, fill out the "Save the Last Word for Me" chart on the following page. Then, share your statement of the poem's theme with that of a classmate. Discuss reasons for your ideas.

Comparing Themes   How might this poem's ending be different if its theme were "Crime Doesn't Pay"? Explain. How would you compare this poem about an outlaw hero who fought a bad sheriff with "The Highwayman"? (See page 161 in *Holt Literature and Language Arts*.) Consider the hero of each poem, the powerful enemy each hero faced, and the outcome of each story.

_____

_____

_____

_____

_____

_____

KEEPING TRACK

Personal Word List   Record the words you learned from this story in your Personal Word List.

Personal Reading Log   Write your reaction to this rhyming tale in your Personal Reading Log. What did you enjoy about reading a story in the form of a poem? Do you think that it is difficult to write a story in this form? Why or why not? Give yourself 2 points on the Reading Meter.

Checklist for Standards Mastery   Use the Checklist for Standards Mastery to mark your progress in mastering the standards. Where did you make the most progress? Where did you make the least progress? How might you improve your grasp of literary concepts?

Robin Hood   *Interactive Reading,* page 84

Interact with a Literary Text

"Save the Last Word for Me" Chart   After reading "Robin Hood," choose a favorite passage that says something to you about the theme, or message, of the story. What does the passage tell you about bravery or the struggle between the poor and the powerful? Copy the passage word for word. Then, write your comments about the passage. Give two reasons why you chose it.

Chosen Passage:

"

"

Comments About the Passage:

The Highwayman

Interact with a Literary Text

Theme Web "The Highwayman" is a narrative poem that tells a story about love, betrayal, and death. Complete the theme web below to help you analyze its theme. Fill in the side boxes first. Then share what you learned about "The Highwayman" by filling in the center box.

What I learned about Bess:

_____
_____
_____
_____
_____
_____

What Bess's actions show about life:

_____
_____
_____

Theme

This poem showed me that:

_____
_____
_____
_____
_____
_____
_____
_____
_____

What I learned about the Highwayman:

_____
_____
_____
_____
_____
_____

What the Highway-man's actions show about life:

_____
_____
_____

What I learned about Tim and the troops:

_____
_____
_____
_____
_____
_____

What Tim's actions show about life:

_____
_____

What I learned from the setting:

_____
_____
_____

What the setting contributes to the story:

_____
_____
_____
_____

Gentlemen of the Road

for use with
Holt Literature and Language Arts,
page 171

CAUSE & EFFECT

Interact with an Informational Text

Cause-and-Effect Charts   A **cause** is a force or an event that makes another event happen. An **effect** is what happens as a result of the cause. A cause may have several effects. For example, a lower speed limit on highways may lead to fewer accidents and more speeding tickets being issued. An effect may have several causes. For example, fewer car accidents may be due to lower speed limits and safer car designs.

As you read "Gentlemen of the Road," think about why things happen and how something that happens causes other things to happen. Then, complete the two charts below with details from the selection.

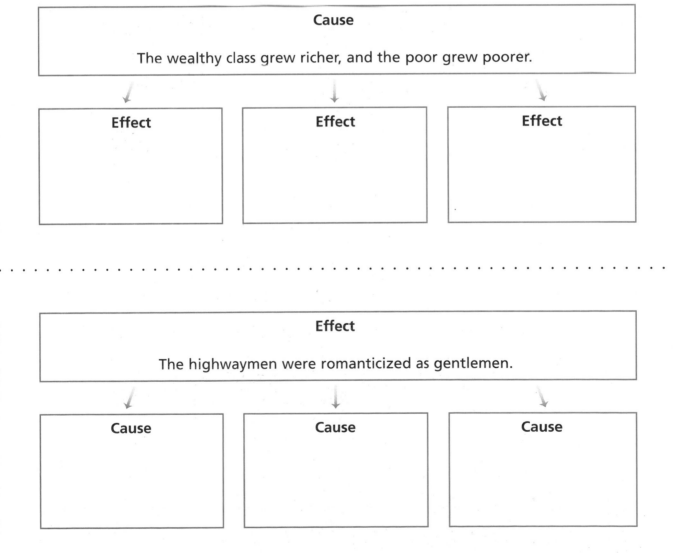

Cause

The wealthy class grew richer, and the poor grew poorer.

| Effect | Effect | Effect |

Effect

The highwaymen were romanticized as gentlemen.

| Cause | Cause | Cause |

THEME

Annabel Lee

Interact with a Literary Text

Theme Chart   A **theme** is an idea or a message about life revealed in a work of literature. Although themes usually are not stated directly, you can make inferences about the theme by thinking about the details in the selection.

As you read "Annabel Lee," fill out the theme chart below with four important details from the poem. Then think about these details, and write a statement that expresses your understanding of the theme of the poem.

Detail

Detail

Detail

Detail

↓

Theme

The Fall of the House of Poe?

Interact with an Informational Text

Cause-and-Effect Chain   A cause-and-effect chain shows a
series of related events. Each event in a chain causes another
event to happen.

Fill in the chart with details from the selection to show the chain
of events. List causes and events that are related, beginning with
the cause listed in box 1.

Cause

Because New York University
in 1999 announced it was planning
to tear down Edgar Allan Poe's
old house . . .

Effect

So . . .

Cause

Because . . .

Effect

So . . .

Cause

Because . . .

Effect

So . . .

User Friendly

for use with
Holt Literature and Language Arts,
page 187

Interact with a Literary Text

Multiple-Effects Chart   A single event may have more than one effect. Fill in the charts below with details from the selection to show the multiple effects that happen because of each cause.

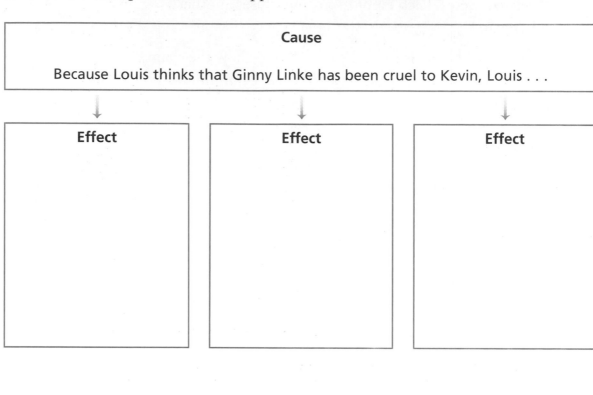

Cause

Because Louis thinks that Ginny Linke has been cruel to Kevin, Louis . . .

| Effect | Effect | Effect |

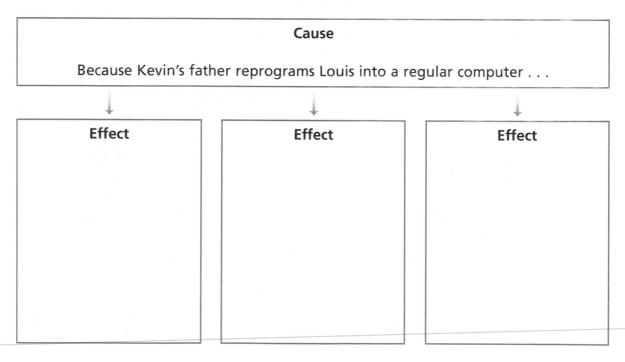

Cause

Because Kevin's father reprograms Louis into a regular computer . . .

| Effect | Effect | Effect |

It Just Keeps Going and Going . . .

Interact with an Informational Text

Cause-and-Effect Links   Sometimes a series of causes and effects creates comedy. For example, say a man slips on a banana peel. Then, because he slipped on the banana peel, he crashes into a wall, causing a flowerpot to fall on his head.

After reading "It Just Keeps Going and Going . . . ," re-read the section that gives the example of a teacher working at his desk. Find the causes and effects that are presented in the passage. Link the causes and effects using the chart below.

Cause		Effect
Because the answer key is wrong,	→	
Because . . .	→	
Because . . .	→	
Because . . .	→	
Because . . .	→	
Because . . .	→	

Echo and Narcissus

Interact with a Literary Text

Thematic Graph   Details in a story can point to its theme. For example, if each character in a story loses something, the theme might have something to say about how losses affect people.

One of the possible themes in "Echo and Narcissus" is stated below. Find six details in the story that support this theme. Write the supporting details in the boxes.

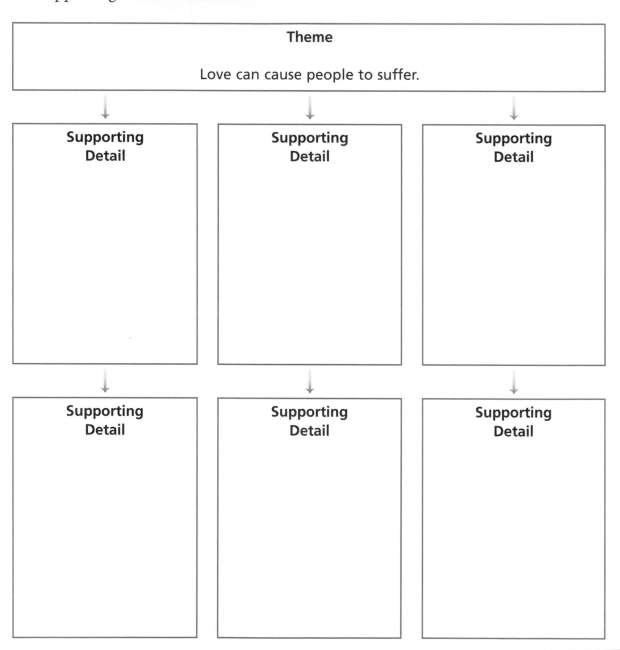

Theme

Love can cause people to suffer.

| Supporting Detail | Supporting Detail | Supporting Detail |
| Supporting Detail | Supporting Detail | Supporting Detail |

Literature

MYTH

The literature of ancient Greece lives on in the form of **myths.** Through these myths we learn about the beliefs and lifestyles of ancient Greeks. Studying the mythological Greek gods who inhabited Mount Olympus gives us a peek into the spirit of ancient times. Understanding Greek literature, art, and music is a way to understand ourselves today.

Heracles was one of the greatest Greek heroes. (You may know him by his Roman name, Hercules.) The ancients liked Heracles so much they included him in many myths. The myth you will read, "The Twelve Tasks of Heracles," tells how Heracles uses his superhuman strength and bravery to accomplish twelve seemingly impossible tasks. This version of the myth is told in comic-book form. After all, Heracles was one of the first superheroes!

Here are some things to know before you read the story:

- This myth is told through drawings and words. Speech balloons tell what the characters say. The captions beneath the drawings describe what is happening.
- Although Heracles was a son of the god Zeus, Heracles himself was not a god.
- In order for Heracles to gain forgiveness from the gods, he had to survive the twelve tasks set by his jealous cousin, King Eurystheus (yōōr·is′thē·əs).

Reading Standard 3.4 Identify and analyze recurring themes across works (for example, the value of bravery, loyalty, and friendship; the effects of loneliness).

THE TWELVE TASKS OF HERACLES

a Greek myth *retold by* Marcia Williams

Heracles was a tough little baby.

Everyone loved him but Hera, Zeus's wife, who sent two snakes to kill him.

But Heracles strangled both of them.

For a while, Hera ignored Heracles.

As he grew up, Heracles became stronger and stronger and stronger.

He married and had many children.

Hera hated him for being so happy.

So one night she put a spell on him. Heracles lashed out with his sword, killing imaginary enemies.

Heracles from *Greek Myths for Young Children* Copyright © 1991 Marcia Williams. Reprinted by permission of Walker Books, Ltd., London. Published in the US by Candlewick Press, Cambridge, Massachusetts.

When he woke from the spell, he saw that he had killed his own children.

Heartbroken, Heracles went to the temple to seek forgiveness.

The priestess said he could make **amends** by serving his old enemy, King Eurystheus.

The king was frightened of Heracles, so he hid in a pot whenever he came near.

And because he hated Heracles, he gave him twelve deadly tasks.

VOCABULARY DEVELOPMENT

amends (ə'mendz') *n.*: something given or done to make up for injury or loss.

INFER

Thought balloons reveal what characters are thinking. Thought balloons have curled edges like a cloud. Who in the third panel on this page has a thought balloon over his head? Underline what he is thinking. Why do you think he is thinking this instead of saying it out loud?

_____

_____

_____

_____

_____

_____

_____

_____

_____

_____

_____

_____

_____

_____

_____

WORD KNOWLEDGE

A **simile** compares two unlike things using *like* or *as*. To what does Heracles compare the dead lion?

_____

_____

_____

_____

_____

_____

_____

_____

VOCABULARY DEVELOPMENT

penetrate (pen'i·trāt') *v.:* pierce into.

• • • • • • Notes • • • • • •

_____

_____

_____

_____

_____

_____

_____

_____

_____

_____

First, Heracles had to kill the lion of Nemea whose hide was so thick that no sword could **penetrate** it.

Next, he had to kill the many-headed Hydra, whose very breath could kill man or beast.

Third, he had to capture the **sacred,** golden-horned deer, an animal as swift as the wind.

The fourth task was to catch a savage boar whose tusks could pierce any armor.

VOCABULARY DEVELOPMENT

sacred (sā′krid) *adj.:* holy; connected with religion.

INTERPRET

Re-read the dialogue in the panels on this page. What do Heracles' words reveal about him?

_____

_____

_____

_____

_____

_____

_____

_____

_____

_____

_____

_____

_____

_____

_____

_____

_____

_____

_____

_____

The Twelve Tasks of Heracles **101**

Underline Heracles' plan to clean the stables of King Augeas. What does the plan reveal about Heracles?

_____
_____
_____
_____
_____
_____
_____

vast (vast) _adj._: very great in size, extent, or amount.

· · · · · · Notes · · · · · ·

_____
_____
_____
_____
_____
_____
_____
_____
_____
_____

Next, Heracles had to clean out the **vast** and filthy stables of King Augeas in a single night.

Then he had to destroy a flock of man-eating birds that hid in a dangerous swamp.

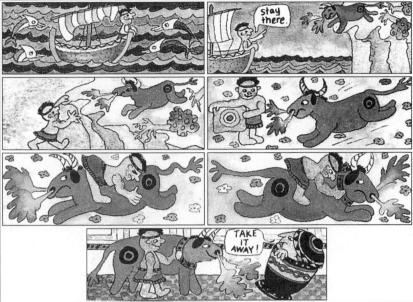

The seventh task was to capture the fire-breathing, marauding bull of Crete.

Next, he had to steal Diomedes' horses, which fed on human flesh.

EVALUATE

Which task so far do you think was the most difficult? Explain.

_____

_____

_____

_____

_____

_____

_____

_____

_____

_____

_____

_____

_____

_____

_____

_____

_____

_____

_____

DECODING TIP

There is no silent *e* in Greek names. *Diomedes* is pronounced (dī′ə·mē′dēz′).

The Twelve Tasks of Heracles **103**

IDENTIFY

Who is Hippolyta? How do you know who she is?

_____

_____

_____

_____

_____

_____

_____

_____

_____

DECODING TIP

Circle the word *Amazon*. Draw lines from the word to the words that help you define *Amazon*.

VOCABULARY DEVELOPMENT

seize (sēz) *v.:* take hold of suddenly or forcibly.

· · · · · · **Notes** · · · · · ·

_____

_____

_____

_____

_____

_____

_____

Then Heracles had to fetch the golden girdle worn by the queen of the Amazon warrior women.

The tenth task was to **seize** the monster Geryon's cattle, guarded by his two-headed dog.

The eleventh, to collect three golden apples protected by a ferocious dragon.

Heracles' twelfth and last task was the most dangerous of all: to fetch the three-headed guard dog, Cerberus, from Hades itself.

PREDICT

Considering what Heracles has been able to do so far and where he is now, do you think that he will accomplish his last labor?

Read the story's captions aloud. Time yourself. Then read them aloud again, trying to improve the smoothness of your delivery.

SAVE THE LAST WORD FOR ME

Do you think that Heracles was well rewarded for his bravery? Underline the sentences in this part of the text that you think are important and helped form your ideas.

_____

_____

_____

_____

_____

_____

_____

_____

_____

_____

_____

_____

_____

_____

_____

_____

_____

_____

His twelve tasks completed, Heracles returned to King Eurystheus.

The king was dismayed to see him alive, and quickly sent him packing.

Then, to avoid angering the gods, Heracles sent Cerberus back to Hades.

At the temple, Heracles was finally pardoned.

He was content at last, and stronger than ever!

And Hera never bothered Heracles again.

OWN THE STORY

Theme   State the theme, or message about life, that is revealed in "The Twelve Tasks of Heracles." Give two reasons for your response.

_____

_____

_____

_____

Comparing Themes   How does the theme of this myth compare to the theme of "Robin Hood"? Discuss your observations with a partner.

_____

_____

_____

_____

_____

_____

_____

KEEPING TRACK

Personal Word List   This selection contained the names of many figures from Greek mythology. Record their names and brief descriptions in your Personal Word List.

Personal Reading Log   As you add this selection to your Personal Reading Log, indicate whether or not you found this story in comic book form easy to read. Give at least two reasons for your response. Then give yourself 2 points on the Reading Meter.

Checklist for Standards Mastery   Use the Checklist for Standards Mastery to see where you need to improve your mastery of the standards.

The Twelve Tasks of Heracles ■ *Interactive Reading,* page 98

Go Beyond a Literary Text

Gods, Goddesses, and Their Realms   In Greek mythology each god ruled a special aspect of Greek life. For example, Heracles' father, Zeus, was the god of the heavens and earth.

To complete the chart below, use reference books, the dictionary, or the Internet to find out what realm each god and goddess ruled.

Gods		Goddesses	
Zeus	god of the heavens and earth	Artemis	
Ares		Athena	
Apollo		Aphrodite	
Hades		Demeter	
Poseidon		Hera	

Now, compare the realms that the gods controlled with the realms the goddesses controlled. What generalization can you make about the roles of gods and goddesses?

_____

_____

_____

_____

BEFORE YOU READ

Many words we use today come to us from Greek mythology. The excerpt from *Words from the Myths* explains the original meaning and the present meaning of some of these words.

Here are some points to know before you read:
- Prometheus (prō·mē′thē·əs) and Epimetheus (ep·ə·mē′thē·əs) are brothers. Zeus, king of the gods, is very angry at Prometheus because Prometheus has just disobeyed Zeus's orders and given humanity the gift of fire. To get revenge on Prometheus and to punish humanity, Zeus tricks Epimetheus, the weaker brother. Here is Zeus's trick.

Reading Standard 2.3 Analyze text that uses the cause-and-effect organizational pattern.

from Words from the Myths

Isaac Asimov

Zeus created a beautiful woman to whom all the gods gave gifts of beauty, grace, wit, melody, and so on. She was called *Pandora* (pan·dôr′ə), from Greek words meaning "all-gifted." She was then given to Epimetheus for a wife. Because of her beauty, Epimetheus accepted her, although Prometheus had warned him against taking any gift from Zeus.

Along with Pandora, Epimetheus received a box which Pandora was forbidden to open. At her first opportunity,
10 she opened the box to see what was in it and out flew the spirits of old age, death, famine, sickness, grief, and all the other ills that **plague** human beings. Only hope was left at

TEXT STRUCTURE

Here Asimov uses causes and effects to explain the story of Pandora's box. Underline the action Pandora takes. What happens because of her action?

_____

_____

_____

VOCABULARY DEVELOPMENT

plague (plāg) *v.:* torment or trouble.

**COMPARE &
CONTRAST**

Use the description of
Pandora to visualize her.
Then, study the painting of
Pandora. How is your vision
of Pandora similar to or
different from Rossetti's?

_____

_____

_____

**WORD
KNOWLEDGE**

Underline the **metaphor** in
line 14. What is misery
compared to here? Why is
this a good way to describe
unhappiness?

_____

_____

_____

_____

_____

**WORD
KNOWLEDGE**

Continually means "happening over and over again."
Knowing this, explain the
torture of Prometheus
(lines 21–22).

_____

_____

_____

Pandora Holding Her Box *by Dante Gabriel Rossetti.*

the bottom of the box and, when finally let out, was all that
kept human beings alive under the weight of their misery.

Thus, anything which is harmless when undisturbed,
but which lets loose many troubles when interfered with, is
called a "Pandora's box."

Not satisfied with having his revenge on humanity,
Zeus also punished Prometheus directly. He chained him

20 to a rock in the Caucasus Mountains which, to the ancient
Greeks, represented the eastern end of the world. There he
was continually tortured by an eagle.

The story of Pandora is actually a moral tale, a kind of fable intended to teach people how to behave. For instance, Epimetheus is a warning against careless action taken without due consideration of possible consequences. Pandora herself is a warning against foolish curiosity.

Many mythical warnings were against the kind of pride which made people consider themselves above the

30 law. Such pride led to **insolent** behavior and a disregard of the rights of others. In the Greek myths, it usually involved defying the gods—the sort of pride the Greeks called "hubris."

When that happened, the gods saw to it that the proud individual was dealt with by *Nemesis,* the goddess of **retribution.** The name comes from Greek words meaning to "distribute." In other words, Nemesis sees to it that matters are distributed evenly. If a person has so much good fortune that he or she becomes **boastful,**

40 proud, and insolent, Nemesis sees to it that this person has a corresponding amount of bad fortune to even things out.

Since most of the Greek myths involve matters evened out by bad fortune, rather than by good fortune, "nemesis" has come to mean, in our language, an unavoidable doom.

Pride is still considered the most serious of the seven deadly sins. It was through pride that Lucifer fell, according to our own stories. We still have this old Greek feeling about pride when we speak of "the jealous gods" who won't allow anyone to be too lucky. That is why we say that "pride

50 goeth before a fall" and knock on wood when talking about how fortunate we are, or how well off. That is supposed to keep off Nemesis.

VOCABULARY DEVELOPMENT

insolent (in′sə·lənt) *adj.:* disrespectful in speech or behavior.

WORD KNOWLEDGE

Underline the word *hubris* (hyo͞o′bris) in line 33. Circle the words in the context that define hubris.

IDENTIFY

What is the effect of hubris?

_____

_____

_____

WORD KNOWLEDGE

Underline the word *nemesis* (nem′ə·sis) in line 43. Circle the words in context that define nemesis. If you say, "Tests are my nemesis," what do you mean?

_____

_____

_____

VOCABULARY DEVELOPMENT

retribution (re′tri·byo͞o′shən) *n.:* punishment for evil done or reward for good done.

boastful (bōst′fəl) *adj.:* inclined to brag.

Asimov tells Arachne's story in a series of causes and effects. Underline the words that tell how Arachne feels about her weaving skill. What does Arachne's pride cause her to do?

_____

_____

_____

Underline the words in context (lines 78–79) that define *arachnoid.* What does that word mean?

_____

_____

_____

_____

An example of such a pride-goeth-before-a-fall myth is the story of *Arachne* (ə·rak′nē). She was a girl of the kingdom of Lydia (in western Asia Minor) who was very skilled at weaving. She was so proud of her skill that she boasted that even Athena, the goddess of the practical arts, including that of weaving, could not do better, and challenged Athena to a contest. (There was hubris.)

60 Athena accepted the challenge and both wove tapestries. Athena wove into hers all sorts of glorious stories about the gods, while Arachne wove into hers unflattering stories about them. Arachne's work was excellent but Athena's was perfect. In anger at Arachne's subject matter, Athena tore Arachne's weaving to shreds and Arachne, struck with terror, hanged herself. (There was nemesis.)

Athena, who was not a cruel goddess, didn't want things to go that far, so she loosened the rope and changed Arachne into a spider. As a spider, Arachne continued 70 spinning threads and weaving beautiful webs, and she also continues to hang from a strand of gossamer as though still trying to hang herself. Of course, "arachne" is the Greek word for "spider" and the idea of the myth surely came from watching spiders at work. But it does teach a moral: Avoid hubris.

In zoology, the name of the girl lives on, since spiders and its relatives are put in the class "Arachnida."

Furthermore, anything as filmy and delicate as a spider's web is said to be "arachnoid." For instance, the 80 brain and spinal cord are enclosed by a double **membrane** for protection. In between the two parts of the double membrane is a third membrane which is very thin and filmy. This is called the "arachnoid membrane."

Greek bowl showing Helios in his chariot.

TEXT STRUCTURE

What cause and effect does Asimov describe in lines 91–97? Circle the sentence that describes the cause, and underline the sentence that describes the effect.

Another example of this sort of myth is that of *Phaethon* (fāʹə·thän), the mortal son of Helios. He was so proud of being the son of the sun god, that he felt he could drive the sun (which was pictured as a gleaming chariot drawn by wild, gleaming horses) across the sky. He tricked his father into promising to let him do so.

90   (That was hubris.)

Phaethon drove the sun but found he could not control the horses, which went out of their course and swooped too near the earth. The Greeks supposed the burning sands of the Sahara showed where the swooping sun chariot had scorched the earth. To save the earth from destruction, Zeus was forced to kill Phaethon with a thunderbolt. (That was nemesis.)

COMPARE & CONTRAST

What character traits do Phaethon and Arachne share? Use the word *hubris* in your answer.

Words from the Myths   **113**

OWN THE TEXT

Finding Causes   Myths often explain how something in our world came to be. According to the myth about Pandora, what caused all the troubles we face in our lives? According to the myth of Phaethon, what caused the Sahara to form?

_____

_____

Comparing Themes   With a partner, discuss how the stories of Arachne and Phaethon are based on the theme "Pride goes before a fall." Find passages in the myths that explain how hubris causes Arachne's and Phaethon's fates.

Cause and Effect Chart   Make a chart like the one that follows. Fill it in with two examples of hubris and its result, nemesis, in these myths.

Cause: Hubris		Effect: Nemesis
Story 1	→	Story 1
Story 2	→	Story 2

Personal Word List   Record the words based on mythological figures in your Personal Word List. Record *hubris* and *nemesis* on your list, with definitions.

Personal Reading Log   As you record this selection in your Personal Reading Log, note how you feel about Pandora's, Arachne's, and Phaethon's fates. Then, give yourself 2 points on the Reading Meter.

Checklist for Standards Mastery   Use the Checklist for Standards Mastery to help improve your mastery of the standards in this chapter.

Go Beyond an Informational Text

Words from Mythology   Words from mythology are present in everyday English. Use the excerpt from *Words from the Myths*, books on mythology, encyclopedias, dictionaries, or the Internet to fill in the meaning and history of some of these words. You may want to enter your findings in your Personal Word List.

Present Word	Meaning of Word	Name from Mythology	Description of Character or Event
arachnida			
echo			
herculean			
hubris			
muse			
narcissistic			
nemesis			
panic			

Literature

BEFORE YOU READ

In this retelling of this myth, you will read about a boy named Phaethon who is not that different from a lot of impatient young boys. There is one thing that makes him special, though. His father is the Greek god Helius!

Before you read, here are a couple of facts to know:

- For a grown man, driving an ordinary chariot and its horses takes a lot of muscle, skill, and experience. Young Phaethon wants to drive Helius's extraordinary chariot, the golden chariot that pulls the sun across the sky.
- *Helius* is the Latin name for Helios, god of the sun.

Reading Standard 3.4 Identify and analyze recurring themes across works (for example, the value of bravery, loyalty, and friendship; the effects of loneliness).

Phaethon

a Greek myth *retold by* **Robert Graves**

IDENTIFY

Personification is a special kind of metaphor in which a nonhuman thing or quality is referred to as if it were human. In the first sentence, circle the name of the nonhuman thing that is personified as the Greek god Helius.

VOCABULARY DEVELOPMENT

chariot (char′ē·ət) *n.*: horse-drawn, two-wheeled cart.

The Sun, whose name was Helius, owned a palace near Colchis in the Far East beyond the Black Sea. He was counted among the smaller gods, because his father had been a Titan. At cockcrow every morning, Helius harnessed four white horses to a fiery **chariot**—so bright that nobody could look at it without hurting his eyes—which he drove across the sky to another palace in the Far West, near the Elysian Fields.° There he unharnessed his team, and when they had grazed, loaded them and the chariot on a golden ferryboat, in which he sailed, fast asleep, round the world by way of the Ocean Stream until he reached Colchis again.

10

° **Elysian** (ē·lizh′ən) **Fields:** area of complete bliss; paradise.

From "Phaëthon's Story" from *Greek Gods and Heroes* by Robert Graves. Copyright © 1957 by Robert Graves. Reprinted by permission of *A. P. Watt Limited on behalf of The Robert Graves Copyright Trust.*

Helius enjoyed watching what went on in the world below, but he could never take a holiday from work.

Phaethon, his eldest son, was constantly asking permission to drive the chariot. "Why not have a day in bed for a change, Father?" Helius always answered, "I must wait until you are a little older." Phaethon grew so impatient and bad-tempered—throwing stones at the palace windows, and pulling up the flowers in the garden—that at last

20 Helius said, "Very well, then, you may drive it tomorrow. But keep a firm hold of the reins. The horses are very **spirited.**" Phaethon tried to show off before his younger sisters, and the horses, realizing that he did not know how to manage the reins, started **plunging** up and down. The Olympians felt icy cold one minute, and the next saw trees and grasses scorching from the heat. "Stop those stupid tricks, boy!" shouted Zeus.

"My team is out of control, Your Majesty," gasped Phaethon.

30 Zeus, in disgust, threw a thunderbolt at Phaethon, and killed him. His body fell into the River Po. The little girls wept and wept. Zeus changed them to poplar trees.

FLUENCY

Read the boxed passage aloud, using different tones of voice for the three characters. You may want to use different colored highlighters to indicate dialogue.

VOCABULARY DEVELOPMENT

spirited (spir′it·id) *adj.:* lively; energetic.

plunging (plun′jin) *v.:* moving violently and rapidly downward or forward.

CAUSE & EFFECT

Pause at line 26. What caused the Olympians to feel these extremes of temperature?

_____

_____

_____

_____

SAVE THE LAST WORD FOR ME

Circle a passage from the story that has special meaning to you. What do you think is the theme, or message, of this myth?

_____

_____

_____

_____

_____

OWN THE STORY

Theme   What lesson is taught through the telling of this tale? If this tale were to be modernized, how would you convey that same lesson? (For example, the sun's chariot could be the family car.) Write your response, and share it with a peer.

_____

_____

_____

_____

Comparing Themes   Compare the theme of "Phaethon" with a story, poem, song, or movie that has a similar theme. Discuss your ideas with a partner.

_____

_____

_____

_____

_____

_____

KEEPING TRACK

Personal Word List   Add the words you learned from this myth to your Personal Word List.

Personal Reading Log   Note other myths you have enjoyed as you record your reactions to this selection in your Personal Reading Log. Give yourself 2 points on the Reading Meter.

Checklist for Standards Mastery   Look through the Checklist for Standards Mastery to see how well you have mastered the standards for this chapter. Where did you make the most improvement? What can you improve?

Phaethon ▪ *Interactive Reading,* page 116

Go Beyond a Literary Text

Comic Strip   A **comic strip** is a story told in pictures and words. Myths have often been turned into comic books or strips. Use the following steps to create your own comic strip based on the myth of Phaethon. The first panel is done for you.

1. Create drawings showing what is happening in each scene.
2. Add speech and thought balloons to help tell the story.
3. Write a caption that describes each scene below your drawing.

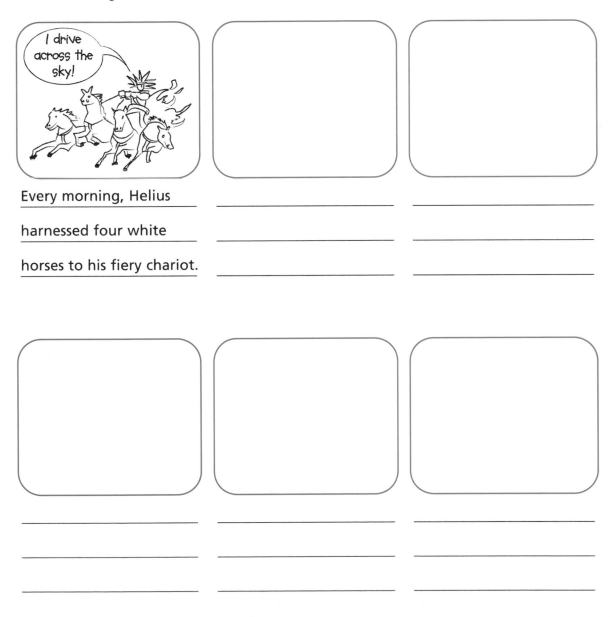

Every morning, Helius

harnessed four white

horses to his fiery chariot.

Chapter 4

Point of View

Who's Talking?

"You're Telling Me!"

LITERARY FOCUS: POINTS OF VIEW

Point of view refers to who is telling us a story. In a story told from the **first-person point of view,** the narrator ("I") is a character in the story and can describe only what he or she sees, knows, and thinks.

In a story told from the **omniscient** (äm·nish′ənt) **point of view,** the narrator can tell us everything about every character and every event. The omniscient narrator is not a character in the story.

In a story told from the **third-person limited point of view,** the narrator, who is not a character in the story, zooms in on one character and tells us what that character sees, knows, and thinks.

A STRATEGY THAT WORKS: "YOU'RE TELLING ME!"

Point of view affects what we know about the characters and their conflicts. For example, a battle may be described one way by the loser and another way by the winner. The point of view makes a difference in the way the story affects us.

"You're Telling Me!" is a strategy that can help you identify and think about point of view.

POINTERS FOR USING "YOU'RE TELLING ME!"

)))➡ As you read, mark up clues that reveal who is telling the story. If the narrator uses *I* and *me,* chances are the narrator is a story character, a first-person narrator. If the narrator uses *he, she,* and *they* to refer to *all* the story characters, the narrator is not taking part in the story and is a third-person narrator.

)))➡ Next, skim the text, and find what the narrator says about the other characters. Does the narrator reveal the thoughts and feelings of all or many of the story characters? If so, the narrator is **omniscient.** If the narrator zooms in on the thoughts and emotions of just a single story character, the narrator is **limited.**

)))➡ Once you've read and marked up the story, ask yourself: How might the story differ if the narrator were different?

Reading Standard 1.3 Clarify word meanings through the use of definition, example, restatement, or contrast.

Reading Standard 2.4 Identify and trace the development of an author's argument, point of view, or perspective in text.

Reading Standard 3.5 Contrast points of view (for example, first and third person, limited and omniscient, subjective and objective) in narrative text, and explain how they affect the overall theme of the work.

> **BEFORE YOU READ**
>
> Familiar stories can take on fresh new life when told from an unexpected point of view. Following are two versions of the fairy tale "Beauty and the Beast." The first version is told from a traditional point of view; the second is told from an unusual point of view. As you read, look for ways in which the point of view of the narrator can affect the story's overall theme and overall impact.

Beauty and the Beast

Mara Rockliff

> **YOU'RE TELLING ME!**
>
> Pause at line 10. Circle the pronouns that the narrator has used so far to describe the story characters. Is this narrator a story character?
>
> _____
>
> _____
>
> _____
>
> _____
>
> _____
>
> _____
>
> _____
>
> _____
>
> _____
>
> _____

Version 1

Once upon a time there lived a merchant with three daughters. All three were lovely, but the youngest was loveliest by far. Her name was Bella, and she was as sweet as she was beautiful.

One day the merchant got ready to leave on a long journey. "What shall I bring you from the city?" he asked his daughters as they stood by the door, watching him saddle his horse.

10 "A golden comb!" said the oldest, tossing her long raven hair.

"A diamond necklace!" said the middle daughter, arching her swanlike neck.

The merchant turned to Bella. "And you, my dear?"

"Just come home safely, Father," she said. "I don't need anything else." But then, noticing her sisters' frowns, she quickly added, "But I do love flowers. You could bring me a rose."

On his first day in the city the merchant bought a
20 comb of gold so pure it was almost white. On his second day he bought a necklace of diamonds that glittered like frozen tears. But not a rose in the city seemed lovely enough for his beautiful Bella.

His heart was heavy as he started home. He stopped in every town along the way, but there wasn't a rose to be found.

Suddenly, up ahead, he saw a fabulous castle. He rode closer. And there, by the castle wall, grew the most **exquisite** rosebush he had ever seen.

30 He looked around, but the castle seemed deserted. Surely, he thought, the owner wouldn't mind if he took just one.

But as he plucked the rose and turned to go, the air split with a terrible roar. "WHO DARES STEAL MY ROSES?"

Before his terrified eyes stood an enormous, hideous beast. The merchant fell to his knees, quaking with fear. "Please spare my life," he said. "If not for my sake, then for the sake of the loving daughter for whom I picked
40 this rose."

"Loving daughter?" growled the beast. "All right, I'll spare you then. But you must bring her to me in three days. Otherwise I'll know you were lying. I will track you down and I will show no mercy."

The merchant begged and pleaded, but the beast was unmoved. "Three days," he repeated.

The two oldest daughters were thrilled to receive their expensive presents. Only Bella noticed the sadness in her

WORD KNOWLEDGE

A **simile** is a comparison between two unlike things which uses the word *like* or *as*. Underline the simile in lines 21 and 22. What two things are being compared?

_____

_____

_____

_____

_____

_____

_____

_____

_____

_____

VOCABULARY DEVELOPMENT

exquisite (cks·kwiz′it) *adj.:* very beautiful, lovely, or delicate.

YOU'RE TELLING ME!

Re-read lines 36–48. Underline what the narrator tells you about the characters' inner feelings.

Pause at line 60. According to this narrator, why does Bella decide to stay with the beast?

_____

_____

_____

_____

INTERPRET

Why might the beast have been "silent a long time" (line 64)?

_____

_____

_____

_____

_____

_____

YOU'RE
TELLING ME!

Re-read lines 73–79. Underline what the narrator tells you about Bella's actions.

VOCABULARY
DEVELOPMENT

exterior (ek·stir′ē·ər) *n.*: outward appearance.

50 father's eyes. Finally she persuaded him to tell her what was wrong.

"You took the rose for me," she said. "I will face the beast for you."

"No!" he cried. But she was determined. So they saddled up the horse and together returned to the castle.

The beast met them at the gate. "You may go," he told the merchant. "But she must stay."

"No!" the merchant cried again.

But Bella looked into the eyes of the beast and saw into his heart. "I will stay," she said.

60 The castle offered every comfort Bella could wish, and the beast was kind. She grew fonder and fonder of him. But as the months passed she pined for her father and sisters. "Please," she asked, "couldn't I visit them just for a week?"

The beast was silent a long time before he replied. "A week," he said. "No more."

Bella was so happy to be home that she forgot all about the waiting beast. A week passed, and then two. It was nearly three weeks when Bella finally returned.

But the castle stood dark and empty. Where was the
70 beast?

At last she found him. He lay next to her rosebush, his eyes closed, his breathing weak and shallow.

"Oh, dear beast!" she cried, cradling him in her arms. "Please, please, don't die. I will never leave you again."

At that, the beast vanished, and a handsome prince sprang to his feet. He'd been under a curse, which Bella had broken by seeing past his fearsome **exterior** and loving the man within. The prince married Bella and brought her family to the castle, and they all lived happily ever after.

Version 2

80

First of all, I was perfectly happy getting turned into a beast. When you're a prince, everyone wants something from you. One minute a bunch of peasants are pounding at the gate, begging you to **slay** some dragon that's laying waste to the village; the next minute it's yet another whiny damsel in distress, expecting to be rescued. Never a moment's peace. But a huge ugly beast, people don't expect so much from. They seemed pleased as punch that I wasn't devouring them—as if I would trade my dinner of rare

90

roast beef in horseradish sauce with tiny red potatoes for some hairy unwashed peasant. Yuck.

So everything was just peachy until that ridiculous traveling salesman came barging into my garden, trampling my petunias and snapping off one of my prize tea roses without so much as a by-your-leave. No respect for private property, that's the problem with merchants today.

Obviously the signs saying KEEP OUT didn't bother him in the least. So I thought I'd try a little reverse psychology. I told him I'd take his life if he didn't bring back his

100

daughter. I thought the bit about bringing his daughter back was a particularly nice touch. Won't be seeing *him* again, I told myself with great **satisfaction** as he hightailed it off my land.

Imagine my shock when he showed up a few days later, daughter in tow. I couldn't believe it when he dumped her on my doorstep and took off.

I believe it now. Oh, boy, do I believe it.

She means well. That's the worst of it. Her type always does. Right from the start it was "Beast, wouldn't wheat

110

germ and fat-free yogurt be a little more heart-healthy than

VOCABULARY DEVELOPMENT

slay (slā) *v.*: kill or destroy in a violent way.

YOU'RE TELLING ME!

Re-read lines 81–91. Who is telling the story? Circle the pronouns that clued you in.

_____

_____

_____

_____

_____

_____

COMPARE & CONTRAST

Re-read lines 92–96. What information can the narrator *not* reveal that is revealed in the first version of the story?

_____

_____

_____

_____

_____

_____

VOCABULARY DEVELOPMENT

satisfaction (sat'is·fak'shən) *n.*: fulfillment of needs, expectations, or wishes.

Re-read lines 108–118. How are Beauty and her beast in this story different from the same characters in the first story?

_____

_____

_____

_____

_____

_____

VOCABULARY DEVELOPMENT

consolation (kän′sə·lā′shən) *n.:* lessening of sadness or disappointment; comfort.

YOU'RE TELLING ME!

What does this narrator say about his life with Bella? Underline the passage. What is the message of this version of the story?

_____

_____

_____

_____

_____

_____

_____

_____

rare roast beef?" And "Look, Beast, I knitted you this lovely hat to keep your head warm while you garden." A knitted hat! Just because I'm a beast doesn't mean I want to go around looking like a complete idiot.

When she said she was going home to her father, all I could think was, Better him than me.

"But I'll be back!" she trilled.

"I'll be waiting," I said glumly.

110 A couple of weeks later I was weeding my petunias
120 when I spotted her marching up the road. As I turned to flee, I stepped on the garden rake. The handle popped up and smacked me in the forehead. I bellowed in pain before I passed out cold.

When I came to, she was wringing her hands and batting her eyes. "Poor Beast," she said. "Poor, poor Beast. I should have known you couldn't go on without me. I'll never leave you again!"

And the next thing I knew—poof—prince time again.

My only **consolation** is, I don't think she's one bit
130 happier than I am. She'd never admit it, of course. Especially not in front of her sisters. But a handsome and universally admired prince just doesn't offer the same scope for her talent as a big ugly beast. Not as much room for improvement. You know?

OWN THE STORIES

Point of View   Compare the messages or themes revealed in the two versions of "Beauty and the Beast." First, fill out the "You're Telling Me!" chart on the following page. Then, get together with a partner to discuss the ways the point of view in each story affected its message.

Changing Perspective   The storyteller has an effect on what information readers are given and how they react to the story. Retell "Beauty and the Beast" from another character's perspective. You may, for example, tell the story from the perspective of one of Bella's sisters. Then, read your retelling to a classmate, and ask for feedback on how the message of the story changed.

_____

_____

_____

_____

_____

_____

_____

_____

KEEPING TRACK

Personal Word List   Record the words you learned from this story in your Personal Word List. Put a star next to your favorite words— words you would like to use in your everyday conversation.

Personal Reading Log   As you add these stories to your Personal Reading Log, jot down your ideas about the different narrators. Then, give yourself 5 points on the Reading Meter.

Checklist for Standards Mastery   Use the Checklist for Standards Mastery to see how well you mastered the standards. What problems, if any, do you have identifying point of view?

Beauty and the Beast

Interactive Reading, page 122

Interact with a Literary Text

"You're Telling Me!" Chart   Fill out the "You're Telling Me!" chart with details about the narrator of each version of "Beauty and the Beast." Then, describe the overall effect the choice of narrator has on each version of the story.

Version 1 Narrator	Version 2 Narrator
What pronouns does the narrator use to describe himself or herself? _____ _____	What pronouns does the narrator use to describe himself or herself? _____ _____
Is the narrator a story character? YES or NO _____	Is the narrator a story character? YES or NO _____
What does the narrator know about other characters' thoughts and feelings? _____ _____ _____	What does the narrator know about other characters' thoughts and feelings? _____ _____ _____
Overall Effect of Choice of Narrator	**Overall Effect of Choice of Narrator**
_____ _____ _____ _____ _____ _____ _____ _____ _____	_____ _____ _____ _____ _____ _____ _____ _____ _____

After Twenty Years

for use with
Holt Literature and Language Arts,
page 225

POINT
OF VIEW/
THEME

Interact with a Literary Text

Questionnaire   This story is told by an omniscient narrator
who knows all the story's secrets. Complete the questionnaire to
examine the way the point of view affects the theme of "After
Twenty Years."

1. What pronouns does the narrator use to describe the story characters?

    _____

    _____

2. Does the narrator reveal the inner thoughts of any of the characters? Explain.

    _____

    _____

3. How might this story differ if it were told by the policeman? List at least
    three points of difference, including what you would know and what you
    would not know.

    • _____

    • _____

    • _____

4. How might this story be different if it were told from Silky Bob's point of view?
    List at least three points of difference, including what you would know and
    what you would not know.

    • _____

    • _____

    • _____

5. Think of the story's theme. How could a new point of view affect the theme?

    _____

    _____

What's *Really* in a Name?

for use with
Holt Literature and Language Arts,
page 233

Interact with an Informational Text

Perspective Chart   We reveal our perspectives, or views, on a subject in almost everything we write. After you read "What's *Really* in a Name?" fill in the chart below. Begin by identifying the position statement, in which the writer reveals her perspective on her subject. (Note: Position statements don't always appear at the beginning of an essay.) Then fill in the Details boxes. Cite the facts, anecdotes, or expert opinions that support the writer's perspective on name-changing.

Detail That Supports Position

_____
_____
_____
_____

Detail That Supports Position

_____
_____
_____
_____

Position Statement or Perspective

_____
_____
_____
_____

Detail That Supports Position

_____
_____
_____
_____

Detail That Supports Position

_____
_____
_____
_____

Bargain

Interact with a Literary Text

"Possibilities" Chart   Work with a partner to complete the following "possibilities" chart. To review the three points of view, read "Point of View: Through Whose Eyes?" on pages 222–223 of *Holt Literature and Language Arts.*

Point of View	What we would know about: Events in Plot	What we would know about: Characters	What we would know about: Theme Change
Omniscient			
Limited third, focus on Slade			
First person, Mr. Baumer			

Yeh-Shen

Interact with a Literary Text

What If? Chart   Stories are told by narrators. Sometimes the choice of narrator has an effect on the story's message or theme. Fill out the chart below to examine how a story's narrator can affect its theme.

What If? . . .

What If . . . **Yeh-Shen narrated the story?** _____ _____ _____	**What might be the story's theme?** _____ _____ _____ _____
What If . . . **the stepmother narrated the story?** _____ _____ _____	**What might be the story's theme?** _____ _____ _____ _____
What If . . . **the king narrated the story?** _____ _____ _____ _____	**What might be the story's theme?** _____ _____ _____ _____

Mirror, Mirror, on the Wall . . .

Interact with an Informational Text

Argument Web   An **argument** is a form of persuasion. Its aim is to convince us to think or act in a certain way. Effective arguments have strong supporting details—such as facts, examples, statistics, and expert quotations. Complete the web that follows to identify the support and type of support for the argument in "Mirror, Mirror, on the Wall. . . ." Identify at least five details that support the writer's argument. The first row has been done for you.

Writer's Argument:

_____

_____

Support	Type of Support
Woman in drugstore thought she looked fat.	Anecdote: real-life example

Names/Nombres

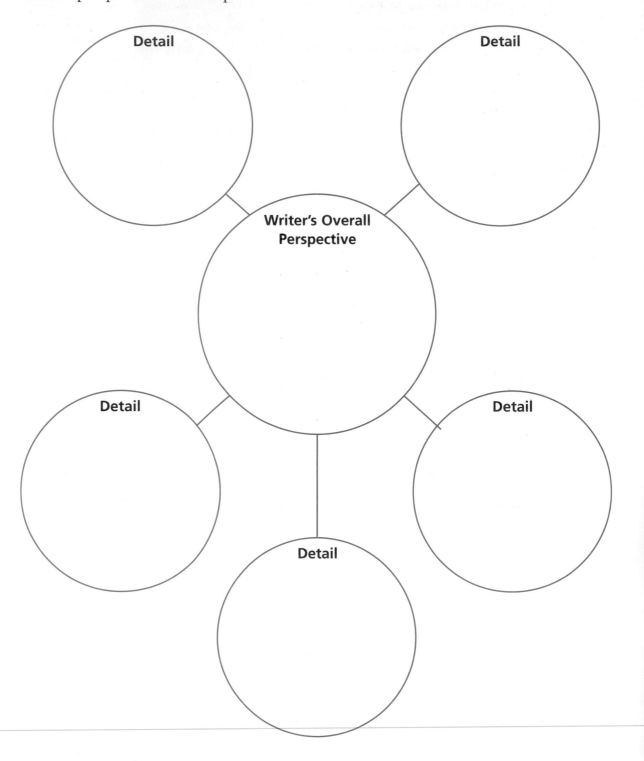

for use with
Holt Literature and Language Arts,
page 262

AUTHOR'S PERSPECTIVE

Interact with a Literary Text

Details Map Fill in the following map with details from "Names/Nombres." Then review those details and identify the writer's perspective on her topic.

Detail

Detail

Writer's Overall Perspective

Detail

Detail

Detail

An Unforgettable Journey

for use with
Holt Literature and Language Arts,
page 271

SUBJECTIVE
POINT
OF VIEW

Interact with a Literary Text

"Actions Through Time" Chart   "An Unforgettable Journey" is an autobiographical narrative that tells about a family's journey from war-torn Laos to Los Angeles, California. This narrator is **subjective:** As she tells her story, she freely reveals her innermost reactions to the story events.

As you read "An Unforgettable Journey," fill in the event column with major events from the story. Then fill out the second column with the narrator's reactions—her inner thoughts, or feelings.

Event	Narrator's Reaction

Exile Eyes

for use with
Holt Literature and Language Arts,
page 279

Interact with an Informational Text

Point-of-View Ladder   When writing to inform, writers use details to support their **points of view.** Fill in this chart to examine the writer's point of view in "Exile Eyes." State the writer's position in the first box. Then, list details the writer gives to support her position. Sum up the writer's conclusion in the last box.

Writer's Position
Supporting Detail
Supporting Detail
Supporting Detail
Supporting Detail
Conclusion

Elizabeth I

for use with
Holt Literature and Language Arts,
page 284

OBJECTIVE
POINT
OF VIEW

Interact with an Informational Text

Fact Listing   A **biography** is the story of someone's life that is told by another person. Some biographies are **subjective**. This means that the writers reveal their own feelings and opinions about their subjects. Most biographies, however, are chiefly **objective**. This means that they present chiefly factual information. They may give opinions, but their opinions are supported by facts.

Fill in the chart below with at least five details from "Elizabeth I." Then, describe each listed item as a fact or an opinion. If an item is an opinion, sum up the support provided by the biographer.

Detail	Fact or Opinion?	Support from Biography

Literature

SHORT STORY

Lensey Namioka has written many books about what it means to be Chinese American. She writes from her own experience. Born in Beijing, China, in 1929, Lensey moved with her family to the United States when she was a young girl. She graduated from college with a degree in mathematics but decided she enjoyed writing more. A few of her twenty-one books are set in Japan, her husband's native country (Namioka is a Japanese name), and still others are set in ancient China. Lensey Namioka lives with her family in Seattle, Washington.

BEFORE YOU READ

This story is from Lensey Namioka's collection of stories called *Yang the Third and Her Impossible Family.* The story has a first-person narrator, Yingmei, who calls the children in the family by their traditional Chinese family names ("Fourth Brother" and "Eldest Brother"). This story is about the cultural differences that cause conflict when the narrator's family attends their first American Thanksgiving Day dinner.

Reading Standard 3.5 Contrast points of view (for example, first and third person, limited and omniscient, subjective and objective) in narrative text, and explain how they affect the overall theme of the work.

Thanksgiving with the Conners

Lensey Namioka

"The Conners are inviting us for Thanksgiving dinner!" yelled Fourth Brother as he hung up the phone.

The Conners are our neighbors here in Seattle, and Matthew Conner is Fourth Brother's best friend. He takes violin lessons from Father, and he also plays in our family string quartet.

Eldest Brother plays first violin, and Second Sister plays viola. I'm the third sister in the Yang family, and I play cello. Fourth Brother plays baseball. He has a terrible ear, and he was relieved when Matthew took his place as the second violin.

We were all happy about the invitation. For weeks, we had been hearing about the American holiday called Thanksgiving. Since coming to this country, we have tried our best to do everything properly, but when Mother heard that preparing a Thanksgiving dinner involved roasting a turkey, she was horrified.

"I can't even roast a pigeon," she cried. "If I tried to wrestle with a turkey, I'd lose!"

We didn't have an oven in China. Almost nobody does. If you want a roast duck or chicken, you buy it already cooked in the store—sometimes chopped into bite-size pieces. When Mother saw the big box under the stove in our Seattle kitchen, she didn't know what it was at first. Even now, months later, she was still nervous about the black cavity and thought of it as a chamber of horrors.

YOU'RE TELLING ME!

Who is telling the story? Underline the sentence that tells you something about the narrator. Then, circle the words that reveal that the story is told from the first-person point of view. Put a box around the phrase that tells you where the story is set.

WORD KNOWLEDGE

The word *cavity* in line 26 is used in an unusual way. Why would the writer describe the oven as a *cavity*?

IDENTIFY

Pause at line 34. What does the narrator say that she wants?

_____

_____

_____

_____

_____

COMPARE & CONTRAST

Underline the words in the last paragraph on this page that describe what the narrator thinks of her mother's dress. How do you think her mother thinks she looks?

_____

_____

_____

_____

_____

_____

_____

VOCABULARY DEVELOPMENT

aggressive (ə·gres′iv) adj.: inclined to start fights or quarrels.

Now we'd learn how real Americans celebrate Thanksgiving. We'd get a delicious meal, like the ones I had seen illustrated in all the papers and magazines.

30   What excited me most was hearing that Holly Hanson and her mother were invited, too. Holly was in the school orchestra with me. She played in the viola section, so I didn't get a chance to talk to her much. But I really wanted to.

When I was little, we had a tin candy box, and on the lid was the picture of a princess with curly blond hair. Holly Hanson looked just like the princess in that picture. She was in a couple of my classes in school, and she always spoke in a soft, unhurried way. I thought that if the

40   princess on the candy box spoke, she would sound just like that.

At the Conners' I would finally get a chance to get acquainted with Holly. But I was nervous, too, because I wanted so much to have my family make a good impression.

When Thanksgiving Day came, the whole Yang family showed up at the Conners' exactly at two o'clock. We'd thought two was a strange time for a dinner party, but Matthew explained that since people stuff themselves

50   at Thanksgiving, eating early gives everybody a chance to digest.

We all tried to look our best for the dinner. Father had on the dark suit he wore for playing in public. Instead of her usual cotton slacks and shirt, Mother wore a dress she had bought at the Goodwill store for three dollars. It was a very nice dress, but on her slender figure, the huge shoulder pads made her look like a stranger—an **aggressive** stranger.

Eldest Brother wore a suit, too. Second Sister and I wore skirts, and Fourth Brother had on his clean blue jeans. I hoped we'd all look presentable when we met Holly and her mother.

Mrs. Hanson and Holly arrived a few minutes after we did, and we were introduced. My parents had told us we should all shake hands with the Hansons. Mrs. Hanson looked a little startled when six Yang hands were extended toward her. Although our etiquette book clearly said shaking hands is the polite thing to do, I decided that in America, children don't usually do it.

Except for that, things seemed to be going pretty well. The dining table looked beautiful, with china plates and tall wine glasses—even for the young people, who drank juice. I carefully studied the way the knives, forks, and spoons were set.

I was delighted when Mrs. Conner seated me next to Holly, but the only thing I could think to say was "I've seen you in the orchestra."

It sounded stupid as soon as I'd said it, but Holly just nodded and murmured something.

The dinner began with Mr. Conner saying some words of thanks for his family's good fortune. It was like a toast at a Chinese banquet, and I thought he sounded very dignified.

Mrs. Conner carried the whole roast turkey into the dining room on a platter, and we all exclaimed at the size of the turkey. It was the largest bird I had ever seen, dead or alive.

Mr. Conner began sharpening a wicked-looking knife. Then he took up the knife and a big fork, and began to cut thin slices of meat from the bird.

YOU'RE TELLING ME!

What reasons does the narrator give for the Yang children's behavior as they are introduced? Underline those reasons.

INFER

Pause at line 79. If the narrator could reveal Holly's thoughts, what might those thoughts be?

Lensey Namioka   **141**

INFER

Who do you think would slice the meat at a Chinese dinner (lines 90–92)?

_____

_____

_____

_____

_____

_____

YOU'RE TELLING ME!

Why are the Yangs embarrassed? What don't they know?

_____

_____

_____

_____

_____

_____

_____

_____

VOCABULARY DEVELOPMENT

savory (sā′vər·ē) adj.: delicious to taste or smell.

90   We Yangs looked at one another in wonder. Instead of complaining about being made to do the slicing, Mr. Conner looked pleased and proud.

After slicing a pile of turkey meat, Mr. Conner started to scoop from the stomach of the bird. I was horrified. Had Mrs. Conner forgotten to dress the turkey and left all the guts behind?

Chicken is an expensive treat in China. When Mother wanted to boil or stir-fry a chicken, she had to buy the bird live to make sure it was fresh. Killing, plucking, and dress-
100   ing the chicken was a gruesome job, and Mother hated it. The worst part was pulling all the guts out of the stomach. Sometimes, when the bird was a hen, she would even find a cluster of eggs inside.

Watching Mr. Conner scooping away, I was embarrassed for him. I exchanged glances with the rest of my family, and I could see that they were dismayed, too.

To my astonishment—and relief—what Mr. Conner scooped out was not the messy intestines. Mrs. Conner had not forgotten to dress the bird after all. She had stuffed the
110   stomach of the bird with a **savory** mixture of bread and onions!

We gasped with admiration, and Mrs. Conner looked pleased. "I hope you like the stuffing. I'm trying out a new recipe."

Mr. Conner placed some slices of turkey meat on each plate, then added a spoonful of the stuffing mixture. Next he ladled a brown sauce over everything. He passed the first plate to Mother.

"Oh, I couldn't take this," Mother said politely. She
120   passed the plate on to Mrs. Hanson.

Mrs. Hanson was jammed up against Mother's shoulder pad at the crowded table. She passed the plate back to Mother. "Oh, no, it's meant for you, Mrs. Yang."

Mother handed the plate back again. "You're so much older, Mrs. Hanson, so you should be served first."

Mrs. Hanson froze. In the silence, I could hear the sauce going *drip, drip* from Mr. Conner's ladle.

"What makes you think so?" asked Mrs. Hanson stiffly. "Just what makes you think I'm older?"

130 "Mom, let's skip it," Holly whispered.

I had already learned that in America it isn't considered an honor to be old. Instead of respecting older people, as we do, Americans think it is pitiful to be old. Mrs. Hanson must have thought that Mother was trying to insult her. Would Mother say something else embarrassing?

She didn't disappoint me. "Well, how old are you, then?" Mother asked Mrs. Hanson.

I **winced.** In school, I had once asked a friend how old our teacher was. We do this a lot. When we meet a stranger, 140 we often ask him how old he is. My friend told me, however, that in America it's rude to ask people's ages. I was really grateful to her for the warning.

After Mother's question, Mrs. Hanson sat completely still. "I am thirty-six," she replied finally, each syllable falling like a chunk of ice.

"Oh, really?" said Mother brightly. "You look much older!"

A whuffling sound came from Matthew and his brother, Eric. Unable to look at the Hansons, I stole a glance at 150 Mr. Conner. His face was bright red, and he seemed to be having trouble breathing. Mrs. Conner was bent over, as if

YOU'RE TELLING ME!

Pause at line 135. Why is it important that the narrator explain this information to readers?

_____

_____

_____

_____

_____

_____

_____

_____

_____

_____

VOCABULARY DEVELOPMENT

winced (winst) *v.*: drew back, with a facial expression of pain or embarrassment.

DECODING TIP

Circle the word *whuffling* (line 148). *Whuffling* is an example of **onomatopoeia**, a word that sounds like what it is. If you say *whuffling* aloud with a lot of breath and force behind it, you will have an idea of what *whuffling* sounds like.

Re-read lines 152–153. What does the narrator reveal here? How does this information make you feel about her?

_____

_____

_____

_____

_____

_____

_____

_____

_____

_____

_____

_____

_____

_____

_____

_____

_____

_____

_____

_____

in pain. I looked down at my plate and wished I could disappear.

Somehow, the dinner went on. Mrs. Hanson finally unclenched her jaw and told Mrs. Conner how delicious the cranberry sauce was. I figured she was referring to the red sticky mound of poisonous-looking berries. I put a berry in my mouth and almost gagged at its sour taste. Next to me, Fourth Brother quietly spat his cranberries into

160   his paper napkin. When he caught my eye, he looked guilty. He wadded up the napkin and stuffed it into his pocket. I hoped he wouldn't forget about it later.

The rest of the food was delicious, though. I thought the stuffing tasted even better than the turkey meat. The good food seemed to relax everybody, and people began to chat. Eldest Brother, who liked to do carpentry, was asking Mr. Conner's advice about various kinds of saws. Mrs. Hanson and Mrs. Conner talked about what kind of cake they were planning to make for the bake sale at the next

170   PTA meeting.

I took a deep breath and turned to Holly. "How do you like the piece we're playing for the winter concert? The violas have a pretty good part."

Holly picked at her cranberries. "I may have to pass up the concert. My viola teacher wants me to play in a recital, and I have to spend all my time practicing for that."

Holly spoke in her usual pleasant voice, but she didn't sound enthusiastic about the recital.

"Do you like your viola teacher?" I asked. "My father

180   teaches viola, as well as violin, you know."

Mrs. Hanson turned her head. "Holly takes lessons from the first violist of the Seattle Symphony!"

I flushed. She sounded as if she thought I was drumming up lessons for my father.

Father looked interested. "Does Holly take lessons from Silverman? He's a marvelous musician! It must be wonderful to be accepted as his pupil!"

Mrs. Hanson's expression softened. "Holly works awfully hard. She can be a regular whirlwind at times!"

190 I stopped worrying. Apparently Mrs. Hanson had got over her anger at being called old, and we Yangs were not **disgracing** ourselves. We all used our knives and forks correctly and waited for permission before helping ourselves from the serving dishes in the middle of the table.

I asked Holly about herself. "Do you have any brothers or sisters?"

"No, there's just Mom and me at home." She added softly, "My parents were divorced three years ago."

I tried to find something sympathetic to say but
200 couldn't think of anything. Holly's expression didn't tell me much. "Do you spend much time with your father?" I finally asked.

"I stay with him during the summer," said Holly. "He has a boat and takes me sailing."

I was impressed. "A boat? Your father must be rich!"

As soon as the words left my mouth, I wished I could take them back. I had forgotten that in America it isn't polite to discuss money. However hard I tried, I just couldn't remember everything.

210 Holly was silent for a moment. Finally she said, "My mom supports the two of us. She works in the records department in a hospital. But Dad pays for my music lessons." She looked curiously at me. "Does your mother work?"

VOCABULARY DEVELOPMENT

disgracing (dis·grās'iŋ) v.: bringing shame or dishonor upon.

YOU'RE TELLING ME!

Pause at line 202. Because the narrator doesn't know what's going on in Holly's mind, we don't know either. What do you guess Holly is feeling?

_____

_____

_____

_____

INTERPRET

Pause at the end of this page. Why are the characters' cultural backgrounds so important to this story?

_____

_____

_____

_____

_____

_____

The narrator doesn't know what kinds of records Mrs. Hanson works with. What mistake does she make (lines 218–220)?

_____

_____

_____

_____

_____

_____

_____

_____

_____

_____

_____

_____

_____

FLUENCY

Read the boxed passage aloud, using expression to show that different characters are speaking. When you read the passage again, smooth out your delivery, and increase your pace.

"No, she spends all her time shopping and cooking," I admitted. Suddenly my mother, with her ridiculous shoulder pads, looked dumpy sitting next to the elegant Mrs. Hanson, who worked with records in a hospital. Were they LP records, cassette tapes, or CDs? I wondered. It sounded
220 like a glamorous job.

"I wish my mother had a job," I said wistfully. Mother had been a professional pianist, but in Seattle she hadn't been able to find work.

At least Second Sister and I earned some money baby-sitting, which is something girls don't do in China. If Chinese parents have to go out, they usually try to get the grandparents to look after the children.

"Do you do any baby-sitting?" I asked.

"I do a little," said Holly. Suddenly she smiled. "What I
230 like best is to baby-sit dogs."

"Baby-sit dogs," I repeated slowly. "You mean dog-sit?"

Holly laughed. I could see *this* was something she really enjoyed talking about. "When my neighbors are busy, I take their dogs for walks," she explained. "I just love animals."

"If Holly had her way, our house would be overflowing with pets," said Mrs. Hanson.

"Did you keep pets in China?" Holly asked me.

I shook my head. "We didn't have room."
240 "We could barely squeeze our family into our Shanghai apartment," said Father, "much less have room for pets."

"Until recently, it was actually illegal to keep a dog in many cities," added Mother. "If a dog was heard barking, the police would come to investigate."

Holly looked shocked. "How about cats, then? Are you allowed to keep cats?"

"Cats are allowed," said Father. "They don't take up much room, and they don't create a sanitation problem in the streets. But keeping them is still a luxury most people can't afford."

"Well, it's different here," said Mrs. Hanson. "Holly and I have a cat and six kittens at the moment."

"If you have a house with a yard, you'd have room enough for a cat," Holly said to me. "Do you live in a house?"

I wondered why she sounded so eager as she asked the question. Before I could say anything, Father answered. "We're renting half of a house, but it would be quite impossible for us to keep a cat. We have so many instruments and piles of sheet music lying around that any kind of pet would be a disaster."

The excitement faded from Holly's face, and I knew our family had disappointed her in some way. I wondered why.

Mrs. Conner began to clear the dinner plates. Matthew and his brother, Eric, jumped up to help her. Fourth Brother also got up, but Mrs. Conner told him to sit down again. "Two helpers are all I need, Sprout. The kitchen isn't big enough for more than that."

"Sprout?" said Father. I knew he loved stir-fried bean sprouts. He looked eagerly around the table and was disappointed when he didn't see any.

I laughed. "Sprout is what everybody calls Fourth Brother, Father."

My American friends call me Mary, the name I picked for myself, since my Chinese name, Yingmei, is too hard for them to remember. In fact I had trouble remembering *American* names when I first came. I still keep a list of new

YOU'RE TELLING ME!

Pause at line 264. Why do *you* think Holly is disappointed?

_____

_____

_____

_____

_____

_____

_____

_____

_____

_____

IDENTIFY

What does Father think of when he hears the word *sprout* (line 274)?

_____

_____

_____

_____

IDENTIFY

Here the story's narrator reveals her name or names. Circle them.

**VOCABULARY
DEVELOPMENT**

determination
(dē·tʉr′min·ā′shən) *n.:*
firmness of purpose.

IDENTIFY

Pause at line 312 on the next
page. Underline the passage
that tells what Chinese people think about being fat.

· · · · · · · Notes · · · · · ·

_____

_____

_____

_____

_____

_____

_____

_____

_____

_____

_____

_____

_____

_____

_____

_____

_____

280 words and phrases for memorizing, and a lot of the entries
are names.

My family could never remember my new American
name, though. When people mentioned Mary, the Yangs
would say, "Who is Mary?" So it was good to see Father
puzzled by Sprout for a change.

Mr. Conner nodded. "Yeah, Sprout is a good name
for the little guy." He added quickly, "The little guy with
the big bat." Mr. Conner was proud of Fourth Brother's
success with baseball, because he was the one who had
coached him.

290 Mr. Conner was right. Sprouts look small and
weedy, but they push up from the earth with a lot of
determination. Fourth Brother is like that.

After the plates were cleared, Mrs. Conner brought in
dessert: ice cream and three different kinds of pies. From
the way their eyes were shining, I guessed that Eric and
Matthew thought this was the best part of the meal.
Personally, I enjoyed the turkey and the stuffing so much
that I didn't feel like eating anything more, especially something sweet.

300 Again, the first slice of pie went to Mother. This time
she didn't try to pass it to Mrs. Hanson. She had learned
her lesson.

Mrs. Hanson looked at the piece of pie served to her.
"Oh, I couldn't eat all this. I've already put on two pounds
this month, and I can't afford to gain another ounce."

"Of course you can afford it!" Mrs. Conner said
heartily. "You're so skinny, you could put on ten pounds
and still look terrific."

Mother was staring at Mrs. Hanson and Mrs. Conner
310 during this exchange. We Chinese think that being fat is

good. It's a sign of good fortune. Thin people are considered unfortunate and miserable.

But I knew that here, being thin is supposed to be attractive. A lot of the girls in school are worried about their weight, and some of them even go on diets.

I saw Mother open her mouth. Don't say it, Mother, I wanted to shout. Don't say it!

But she did. Radiating good will, Mother said, "Why, you're not skinny at all, Mrs. Hanson. You're actually quite fat!"

320

INTERPRET

What does Mother want to express to Mrs. Hanson? What does she actually say?

_____

_____

_____

_____

_____

_____

OWN THE STORY

PRACTICING THE STANDARDS

Point of View   Take a portion of the scene at the Thanksgiving dinner, and let Mrs. Conner tell the story. Then, take the same scene, and tell it from the point of view of an omniscient narrator—one who can explain everything to us and tell us all about all the characters. Finally, retell the scene from the third-person limited point of view. You might zoom in on Holly. Here are some openers:

Mrs. Conner: I carried the whole roast turkey into the dining room on a platter. I hoped my guests would like turkey. . . .

Omniscient narrator: Mrs. Conner carried the whole roast turkey into the dining room on a platter. Little did she know that a year from that day she would be eating squid at the Yangs. . . .

Third-person limited: Holly was uncomfortable at the table because her mother and Mrs. Yang just seemed to keep blundering into problems. She also was worried about her dad. She thought Yingmei, the narrator, might be a friend who would listen to her worries. But Holly was shy, even though she didn't look it. . . .

_____

_____

_____

_____

_____

_____

_____

_____

_____

_____

_____

_____

_____

_____

_____

_____

_____

KEEPING TRACK

Personal Word List   Add the new words you encountered to your Personal Word List. Put a star next to any words that you think you might use soon.

Personal Reading Log   Did you think the first-person narrator was funny? Note other humorous stories told from the first-person point of view you have enjoyed. Give yourself 6 points on the Reading Meter.

Checklist for Standards Mastery   Point of view can be a difficult concept. Be sure you understand the three types of point of view. Use the Checklist for Standards Mastery to see how far you have come in mastering the standards.

Thanksgiving with the Conners
Interactive Reading, page 139

Go Beyond a Literary Text

Cartoon Strip   Cartoonists use a series of illustrations and words to tell a story. Speech balloons in cartoons show what the characters are saying, and thought bubbles show what characters are thinking. Illustrate a scene from this story in a series of cartoon panels. As a starting point, you might choose an exchange between Yingmei's mother and Mrs. Hanson. Use speech balloons to show what the characters are saying and thought bubbles to show what they are thinking.

Speech balloon   **Thought bubble**

ETIQUETTE GUIDE

BEFORE YOU READ

Etiquette (et′i·kit) is a word meaning "manners." An etiquette guide tells you how to behave properly in different types of social situations. What is the "correct" way to put a soup spoon in your mouth? How do you know which knife to use? How do you use chopsticks? Read on to find entertaining information on these subjects.

Here are a few points to know before you begin reading:

- The author, Judith Martin, uses the pseudonym Miss Manners to refer to herself.
- Martin explains why she holds her opinions and tries to persuade readers that her view is correct.

Reading Standard 2.4
Identify and trace the development of an author's argument, point of view, or perspective in text.

from Miss Manners' Basic Training: Eating

Judith Martin

TEXT STRUCTURE

Most of the text uses a question-and-answer format in the form of letters to and from Miss Manners. Circle the greeting in each letter from Miss Manners. How does Miss Manners address her readers? How do you feel about this greeting?

_____

_____

_____

American and European Styles

Dear Miss Manners—Is it acceptable in the United States to use the European method of dining with the knife in the right hand and the fork in the left, cutting the food as you eat it?

Gentle Reader—Is it acceptable for someone in the United States to speak with, say, an English or French accent?

    Certainly, if that person is a foreigner or foreign-born. Eating European style (keeping the fork in the left hand

10   and packing food onto the back of it with the knife) rather

American style of eating.

European style of eating.

IDENTIFY

Pause at line 15. How does the writer feel about Americans who use the European method of eating? Underline the answer.

VOCABULARY DEVELOPMENT

affected (ə·fekt′id) *adj.:* artificial; pretending to be something you are not.

incident (in′sə·dənt) *n.:* minor disturbance.

INFER

What do you think Miss Manners means by "without incident" (line 28)?

_____

_____

_____

_____

_____

_____

_____

_____

_____

_____

_____

_____

_____

than American style (switching the fork to the right hand after cutting and bringing food to the mouth with the fork facing upward) is acceptable in the United States for foreigners and the foreign-born. In anyone else, it is considered **affected.**

Chopsticks

Chopstick usage varies in different countries, as indeed do the implements[1] themselves. Here is the basic technique considered acceptable when practiced by Westerners:

20   Chopsticks are held as if you were using two pencils at once, except that the lower one is gripped between the thumb, at about knuckle level, and the end of the ring finger, while the upper chopstick is gripped between the end of the thumb and the end of the forefinger, with the assistance of the middle finger. This should provide enough leverage to grasp food by moving the upper chopstick down so that the tips hold it securely enough to get it to the mouth without **incident.**

---

1. **implements:** tools.

Pause at line 32. In this passage the writer refers to Miss Manners in the third person. Rewrite this line of text so that the writer refers to herself in the first person.

_____

_____

_____

_____

WORD
KNOWLEDGE

What do you guess *ineptitude* means in line 36? Check the context.

_____

_____

_____

_____

_____

_____

VOCABULARY
DEVELOPMENT

cultivate (kul′tə·vāt′) *v.:* develop or acquire.

communal (kə·myo̅o̅n′əl) *adj.:* belonging to a group.

Of course, a lot depends on what we mean by "it."
30 Grains of rice? Slippery noodles? Tiny tofu squares that collapse under pressure?

This may be the place for Miss Manners to mention that one may properly ask for a fork when dining in an Asian restaurant in the West—although they are usually already provided by restaurateurs, who have no desire to witness or clean up after ineptitude. Tourists attempting a difficult foreign custom should **cultivate** a look of appealing stupidity that will give their mistakes a sort of childish charm.

40 Things you may not do with your chopsticks include stabbing (food or people), putting the parts that have been in your mouth into a **communal** bowl (Chinese restaurants provide a spoon to get around this practice, and the Japanese method is to reverse one's sticks), parking them in the bowl crossed or pointing across the table (they are left on a chopstick holder or on the paper container in which they came), or doing any of those other nasty things imaginative children of all nations come up with.

An East-West trade-off.

The Soup Spoon

50 Dear Miss Manners—Where do you place your mouth and lips in relation to a soup spoon? A friend and I have a difference of opinion. I say you sip from the side, but if it's a thick type of soup with lots of items in it (such as pieces of vegetables), you place the tip of the spoon in your mouth so you can consume the liquid and whatever else at the same time.

Gentle Reader—Yours would be an excellent solution if the journey of food to mouth were merely a transportation problem, to be figured out on a practical basis. But if that

60 were the case, Miss Manners would also have to listen to more efficient movers, who might point out that picking things out of the soup with the fingers would be even more practical, provided that the soup wasn't scalding.

One always pours soup, even goody-laden soup, into the mouth from the side of an oval soup spoon. Perhaps Miss Manners can make up for this bad news by telling you about the gumbo[2] spoon: It's large, it's proper for soups with a lot of things in them, and it's round, so it is less obvious if you slip from side to tip.

70 ## Extra Spoons (and Some Plates)

Dear Miss Manners—My boyfriend insists that when we are having company (unless it's a picnic), a spoon is to be set, along with whatever other flatware[3] is needed, even when there is nothing being served that requires a spoon. The dinner in question consisted of green salad, grilled halibut, wild rice, and bread. In addition, he felt that bread

---

2. **gumbo:** thick soup made with okra.
3. **flatware:** knives, forks, and spoons.

Underline Miss Manners' advice about eating soup. Do you agree with her?

INFER

Why does Miss Manners ask
about dessert (line 91)?

_____

_____

_____

_____

_____

_____

_____

_____

_____

_____

_____

_____

_____

_____

_____

_____

plates weren't necessary, as that created too many dishes on
the table, in addition to dinner and salad plates.

80   Gentle Reader—Miss Manners appreciates the interest that
both of you take in the properly set table and the opportunity she has to side graciously with both of you.

She is with you on the spoon. Contrary to popular
fears, table settings are not tricks to **humiliate** people who
can't see a relationship between the flatware and the food.
The two are directly connected: What is set out is there
to be used and is even placed (outside to inside) in order
of use. A spoon is not set out unless it is needed—for
grapefruit at breakfast, for example, or for soup at dinner.
A dessert spoon would be placed above the plate, parallel

90   to the table's edge. (Which reminds Miss Manners—
you didn't have any dessert, did you? Are all your friends
on diets?)

However, she is with the gentleman in thinking that
three plates for each person would make the table look like
a china shop. Bread can always be placed on the edge of the
main plate, or on the tablecloth (yes, surprisingly enough—
as long as there is no butter involved to make grease stains).
You could also serve the salad as a separate course.

The Knife

100   Dear Miss Manners—My niece, an educated and charming
person, holds her knife and fork in a most awkward fash-
ion. She holds her knife vertically while cutting her meat.
Please comment.

Gentle Reader—She tries to cut meat while holding her knife in a completely vertical position? The poor lady. She will probably starve to death.

Packing the Fork

110 | Dear Miss Manners—Is a person allowed to eat a small portion of potato and meat together from the same forkful of food, or must they always be consumed separately?

Gentle Reader—Making a food package on the fork, such as using mashed potatoes to cement meat and peas onto it, is considered distasteful in America—to other diners, that is. However, those who find it tasty may absentmindedly allow the prongs of a meat-laden fork to drift idly into the potatoes on its way to the mouth. Or they can learn how to park meat in a discreet corner of the cheek until the potato delivery arrives on the next fork run.

FLUENCY

Read the boxed passage aloud. What *tone* or feeling will you convey? Circle or underline words that you stumbled over. Then, read the passage again, paying careful attention to those problem words.

INTERPRET

What is Miss Manners' tone in lines 111–118—is she serious or humorous? Underline the words that give you a clue.

_____

_____

_____

_____

_____

_____

_____

_____

_____

_____

_____

_____

_____

_____

OWN THE TEXT

Perspective   Which sentence describes Miss Manners' **perspective,** or point of view, on manners?

1. She is very serious and uptight about them.
2. She is relaxed and informal.
3. She mocks manners at the table.
4. She is serious but good-humored.

Decide on Miss Manners' perspective, and write three sentences defending your answer. Use details from the text to support your opinion.

_____

_____

_____

_____

_____

_____

Personal Word List   Add the new words you came across in this text to your Personal Word List.

Personal Reading Log   What did you think of these letters? Could you use any of Miss Manners' information? Write your ideas about etiquette in your Personal Reading Log, and give yourself 4 points on the Reading Meter.

Checklist for Standards Mastery   Use the Checklist for Standards Mastery to see how far you have come in mastering the standards.

from Miss Manners' Basic Training: Eating

Go Beyond an Informational Text

Advice Column   Advice columns are popular newspaper features. Readers send in questions that the columnist answers. Some advice columns focus on specific subjects, such as love, dieting, or etiquette.

Create a title for an advice column, and write the columnist's byline. Then, write a letter from "a reader" that asks a question. Answer the question in a letter from "the columnist."

Column Title _____

Byline _____

Dear _____

Dear _____

BEFORE YOU READ

"China's Little Ambassador" is about Shirley, a young Chinese immigrant, and her first days at a school, P.S. 8, in New York City. Unlike the narrator in "Thanksgiving with the Conners," Shirley has not had a whole year to learn about a new culture. What will an American school seem like to her?

Here are some points to know before you read the story:

- This is the third chapter of a book with an interesting title: *In the Year of the Boar and Jackie Robinson.*
- The story is told in the third-person limited point of view. The narrator knows everything that is going on but zooms in and tells the story from Shirley's point of view. We feel as if we were right in Shirley's head.
- Traditionally the Chinese count themselves as one year old on the day they are born.

Reading Standard 3.5 Contrast points of view (for example, first and third person, limited and omniscient, subjective and objective) in narrative text, and explain how they affect the overall theme of the work.

China's Little Ambassador

Bette Bao Lord

YOU'RE TELLING ME!

Pause at line 6. What does Shirley wish she had done? Who tells you this?

_____

_____

_____

_____

_____

Shirley sat in the principal's office at P.S. 8. Her mother and the schoolmistress were talking. Shirley didn't understand a word. It was embarrassing. Why hadn't she, too, studied the English course on the records that Father had sent? But it was too late now. She stopped trying to understand. Suddenly, Mother hissed, in Chinese, "Stop that or else!"

Shirley snapped her head down. She had been staring at the stranger. But she could not keep her eyes from rolling up again. There was something more foreign about the

10   principal than about any other foreigner she had seen so

"China's Little Ambassador" by Bette Bao Lord from *In the Year of the Boar and Jackie Robinson.* Copyright © 1984 by Bette Bao Lord. Reprinted by permission of *HarperCollins Publishers.*

far. What was it? It was not the blue eyes. Many others had them too. It was not the high nose. All foreign noses were higher than Chinese ones. It was not the blue hair. Hair came in all colors in America.

Yes, of course, naturally. The woman had no eyelashes. Other foreigners grew hair all over them, more than six Chinese together. This woman had none. Her skin was as bare as the Happy Buddha's belly, except for the neat rows of stiff curls that hugged her head.

20   She had no eyebrows, even. They were penciled on, and looked just like the character for man, ∧. And every time she tilted her head, her hair moved all in one piece like a hat.

"Shirley."

Mother was trying to get her attention. "Tell the principal how old you are."

Shirley put up ten fingers.

While the principal filled out a form, mother argued excitedly. But why? Shirley had given the correct answer.

30 She counted just to make sure. On the day she was born, she was one year old. And two months later, upon the new year, she was two. That was the Year of the Rabbit. Then came the Dragon, Snake, Horse, Sheep, Monkey, Rooster, Dog, and now it was the year of the Boar, making ten. Proof she was ten.

Mother shook her head. Apparently, she had lost the argument. She announced in Chinese, "Shirley, you will enter fifth grade."

"Fifth? But, Mother, I don't speak English. And besides,

40 I only completed three grades in Chungking."

"I know. But the principal has explained that in America everyone is assigned according to age. Ten years

YOU'RE TELLING ME!

Pause at line 19. What have you learned about Shirley's background and knowledge?

_____

_____

_____

_____

_____

_____

_____

_____

PREDICT

Pause at line 35. Think about how Shirley is counting the years since the day she was born. How old is she really? How could this be a problem for Shirley?

_____

_____

_____

_____

_____

_____

_____

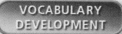

obediently (ō·bē′dē·ənt′lē)
adv.: in a dutiful manner.

Re-read lines 59–65. What
does Shirley think the
teacher's wink means?
(Did you know what the
teacher was doing?)

_____

_____

_____

_____

_____

_____

_____

_____

_____

_____

_____

_____

_____

_____

_____

old means fifth grade. And we must observe the American rules, mustn't we?"

Shirley nodded **obediently.** But she could not help thinking that only Shirley had to go to school, and only Shirley would be in trouble if she failed.

Mother stood up to leave. She took Shirley by the hand. "Remember, my daughter, you may be the only
50   Chinese these Americans will ever meet. Do your best. Be extra good. Upon your shoulders rests the reputation of all Chinese."

All five hundred million? Shirley wondered.

"You are China's little ambassador."

"Yes, Mother." Shirley squared her shoulders and tried to feel worthy of this great honor. At the same time she wished she could leave with Mother.

Alone, the schoolmistress and Shirley looked at each other. Suddenly the principal shut one eye, the right one,
60   then opened it again.

Was this another foreign custom, like shaking hands? It must be proper if a principal does it, Shirley thought. She ought to return the gesture, but she didn't know how. So she shut and opened both eyes. Twice.

This brought a warm laugh.

The principal then led her to class. The room was large, with windows up to the ceiling. Row after row of students, each one unlike the next. Some faces were white, like clean plates, others black like ebony. Some were in-between
70   shades. A few were spotted all over. One boy was as big around as a water jar. Several others were as thin as chopsticks. No one wore a uniform of blue, like hers. There were sweaters with animals on them, shirts with stripes and

shirts with squares, dresses in colors as **varied** as Grand-granduncle's paints. Three girls even wore earrings.

While Shirley looked about, the principal had been making a speech. Suddenly it ended with "Shirley Temple Wong." The class stood up and waved.

Amitabha! They were all so tall. Even Water Jar was a head taller than she. For a fleeting moment she wondered if Mother would consider buying an ambassador a pair of high-heeled shoes.

"Hi, Shirley!" The class shouted.

Shirley bowed deeply. Then, taking a guess, she replied, "Hi!"

The teacher introduced herself and showed the new pupil to a front-row seat. Shirley liked her right away, although she had a most difficult name, Mrs. Rappaport. She was a tiny woman with dainty bones and fiery red hair brushed skyward. Shirley thought that in her previous life she must have been a bird, a cardinal perhaps. Yet she **commanded** respect, for no student talked out of turn. Or was it the long mean pole that hung on the wall behind the desk that commanded respect? It **dwarfed** the bamboo cane the teacher in Chungking had used to punish Four Hands whenever he stole a trifle from another.

Throughout the lessons, Shirley leaned forward, barely touching her seat, to catch the meaning, but the words sounded like gurgling water. Now and then, when Mrs. Rappaport looked her way, she opened and shut her eyes as the principal had done, to show friendship.

At lunchtime, Shirley went with the class to the school cafeteria, but before she could pick up a tray, several boys and girls waved for her to follow them. They were smiling, so she went along. They snuck back to the classroom to

80

90

100

VOCABULARY DEVELOPMENT

varied (ver'ēd) *adj.:* made up of different kinds.

WORD KNOWLEDGE

Amitabha in line 79 is the most common name of the Buddha of Infinite Light and Infinite Life.

VOCABULARY DEVELOPMENT

commanded (kə·mand'id) *v.:* gave orders.

dwarfed (dwôrft) *v.:* caused to appear small by comparison.

· · · · · · **Notes** · · · · · ·

VOCABULARY DEVELOPMENT

escapade (es′kə·pād′) *n.:* reckless act.

· · · · · · Notes · · · · · ·

pick up coats, then hurried out the door and across the schoolyard to a nearby store. Shirley was certain they should not be there, but what choice did she have? These were now her friends.

110   One by one they gave their lunch money to the store owner, whom they called Mr. P. In return, he gave each a bottle of orange-colored water, bread twice the size of an ear of corn oozing with meat balls, peppers, onions, and hot red gravy, and a large piece of brown paper to lay on the icy sidewalk and sit upon. While they ate, everyone except Shirley played marbles or cards and traded bottle caps and pictures of men swinging a stick or wearing one huge glove. It was the best lunch Shirley had ever had.

And there was more. After lunch, each of them was
120   allowed to select one item from those displayed under the glass counter. There were paper strips dotted with red and yellow sugar tacks, chocolate soldiers in blue tin foil, boxes of raisins and nuts, envelopes of chips, cookies as big as pancakes, candy elephants, lollipops in every color, a wax collection of red lips, white teeth, pink ears, and curly black moustaches. Shirley was the last to make up her mind. She chose a hand, filled with juice. It looked better than it tasted, but she did not mind. Tomorrow she could choose again.

130   But when she was back in her seat, waiting for Mrs. Rappaport to enter the classroom, Shirley's knees shook. What if the teacher found out about her **escapade?** There would go her ambassadorship. She would be shamed. Her parents would lose face. All five hundred million Chinese would suffer. Round and round in her stomach the meat balls tumbled like pebbles.

Then Mrs. Rappaport came in. She did not look pleased. Shirley flinched when the teacher went straight to the long mean pole. For the first time her heart went out to

140 Four Hands. She shut her eyes and prayed to the Goddess of Mercy. Oh Kwan Yin, please don't let me cry! She waited, listening for Mrs. Rappaport's footsteps to become louder and louder. They did not. Finally curiosity overcame fear and she looked up. Mrs. Rappaport was using the pole to open a window!

The lessons continued. During arithmetic, Shirley raised her hand. She went to the blackboard and wrote the correct answer. Mrs. Rappaport rewarded her with a big smile. Shirley opened and shut her eyes to show her

150 pleasure. Soon, she was dreaming about candy elephants and cookies the size of pancakes.

Then school was over. As Shirley was putting on her coat, Mrs. Rappaport handed her a letter, obviously to be given to her parents. Fear returned. Round and round, this time like rocks.

She barely greeted her mother at the door.

"What happened?"

"Nothing."

"You look sick."

160 "I'm all right."

"Perhaps it was something you ate at lunch?"

"No," she said much too quickly. "Nothing at all to do with lunch."

"What then?"

"The job of ambassador is harder than I thought."

YOU'RE TELLING ME!

Underline the lines where you learn how Shirley feels about "the long mean pole" (line 139). What do you think this passage would be like if Mrs. Rappaport were the narrator?

Lines 166–168 describe
Shirley's worries and fears.
What *don't* we know
because of this limited point
of view?

_____

_____

_____

At bedtime, Shirley could no longer put off giving up the letter. Trembling, she handed it to Father. She imagined herself on a boat back to China.

He read it aloud to Mother. Then they both turned to
170 her, a most quizzical look on their faces.

"Your teacher suggests we take you to a doctor. She thinks there is something wrong with your eyes."

OWN THE STORY

PRACTICING THE STANDARDS

Point of View   Choose a passage from the story, and rewrite it from the point of view of Shirley's teacher or one of Shirley's classmates. You can use *I* or the third-person limited point of view, zooming in on the character you choose.

_____

_____

_____

_____

KEEPING TRACK

Personal Word List   Record new words in your Personal Word List. Put a star next to words that are particularly descriptive.

Personal Reading Log   As you add this story to your Personal Reading Log, tell why you would or would not recommend it to a friend. Give yourself 3 points on the Reading Meter.

Checklist for Standards Mastery   Use the Checklist for Standards Mastery to see how much you have learned.

China's Little Ambassador

Interactive Reading, page 160

Go Beyond a Literary Text

Chinese Calendar   The Chinese calendar that Shirley uses to calculate her age is a lunar calendar; it follows the cycle of the moon. The Chinese give each year an animal name in a twelve-year cycle. The cycle begins with the year of the rat.

Use your library or the Internet to find the animal names of each year in the Chinese calendar cycle. Complete the lunar calendar below by writing the names of the animals in order. Then find out what year in the cycle we are in now, and label the calendar with the dates for the next twelve years. Use the calendar to find out what animal year it is now and what animal year you were born in. The year 2001 has been done for you.

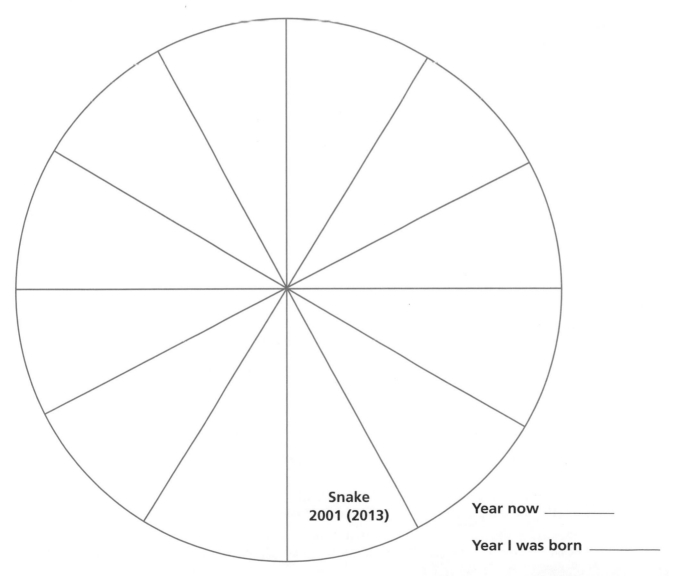

Snake
2001 (2013)

Year now _____

Year I was born _____

Chapter 5

Worlds of Words
Prose and Poetry

Strategy Launch: "Text Reformulation"

LITERARY FOCUS: PROSE

Most of what you read is prose writing presented in sentence-and-paragraph form. There are two main types of **prose.** *Fiction* is prose about made-up characters and events. *Nonfiction* is prose that deals with real people and real events—with facts. Within these two categories are several forms of prose, such as the short story, novel, and essay. Each type of prose is written for a purpose and has certain characteristics.

A STRATEGY THAT WORKS: "TEXT REFORMULATION"

Suppose you have read a short story that is set in a town destroyed by a volcano. You can use the "Text Reformulation" strategy to help you analyze the story and to see how it differs from another prose form.

POINTERS FOR USING "TEXT REFORMULATION"

Here is a two-step strategy that will help you identify and analyze the characteristics of various types of prose:

First Step: As you read, identify the text patterns and elements that are characteristic of that type of prose. Here are some strategies that can help you identify text patterns:

- ⟫➡ Reformulate a plot by restating its events in pairs of sentences. One begins "Fortunately" and the next begins "Unfortunately."

- ⟫➡ Use the "If/Then" pattern to identify cause-and-effect patterns.

- ⟫➡ Use "Who/What/When/Where/Why/How" questions to identify facts in an article.

Second Step: After you read, reformulate the text as another type of prose. For example, if you've read a short story about a volcano eruption, you could reformulate it as a news article using "Who/What/When/Where/Why/How" questions. Reformulating text will help you understand and appreciate how the elements in the original text work together to create a whole.

Reading Standard 1.1
Identify idioms, analogies, metaphors, and similes in prose and poetry.

Reading Standard 2.2 (Grade 6 Review)
Analyze text that uses the compare-and-contrast organizational pattern.

Reading Standard 2.4 (Grade 6 Review)
Clarify an understanding of texts by creating outlines, logical notes, summaries, or reports.

Reading Standard 3.1
Articulate the expressed purposes and characteristics of different forms of prose (for example, short story, novel, novella, essay).

Practice Read

The **short story** is a form of fiction that usually follows this pattern: A character wants something very badly, takes action to get it, and runs into problems or conflicts. The story builds to a climax when the conflict is resolved one way or another. The very title of this short story suggests a conflict.

The Competitors

Meish Goldish

VOCABULARY DEVELOPMENT

preliminaries
(prē·lim′ə·ner′ēz) *n.:* contests or matches that take place before the main one.

TEXT REFORMULATION

Underline the words that tell what Tanya wants and the problem she faces. Write an "Unfortunately" sentence explaining her problem.

_____

_____

_____

_____

_____

_____

Tanya was so busy daydreaming about the upcoming track meet that she didn't even hear Mr. Martin call her name.

"Tanya," Mr. Martin repeated in an annoyed tone. "The class is waiting for your answer."

Tanya came to. She shook her head and said, "I'm sorry, Mr. Martin. What was the question?"

A snicker came from Suki, the student sitting directly behind Tanya. Tanya turned around and hissed, "Not so funny! We'll see who's laughing after the track
10 **preliminaries.**"

"Tanya, please see me after class," Mr. Martin said sternly. Tanya turned back in her seat, but not before she saw the smirk on Suki's face.

Great, Tanya thought. Now I'm in trouble with Mr. Martin. And this is the one class I have trouble in.

Tanya knew that to stay on the school track team, she needed to maintain a B average. Getting good grades in Mr. Martin's math class was like cracking walnuts with your

bare hands. It was a tough job. Tanya couldn't afford to
20 slack off.

When the bell rang, Tanya remained in her seat until
all the other students had left the room. Mr. Martin sat
down near her and asked, "So what's the problem, Tanya?
Your concentration these past few days has been lacking, to
say the least."

Tanya paused. "I guess it's the pressure of the
upcoming track meet," she sighed. "I know it's no excuse.
But the state competition is in two weeks, and only one
pair of runners can represent each school in the relay
30 race. I want to be there with my running partner, Luisa.
But first we've got to beat out other running partners
from school in the prelim—"

Mr. Martin interrupted her before she could finish.
"Tanya," he said, "I think you should focus on your school
work for the moment. You've got a big exam coming up in
two weeks. If you don't do well, it will really affect your
grade. That's why I'm assigning you a tutor."

"A tutor?" Tanya said, shocked. "I can't afford a tutor!"

Mr. Martin smiled. "It's not a paid tutor, Tanya. It's a
40 student-to-student thing. You'll be tutored by one of your
classmates."

"Who?" Tanya asked.

"Suki Midori," Mr. Martin replied.

Tanya's face turned red. "Suki?" she gasped. "No way,
Mr. Martin. You can't do that! First of all, we don't even like
each other. Second of all, she's my competitor in the track
preliminaries. Third, we've got nothing in common. We
hardly know each other!"

"All the more reason to study together," Mr. Martin
50 replied. "Suki is one of my best students. She really

IDENTIFY

Pause at line 32. Underline the words that tell what Tanya wants and the problems she must resolve in order to get it.

TEXT REFORMULATION

Pause at line 41. Underline the passage that shows how Mr. Martin plans to solve Tanya's math problem. Then write a sentence that begins with "Fortunately, . . ." to follow the "Unfortunately" sentence you wrote before.

_____

_____

TEXT REFORMULATION

Pause at line 49. Write a sentence beginning with "Unfortunately, . . ." to follow the "Fortunately" sentence that you just wrote. Now we know one of the conflicts in this story.

_____

_____

_____

_____

_____

_____

understands the material. So you'll be getting great help, Tanya. Plus, you'll have a chance to get to know each other."

Great, Tanya thought. It's not bad enough I have to put up with Suki in school. It's not bad enough that she's my chief competition in the track preliminaries. Now I'm going to have to study with her after school as well. That's like being stuck out in the rain all day, and then coming home to a leaky ceiling!

That night, Tanya received a phone call.

60   "Hi, Tanya," the voice said. "It's Suki Midori. Is now a good time to come over and tutor you? It's good for me."

Tanya was tempted to say that the best time would be never, but she knew that wouldn't be very smart. She had to think of her math score.

"Now is fine," Tanya said in her sweetest voice. "Do you know where I live?"

"Sure," laughed Suki. "My house is just behind yours, one block over."

Tanya hung up and went to get her math book. Great,

70   she thought. Not only is Suki right behind me in math class, she's also behind me in the neighborhood. Just what I need.

When the doorbell rang, Tanya walked downstairs and opened the front door. Suki stood there, all smiles.

"Come on in," Tanya said with forced cheerfulness. "We can study in my bedroom. It'll be quiet there."

The girls entered Tanya's bedroom. On the wall, the large poster of Cheryl Toussaint immediately caught Suki's eye.

80   "Oh, my gosh!" Suki cried. "You have the exact same poster that I have on my wall! Cheryl Toussaint is my idol!"

"She is?" Tanya responded, a little annoyed.

PREDICT

Pause at line 82. At this point in the story, what do you predict will happen next?

"You bet," said Suki. "My grandmother first told me about her when I got interested in running. About how Cheryl ran in the 1972 Olympics and won a silver medal in the relay finals."

Tanya gave in a little. "Cheryl Toussaint is my idol, too!"

"She inspires me," Suki said.

Suki's comment hit Tanya like a hammer. How could
90   she admire the same person that I do? Tanya wondered. But rather than ask any more questions, Tanya decided it was safer to stick to math.

For the next two hours, Suki reviewed all the lessons Mr. Martin had taught in the past week. Tanya couldn't believe how clear Suki made everything seem. Even though Tanya didn't like Suki, she had to admit she was a very good teacher.

At the end of the session, Suki said, "So, when should we meet again?"

100   "Let's meet Wednesday night. No, wait, make it Thursday night. Wednesday night I want to get to bed early, because our track preliminary is the following morning."

"Good idea," Suki agreed. "My running partner and I are competing in the same meet, you know."

"I know," said Tanya, with a twisted smile.

Every day after school, Tanya and Suki practiced on the school running track with their partners. Ordinarily, Tanya wouldn't have talked to Suki during practice. But now that Suki was tutoring her, things were different. Tanya couldn't
110   ignore Suki like she usually did. But more than that, Tanya didn't want to ignore her. She couldn't help but think about how Suki had a Cheryl Toussaint poster on her wall. It made her see Suki in a totally different way.

INFER

Pause at line 113. How is Tanya changing? Underline the sentences that provide clues.

VOCABULARY DEVELOPMENT

poised (poizd) *adj.:* balanced; steady.

adjacent (ə·jā′sənt) *adj.:* near; close by.

WORD KNOWLEDGE

Similes compare two different things using a specific comparison word, such as *like, as, than,* or *resembles.* Underline the two similes in the paragraph beginning at line 128. What is compared to what?

_____

_____

_____

_____

_____

_____

_____

_____

_____

_____

_____

_____

_____

_____

On Thursday morning, the track team assembled for the preliminary meet. When it was time for the relay race, Tanya's partner, Luisa, stood **poised** at the starting line. Next to her, in the **adjacent** lane, was Suki's running partner, Kelly. Tanya and Suki stood at the far end of the track, each ready to grab the baton from their partner in

120 order to finish the race.

When the coach fired the starter's pistol, Luisa and Kelly each took off like a shot. The crowd cheered.

Before long, Tanya and Suki could see their running partners approaching. Suki rubbed her hands on her shorts, so her sweaty palms wouldn't let the baton slip when Kelly passed it to her. Tanya stood with her heart pounding, ready to grab Luisa's baton.

Finally, the runners approached. They were just about neck and neck when they reached the transfer point. Luisa

130 slammed her baton into Tanya's hand, and Tanya took off like a bullet. Five seconds later, Suki grabbed the baton from Kelly and began to dash like a cheetah, staying right on Tanya's heels.

Run, girl, run! Tanya told herself. You can do it! Stay ahead and focus on the finish line! Concentrate!

Suddenly, the unexpected occurred. The baton slipped from Tanya's hand and fell to the ground. For a split second, Tanya panicked. She knew she couldn't win the race without the baton in her hand. But she also knew that

140 stopping to pick it up would waste precious seconds, with Suki hot on her heels.

Suddenly, before Tanya could think anymore, she felt the baton slamming into her palm. Suki was handing it to her! Tanya was so startled that she almost dropped the baton a second time. But when she saw Suki fly in front of her, Tanya snapped out of it, and the race continued.

The onlookers screamed as Tanya and Suki neared the finish line. Tanya's heart pounded harder and louder as she approached the end. From the corner of her eye, she could

150   see Suki alongside her. Neither runner was willing to give an inch. Their legs and lungs pumped desperately as they crossed the finish line together.

"Who won?" the onlookers began to yell. "Who won? Who won?"

The judges declared that Tanya and Suki had tied. After a few seconds, an argument broke out.

"We should be the winner!" Kelly shouted to the judges. "Suki stopped to give Tanya her baton. If she'd kept going instead, she'd have beat Tanya by a mile!"

160   "So what?" Luisa objected. "No one forced Suki to stop and help Tanya. She shouldn't have done it! This is a competition, not a Girl Scout help-a-thon. Tanya should be the winner, just for following the rules!"

The judges repeated their decision: The race was a tie.

Kelly turned to one of the judges and shouted, "That stinks!"

Luisa turned to another judge and said, "You judges should quit!"

The judge blew a whistle and jerked his thumb at Kelly

170   and Luisa, **ejecting** them from the field.

"You're both out of the meet!" the judge shouted. "Poor sportsmanship!"

Kelly and Luisa picked up their bags of running gear and stormed off the field.

TEXT REFORMULATION

Pause at line 146. Write three "Fortunately/Unfortunately" sentences telling what has happened so far.

_____

_____

_____

_____

_____

_____

TEXT REFORMULATION

Pause at line 170. Underline the names of the characters who cause another problem. Write an "Unfortunately" sentence to describe what happens.

_____

_____

_____

_____

_____

VOCABULARY DEVELOPMENT

ejecting (ē·jekt′iŋ) v.: throwing out; driving out.

Write a "Fortunately" state-
ment to describe the story's
resolution, or outcome.

_____

_____

_____

_____

_____

_____

INFER

Do you think this story was
written to teach a lesson?
Answer, and explain your
answer.

_____

_____

_____

_____

_____

_____

_____

_____

_____

_____

_____

For a moment, all was quiet. Tanya and Suki just stared at each other, unsure of what to say. Then their coach came over.

"Girls, your running partners are both off the team. I'm sorry, but I can't have poor attitudes like theirs. Now,

180 nobody will be able to represent the school in the state competition."

Panic spread on Tanya's and Suki's faces. Suddenly, Tanya had an idea.

"Coach, what if Suki and I run as partners in the meet?"

Suki looked shocked and then pleased.

"It's fine with me if it's okay with Suki," the coach responded.

Suki held out her hand and shook Tanya's.

190 "It's fine with me," Suki said.

Later, Suki and Tanya walked home together. Tanya asked, "Suki, why did you pick up my baton?"

Suki put her arm around Tanya and laughed, "I guess I've learned to admire anyone who can beat me. Now let's go. We've got a math test to study for!"

OWN THE STORY

Forms of Fiction   Use the chart on the next page to list the main events of this short story as a series of "Fortunately/Unfortunately" events.

Clarify Texts   Summarize the main events of this short story. Use the terms *characters, conflicts, climax,* and *resolution.* Include the story's title and author in your summary. At the end of your summary, tell what you thought of the story and the lessons it taught.

_____

_____

_____

_____

_____

_____

_____

_____

_____

_____

KEEPING TRACK

Personal Word List   Record the words you learned from this story in your Personal Word List. Also add similes and metaphors from the story to your list.

Personal Reading Log   As you record this story in your Personal Reading Log, write down your thoughts about the short story form. Do you enjoy short stories? Why or why not? Then, give yourself 4 points on the Reading Meter.

Checklist for Standards Mastery   Use the Checklist for Standards Mastery to see which standards you have mastered. Where did you do the best? Where can you improve?

The Competitors ■ *Interactive Reading,* page 170

Interact with a Literary Text

"Fortunately/Unfortunately" Pattern   Fill out the graphic organizer below to reformulate the conflicts, climax, and resolution in "The Competitors." Complete the patterned sentences with details from the story.

Unfortunately, Mr. Martin asked Tanya to stay after class.
Fortunately,
Unfortunately,

↓

Unfortunately, Tanya didn't think she had anything in common with Suki.
Fortunately,

↓

Unfortunately, Tanya dropped the baton during the race.
Fortunately,

↓

Fortunately, the race was a tie.
Unfortunately,

↓

Unfortunately, Kelly and Luisa were thrown out of the track meet because of poor sportsmanship.
Fortunately,

Amigo Brothers

for use with
Holt Literature and Language Arts,
page 309

Interact with a Literary Text

Text Reformulation   Text reformulation means that you recast a selection in another form. Since the short story "Amigo Brothers" is full of action, it would be an excellent candidate for reformulation as a TV drama.

To reformulate the story as a TV drama, you first have to know how TV dramas are set up. On page 69 of *Holt Literature and Language Arts*, you will find a TV drama called *The Monsters Are Due on Maple Street*. Refer to the structure of that play as you reformulate "Amigo Brothers."

This chart will help you block out the story into scenes of a play. Be sure you make clear the causes of the boys' actions and decisions. Be sure you also make clear the effects of other actions and decisions.

Scene 1

Characters
Setting
Problem
Main events
Situation at end of scene

Scene 2

Characters
Setting
Problem
Main events
Situation at end of scene

Scene 3

Characters
Setting
Problem
Main events
Situation at end of scene

When you have blocked out the story into scenes, put an asterisk beside the scene that will contain the story's **climax,** or most exciting and suspenseful moment.

Right Hook—Left Hook: The Boxing Controversy

Interact with an Informational Text

Pro-and-Con Chart   This article presents two opinions on the sport of boxing. List the positive and negative aspects of the debate in this pro-and-con chart. (*Pro* means "for" and *con* means "against.") Which side are you on?

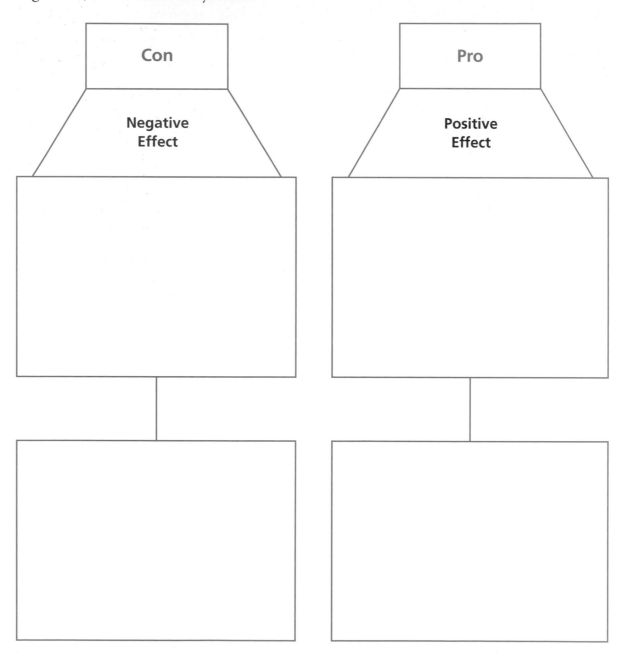

Con

Negative Effect

Pro

Positive Effect

from **Barrio Boy**

Interact with a Literary Text

Main-Idea Graphic   Most nonfiction prose pieces are written to present a main idea. Sometimes main ideas are directly stated. More often you have to think about the key details in a text and infer the main idea that all the details add up to. Fill out the following graphic with key details from *Barrio Boy*. What main idea do they add up to? Write the main idea in the middle box. Then write a key statement from the text that supports the main idea.

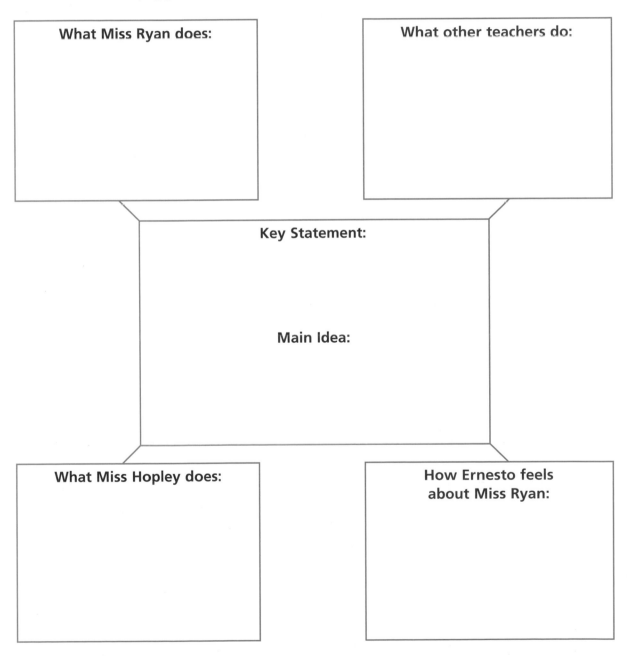

What Miss Ryan does:

What other teachers do:

Key Statement:

Main Idea:

What Miss Hopley does:

How Ernesto feels about Miss Ryan:

Song of the Trees

for use with
Holt Literature and Language Arts,
page 333

Interact with a Literary Text

Story Map   Make a story map outlining the plot of *Song of the Trees* using the graphic organizer below.

Main Characters
Conflicts

Event
Event
Event
Event
Climax
Resolution

Fish Cheeks

Interact with a Literary Text

Events Chart   In the essay "Fish Cheeks," the topic is a Christmas dinner. The events in this essay are told in chronological order, the order in which they happened. As with all essays, this one is told to make a point.

The narrator's mother invites Robert's family for Christmas dinner.

Event

Event

Event

Event

Event

Event

What is the writer's point?

A Mason-Dixon Memory

for use with
Holt Literature and Language Arts,
page 358

Interact with an Informational Text

Comparison Chart   In "A Mason-Dixon Memory," Clifton Davis describes two experiences with discrimination. To see how the experiences are alike and to come up with the main idea of the essay, fill in the chart below.

	Experience	Friends' Response
Dondré Green	Member of: Segregated place: Coach Murphy's decision:	What friends say and do: Green's reaction to friends:
Clifton Davis	Member of: Segregated place: Chaperone's decision:	What friends say and do: Davis's reaction to friends:

Buddies Bare Their Affection for Ill Classmate

Interact with an Informational Text

Summary Chart   Summarizing a text can help you remember its key details and determine its main idea. In a summary, you use your own words to restate the main events or main details of the text. A summary is always much shorter than the text itself.

Fill out the chart that follows with details from "Buddies Bare Their Affection. . . ." Then write a summary of the article and its main idea in the boxes at the right.

Key Details

Thirteen boys shave their heads so that no one can tell who in class has cancer.
Ian O'Gorman had started chemotherapy to treat his disease.
Ian decided to

Summary

Thirteen boys and their teacher shave their heads so that

Main Idea

When the Earth Shakes

for use with
Holt Literature and Language Arts,
page 371

Interact with an Informational Text

KWL Chart   Completing a KWL chart like the one below is
an especially good way to check your understanding of a scientific
text like "When the Earth Shakes." In the "What I Know" column,
write what you already know about the topic of earthquakes. Write
what you want to know in the "What I Want to Know" column.
As you read the article, write information you learn in the "What
I Learned" column.

What I Know	What I Want to Know	What I Learned

The Elements of Poetry

for use with
Holt Literature and Language Arts,
page 383

FORMS OF POETRY

Interact with a Literary Text

Poetry Comparison Chart   Filling in a chart like the one that follows will help you compare the ways several poems use figures of speech and sound effects. In the last column, sum up the theme of each poem—what it reveals to you about our lives.

Poem Title	Figures of Speech	Sound Effects	Theme
I'm Nobody			
I Am of the Earth			
Early Song			
Madam and the Rent Man			
The Runaway			
maggie and milly and molly and may			

Literature

AUTHOR STUDY

Patricia Lauber loved stories from an early age. By the second grade, she says she knew she was going to be a writer. Lauber is fascinated by how nature both destroys and rebuilds. In 1987, *Volcano: The Eruption and Healing of Mount St. Helens* became a Newbery Honor Book. Lauber brings patience and persistence to her work. To report on what happened to the land around Mount St. Helens after the volcano, Lauber had to wait years to see if the plants and animals would come back.

Lauber has written many prize-winning nonfiction books for young adults. Her topics include robots, dinosaurs, cave paintings, hurricanes, penguins, and rivers.

BEFORE YOU READ

Here are a few facts to know before you read this chapter from Lauber's book:

- The volcano Mount St. Helens in the state of Washington erupted on May 18, 1980.
- Mount St. Helens had been an active volcano for thousands of years, although prior to 1980 it had not erupted since the 1850s.
- The eruption that spring killed 57 people and countless plants and animals. It spread destruction over 230 square miles and left the mountain 1,200 feet lower than it had been.

Reading Standard 2.4 **(Grade 6 Review)** Clarify an understanding of texts by creating outlines, logical notes, summaries, or reports.

from Volcano

The Eruption and Healing of Mount St. Helens

Patricia Lauber

The Volcano Wakes

For many years the volcano slept. It was silent and still, big and beautiful. Then the volcano, which was named Mount St. Helens, began to stir. On March 20, 1980, it was shaken by a strong earthquake. The quake was a sign of movement inside St. Helens. It was a sign of a waking volcano that might soon erupt again.

Mount St. Helens was built by many eruptions over thousands of years. In each eruption hot rock from inside the earth forced its way to the surface. The rock was so hot
10 that it was molten, or melted, and it had gases trapped in it. The name for such rock is magma. Once the molten rock reaches the surface, it is called lava. In some eruptions the magma was fairly liquid. Its gases escaped gently. Lava flowed out of the volcano, cooled, and hardened. In other eruptions the magma was thick and sticky. Its gases burst out violently, carrying along sprays of molten rock. As it blasted into the sky, the rock cooled and hardened. Some of it rained down as ash—tiny bits of rock. Some rained down as pumice—frothy rock puffed up by gases.

20 Together the lava flows, ash, and pumice built a mountain with a bowl-shaped crater at its top. St. Helens grew to a height of 9,677 feet, so high that its peak was often hidden by clouds. Its big neighbors were built in the same

From *Volcano: The Eruption and Healing of Mount St. Helens* by Patricia Lauber. Copyright © 1986 by Patricia Lauber. Reprinted by permission of *Simon & Schuster Books for Young Readers, an imprint of Simon & Schuster Children's Publishing Division.*

IDENTIFY

Most scientific texts clearly state the main ideas or topics. Underline the main idea of the first paragraph.

WORD KNOWLEDGE

The second paragraph introduces several geology terms. Underline the context clue that defines *magma* for you.

Underline the context clue that defines *lava* for you.

Underline the context clue that defines *pumice* for you.

CLARIFY TEXT

Underline the detail that tells how high Mount St. Helens grew. Write the main idea contained in paragraphs 2 and 3.

_____

_____

_____

_____

_____

_____

Notice the cross-section diagram of the mountain. The illustration shows in pictures what the writer explains in words. It helps explain how the mountain has been built up and how the magma travels to the crater. Circle the path the magma takes to reach the surface.

WORD
KNOWLEDGE

In line 31, underline the words "the volcano slept." In this context, *slept* does not have a scientific meaning. The writer is using *personification* to compare the volcano to a sleeping person. In other words, the volcano was not active. **Personification** means "giving a human characteristic to something that is not human." Look for other examples of personification as you read this text.

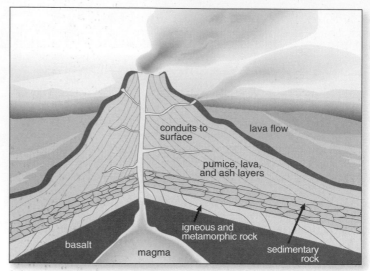

A volcano is a place where hot, molten rock from inside the earth comes to the surface. Mount St. Helens was built by many eruptions over thousands of years.

way. Mount St. Helens is part of the Cascade Range, a chain of volcanoes that runs from northern California into British Columbia.

In the middle 1800s, a number of small eruptions took place. Between 1832 and 1857, St. Helens puffed out clouds of steam and ash from time to time. It also gave off small

30 flows of lava. Then the mountain fell still.

For well over a hundred years the volcano slept. Each spring, as winter snows melted, its slopes seemed to come alive. Wildflowers bloomed in meadows. Bees gathered pollen and nectar. Birds fed, found mates, and built nests. Bears lumbered out of their dens. Herds of elk and deer feasted on fresh green shoots. Thousands of people came to hike, picnic, camp, fish, paint, bird-watch, or just enjoy the scenery. Logging crews felled tall trees and planted seedlings.

40 These people knew that Mount St. Helens was a volcano, but they did not fear it. To them it was simply a

green and pleasant mountain, where forests of firs stretched up the slopes and streams ran clear and cold.

The mountain did not seem so trustworthy to geologists (scientists who study the earth). They knew that Mount St. Helens was dangerous. It was a young volcano and one of the most active in the Cascade Range. In 1975, two geologists finished a study of the volcano's past eruptions. They predicted that Mount St. Helens would

50   erupt again within 100 years, perhaps before the year 2000.

The geologists were right. With the earthquake of March 20, 1980, Mount St. Helens woke from a sleep of 123 years. Magma had forced its way into the mountain, tearing apart solid rock. The snapping of that rock set off the shock waves that shook St. Helens. That quake was followed by many others. Most of them were smaller, but they came so fast and so often that it was hard to tell when one quake ended and another began.

Mount St. Helens spouting volcanic steam, April 1980.

WORD KNOWLEDGE

Underline the context clue in line 45 that defines *geologists* for you.

CLARIFY TEXT

Underline the main ideas that explain why geologists felt Mount St. Helens might soon erupt. Write a summary about what happened when it did erupt.

RETELL

The paragraph beginning on line 64 describes the effects of the earthquakes that shook Mount St. Helens, beginning on March 20. Underline two details that tell what happened. Then write the details in your own words.

_____

_____

_____

_____

_____

_____

_____

_____

_____

IDENTIFY

What were the effects of the eruption? Underline some facts in lines 86–92.

_____

_____

_____

_____

_____

_____

_____

60 On March 27, people near Mount St. Helens heard a tremendous explosion. The volcano began to blow out steam and ash that stained its snow-white peak. Small explosions went on into late April, stopped, started again on May 7, and stopped on May 14.

The explosions of late March opened up two new craters at the top of the mountain. One formed inside the old crater. The other formed nearby. The two new craters grew bigger. Soon they joined, forming one large crater that continued to grow during the next few weeks. Meanwhile, the north face of the mountaintop was swelling and crack-
70 ing. The swelling formed a bulge that grew outward at a rate of five to six feet a day.

Geologists were hard at work on the waking volcano. They took samples of ash and gases, hoping to find clues to what was happening inside. They placed instruments on the mountain to record earthquakes and the tilting of ground. They kept measuring the bulge. A sudden change in its rate of growth might be a sign that the volcano was about to erupt. But the bulge grew steadily, and the ash and gases yielded no clues.

80 By mid-May, the bulge was huge. Half a mile wide and more than a mile long, it had swelled out 300 feet.

On Sunday morning, May 18, the sun inched up behind the Cascades, turning the sky pink. By 8:00 A.M. the sun was above the mountains, the sky blue, the air cool. There was not one hint of what was to come.

At 8:32, Mount St. Helens erupted. Billowing clouds of smoke, steam, and ash hid the mountain from view and darkened the sky for miles.

The eruption went on until evening. By its end a
90 fan-shaped area of destruction stretched out to the north,

covering some 230 square miles. Within that area 57 people and countless plants and animals had died.

Geologists now faced two big jobs. One was to keep watch on the mountain to find out if more eruptions were building up. If so, they hoped to learn how to predict the eruptions.

The other job was to find out exactly what had happened on May 18. Most volcanic eruptions start slowly. Why had Mount St. Helens erupted suddenly? What events had caused the big fan-shaped area of destruction? What had become of the mountaintop, which was now 1,200 feet lower?

The answers to these questions came slowly as geologists studied instrument records and photographs, interviewed witnesses, and studied the clues left by the eruption itself. But in time they pieced together a story that surprised them. This eruption turned out to be very different from the ones that built Mount St. Helens.

100

Mount St. Helens partially covered with volcanic ash, April 1980.

IDENTIFY

What surprised the scientists? Write the most important idea found in the last paragraph on this page.

VOCABULARY DEVELOPMENT

avalanche (av′ə·lanch′) *n.:*
mass of snow, earth, or
rocks sliding suddenly
down a mountain.

FLUENCY

Time yourself as you read the
boxed paragraph silently.
Your goal is to read at a
normal rate and to under-
stand what you are reading.
After you read, ask yourself
what the main point of the
paragraph is.

_____

_____

_____

_____

_____

_____

_____

_____

_____

_____

VOCABULARY DEVELOPMENT

scalding (skäld′iŋ) *adj.:*
boiling hot.

Violent eruption of Mount St. Helens, showing ash cloud.

The Big Blast

110 The May 18 eruption began with an earthquake that
triggered an **avalanche.** At 8:32 A.M., instruments that
were miles away registered a strong earthquake. The pilot
and passengers of a small plane saw the north side of the
mountain rippling and churning. Shaken by the quake,
the bulge was tearing loose. It began to slide, in a huge
avalanche that carried along rock ripped from deep inside
Mount St. Helens.

The avalanche tore open the mountain. A **scalding**
blast shot sideways out of the opening. It was a blast of
120 steam, from water heated by rising magma.

Normally water cannot be heated beyond its boiling
point, which is 212 degrees Fahrenheit at sea level. At boiling point, water turns to a gas, which we call steam. But if
water is kept under pressure, it can be heated far beyond its
boiling point and still stay liquid. (That is how a pressure
cooker works.) If the pressure is removed, this superheated

water suddenly turns, or flashes, to steam. As steam it takes up much more room—it expands. The sudden change to steam can cause an explosion.

130   Before the eruption Mount St. Helens was like a giant pressure cooker. The rock inside it held superheated water. The water stayed liquid because it was under great pressure, sealed in the mountain. When the mountain was torn open, the pressure was suddenly relieved. The superheated water flashed to steam. Expanding violently, it shattered rock inside the mountain and exploded out the opening, traveling at speeds of up to 200 miles an hour.

      The blast flattened whole forests of 180-foot-high firs. It snapped off or uprooted the trees, scattering the trunks
140 as if they were straws. At first, this damage was puzzling. A wind of 200 miles an hour is not strong enough to level forests of giant trees. The explanation, geologists later discovered, was that the wind carried rocks ranging in size from grains of sand to blocks as big as cars. As the blast roared out of the volcano, it swept up and carried along the rock it had shattered.

The blast leveled forests of huge firs. The tiny figures of two scientists (lower right) give an idea of the scale.

WORD KNOWLEDGE

A **simile** is a comparison of two unlike things that uses a word such as *like, as,* or *than.* Scientific writers often use comparisons to explain complex events. What does the writer compare Mount St. Helens to in line 130? Circle the simile.

IDENTIFY

Usually a volcano erupts from the top of the crater. What was different about this eruption on May 18?

_____

_____

_____

_____

IDENTIFY

What question about the eruption is the writer answering in the paragraph beginning at line 138?

_____

_____

_____

_____

_____

_____

DECODING TIP

Draw a line between the two words in the compound word *sandblasted* in line 151. Literally the word means "blasted by sand." Think of sandpaper. How do you think sandblasted tree stumps would look?

_____

_____

_____

_____

_____

_____

_____

_____

_____

_____

_____

_____

VOCABULARY
DEVELOPMENT

scorched (skôrcht) *v.:* burned.

IDENTIFY

Underline the details on this page that describe the destruction caused by the "stone wind."

An eruption on March 19, 1982, melted snow and caused this mudflow. The smaller part of the flow went into Spirit Lake (lower left), while the larger part traveled down the Toutle River.

The result was what one geologist described as "a stone wind." It was a wind of steam and rocks, traveling at high speed. The rocks gave the blast its great force. Before it,

150 trees snapped and fell. Their stumps looked as if they had been sandblasted. The wind of stone rushed on. It stripped bark and branches from trees and uprooted them, leveling 150 square miles of countryside. At the edge of this area other trees were left standing, but the heat of the blast **scorched** and killed them.

The stone wind was traveling so fast that it overtook and passed the avalanche. On its path was Spirit Lake, one of the most beautiful lakes in the Cascades. The blast stripped the trees from the slopes surrounding the lake and

160 moved on.

Meanwhile the avalanche had hit a ridge and split. One part of it poured into Spirit Lake, adding a 180-foot layer of rock and dirt to the bottom of the lake. The slide of avalanche into the lake forced the water out. The water sloshed up the slopes, then fell back into the lake. With it came thousands of trees felled by the blast.

The main part of the avalanche swept down the valley of the North Fork of the Toutle River. There, in the valley, most of the avalanche slowed and stopped. It covered 24 square miles and averaged 150 feet thick.

The blast itself continued for 10 to 15 minutes, then stopped. Minutes later, Mount St. Helens began to erupt upward. A dark column of ash and ground-up rock rose miles into the sky. Winds blew the ash eastward. Lightning flashed in the ash cloud and started forest fires. In Yakima, Washington, some 80 miles away, the sky turned so dark that street lights went on at noon. Ash fell like snow that would not melt. This eruption continued for nine hours.

Shortly after noon the color of the ash column changed. It became lighter, a sign that the volcano was now throwing out mostly new magma. Until then much of the ash had been made of old rock.

At the same time, the volcano began giving off huge flows of pumice and ash. The material was very hot, with temperatures of about 1,000 degrees Fahrenheit, and it traveled down the mountain at speeds of 100 miles an hour. The flows went on until 5:30 in the afternoon. They formed a wedge-shaped plain of pumice on the side of the mountain. Two weeks later temperatures in the pumice were still about 780 degrees.

Finally, there were the mudflows, which started when heat from the blast melted ice and snow on the mountaintop. The water mixed with ash, pumice, ground-up rock, and dirt and rocks of the avalanche. The result was a thick mixture that was like wet concrete, a mudflow. The mudflows traveled fast, **scouring** the

IDENTIFY

What started to happen right after the blast stopped (line 172)? Underline the answers.

· · · · · · **Notes** · · · · · ·

IDENTIFY

In line 195, what comparison does the writer use to help you picture the mudflow?

VOCABULARY DEVELOPMENT

scouring (skour′iŋ) v. used as adj.: removing as if by cleaning and scraping; sweeping away.

Underline the example of **personification** in the middle paragraph. Explain what is meant.

_____

_____

_____

_____

_____

_____

_____

_____

_____

_____

_____

_____

_____

_____

_____

_____

_____

_____

_____

_____

_____

_____

Arnica flowers blooming on the Lang Ridge in 1984, four years after the eruption of Mount St. Helens.

landscape and sweeping down the slopes into river valleys. Together their speed and thickness did great damage.

200   The largest mudflow was made of avalanche material from the valley of the North Fork of the Toutle River. It churned down the river valley, tearing out steel bridges, ripping houses apart, picking up boulders and trucks and carrying them along. Miles away it choked the Cowlitz River and blocked shipping channels in the Columbia River.

When the sun rose on May 19, it showed a greatly changed St. Helens. The mountain was 1,200 feet shorter than it had been the morning before. Most of the old top had slid down the mountain in the avalanche. The rest had

210 erupted out as shattered rock. Geologists later figured that the volcano had lost three quarters of a cubic mile of old rock.

The north side of the mountain had changed from a green and lovely slope to a fan-shaped wasteland.

At the top of Mount St. Helens was a big, new crater with the shape of a horseshoe. Inside the crater was the vent, the opening through which rock and gases erupted from time to time over the next few years.

In 1980, St. Helens erupted six more times. Most of
220 these eruptions were explosive—ash soared into the air, pumice swept down the north side of the mountain. In the eruptions of June and August, thick, pasty lava oozed out of the vent and built a dome. But both domes were destroyed by the next eruptions. In October the pattern changed. The explosions stopped, and thick lava built a dome that was not destroyed. Later eruptions added to the dome, making it bigger and bigger.

During this time, geologists were learning to read the clues found before eruptions. They learned to predict
230 what St. Helens was going to do. The predictions helped to protect people who were on and near the mountain.

Among these people were many natural scientists. They had come to look for survivors, for plants and animals that had lived through the eruption. They had come to look for colonizers, for plants and animals that would move in. Mount St. Helens had erupted many times before. Each time life had returned. Now scientists would have a chance to see how it did. They would see how nature healed itself.

IDENTIFY

Underline the main idea in lines 219–227. Write two details that support the main idea.

_____
_____
_____
_____
_____
_____
_____
_____

INFER

What impression do you think the writer wants to give in the last paragraph?

_____
_____
_____
_____
_____
_____
_____
_____
_____
_____
_____

OWN THE TEXT

Clarify Text   Work with a partner to write a summary of this account of a volcanic eruption. Be sure to refer to the notes you made as you were reading. Exchange summaries with another pair of students, and compare your work. Rate the completeness of each summary. Use a score of 1–4, with 4 the highest score.

Here are the criteria you should use when you evaluate a summary:
1. The summary should cite the title and author of the text.
2. It should state the topic of the text.
3. It should state all the key details in the text.
4. It should sum up the main idea or main point of the text.

Before you write your summary, fill out the graphic organizer on the next page. It will help you identify the sequence of events that led up to the eruption and those that followed it.

_____

_____

_____

_____

_____

KEEPING TRACK

Personal Word List   Add the new words about geology you encountered to your Personal Word List. Be alert for new words about geology in newspapers, in magazines, and on television.

Personal Reading Log   As you record this reading in your Personal Reading Log, include your summary. Then, give yourself 5 points on the Reading Meter.

Checklist for Standards Mastery   Use the Checklist for Standards Mastery to see how far you have come in mastering the standards.

Interact with a Literary Text

Sequence Chart   Fill in the sequence chart that follows to show the order of events described in this account of the eruption of Mount St. Helens. Be sure to refer to the notes you took as you read the text. Use dates as often as you can to make the sequence clear.

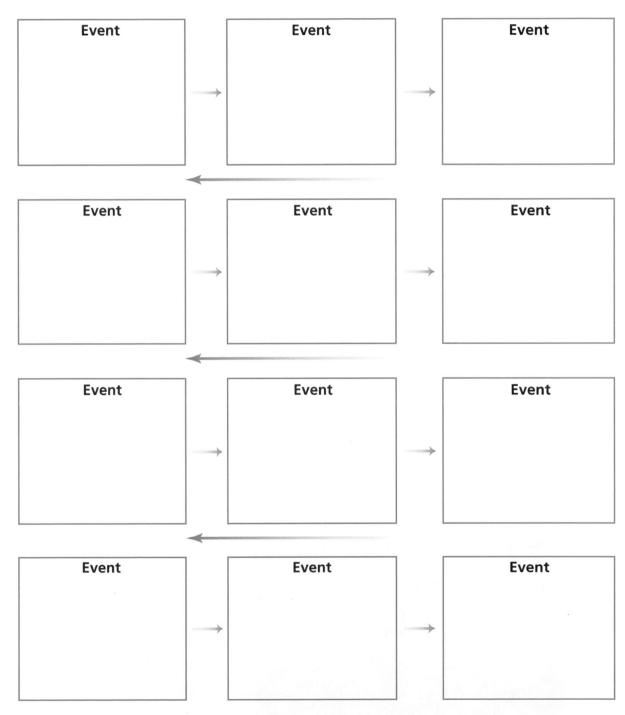

Event	Event	Event
Event	Event	Event
Event	Event	Event
Event	Event	Event

The volcano Popocatépetl (pō·pō'kä·te'pet'l) near Mexico City is one of the world's most dangerous volcanoes. The reporter Tim Weiner was on the scene during one of its most recent eruptions, on December 18, 2000. Weiner filed this eyewitness report the day after the eruption.

Here are some things to know before you read the article:

• On December 18, 2000, Popocatépetl erupted in its strongest explosion in over a thousand years.

• Popocatépetl is 17,945 high and can be seen by about thirty million people, most of whom live in Mexico City.

• The name *Popocatépetl* means "smoking mountain" in the Nahuatl language, the language of the ancient Aztec people.

Reading Standard 2.2 (Grade 6 Review) Analyze text that uses the compare-and-contrast organizational pattern.

Reading Standard 2.4 (Grade 6 Review) Clarify an understanding of texts by creating outlines, logical notes, summaries, or reports.

from The New York Times on the Web

Mexicans Resist Flight from "Friendly" Volcano

Tim Weiner

Residents of communities near the base of the volcano Popocatépetl try to keep warm as the volcano spews ash and smoke in the background.

Location: _____

Mexico City, Dec. 19—Every thousand years or so, the great Popocatépetl explodes with killing force, and as it rumbled and puffed this weekend, government officials monitoring geophysicists' instruments pleaded with thousands of villagers under the volcano to flee.

Few did. People fought to stay put, even after it erupted violently throughout Monday night and this morning, flinging glowing five-foot rocks for miles, in
10 what is believed to be its biggest bang in more than a millennium. They felt strongly that the volcano— their volcano, **revered** as the god of rain and giver of rich soil—was more **benevolent** a force than their government.

"The people in the villages consider Popo a friendly volcano, the beating heart of the land," said Homero Aridjis, a poet, former diplomat, and president of PEN, the international writers' association. "It's our Indian beliefs against European science."
20 Maybe they were right: Though the mountain is hurling incandescent bombs, potentially threatening everyone for 20 miles around, it has killed no one yet. But this clash of verities versus technology—or human nature against nature—is an old story. And since the volcano still is capable of an immense explosion, it is far from over.

Scientists and the government warned today that a full-blown eruption, pouring rivers of lava down Popocatépetl's slopes, could come at any time. The

TEXT STRUCTURE

Underline the place and date of this article. Newspaper articles usually include a title, the place where the report is filed, the date, and a byline, or the line that gives the writer's name.

VOCABULARY DEVELOPMENT

revered (ri·vird′) *v.* used as *adj.:* adored; loved.

benevolent (bə·nev′ə·lənt) *adj.:* kindly; good.

INFER

How do the villagers feel about the volcano?

_____

_____

_____

_____

_____

_____

_____

_____

WORD KNOWLEDGE

Something that glows with intense heat is *incandescent* (in′kən·des′ənt).

VOCABULARY DEVELOPMENT

metropolis (mə·träp′ə·lis) *n.*: main city of a country, state, or region.

abrasive (ə·brā′siv) *adj.*: causing rubbing off or scraping; rough.

evacuation (ē·vak′yōō·ā′shən) *n.*: removal from, often because of danger.

FLUENCY

The writer quotes three different people to support one of the main ideas in his story. Read the boxed passage aloud, using expression to show that three different people are speaking.

WORD KNOWLEDGE

Use context clues to guess at the meaning of *antiquities* in line 51.

_____

_____

_____

_____

_____

_____

_____

_____

Back   Forward   Reload   Home   Search

Location: _____

30 volcano, less than 40 miles east of Mexico City and its nearly 20 million people, fumed billows of gray ash all day. The wind carried it south, sparing the **metropolis** and its international airport a coat of **abrasive** soot.

All day Monday and today, government sound trucks went through villages near the volcano, blaring warnings. Church bells rang out danger and army commanders appeared with evacuation orders. But thousands resisted the call. Vicente Jiménez, a

40 26-year-old corn farmer from Santiago Xanitzintla, about seven miles from the flaming crater, heard all the alarms and was unmoved.

"We never left," he said today. "We don't feel comfortable leaving our homes and everything we own in the hands of the authorities. For many people leaving was hard enough, but leaving our homes in the hands of the police is even harder."

A fellow farmer who stayed behind, Adolfo Castro, 55, said, "This is a very old village. The church

50 is important to us, and there was no one guarding it. There are antiquities inside that go back centuries."

An army commander charged with carrying out **evacuation** today shook his head. "It's too late to be fighting with these people," he said. "They've shut themselves in behind four locks. They are older people who will never leave."

More than 20,000 people appeared to have turned down the government's offers of transportation, food, and shelter. "Their resistance is

60 reasonable, based on their experience," said Luis
González y González, a historian at the National
College. "The people have nothing to identify with
but their families and their land."

After nearly seven decades of deep sleep,
17,945-foot Popocatépetl (pronounced poh-poh-
kah-TEH-peh-tel), became active again in December
1994. Since then, government scientists have erected
a world-class monitoring network of sensors around
it, measuring its internal pressure and recording its

70 smallest tremors.

The Mexican government also set up 1,232
shelters with room for more than 300,000 people.
It accurately predicted the eruption, broadcast the
warning clearly, and yet could not persuade people
to leave through reason alone.

Part of the resistance lies in village traditions.
People call the volcano Don Gregorio, or Don Goyo
for short, and see him as a living, giving creature.
Shamans in the villages communicate with him and

80 insist he will not hurt people unless people hurt him.

"People here still carry gifts up the mountain, a
stewpot of turkey with mole, a basket of fruits," said
Tomás Jiménez, Vicente's father, who said his family
has lived in Santiago Xanitzintla for centuries. "They
ask for a better harvest or more rain."

Part of the fight against flight has an even deeper
foundation, though.

DECODING TIP

Draw a vertical line between the root word *resist* and the suffix *-ance*. The suffix means "process or action of." What does *resistance* mean?

_____

_____

_____

_____

_____

_____

_____

_____

_____

_____

_____

_____

_____

_____

_____

WORD KNOWLEDGE

You saw in the article about Mount St. Helens that the writer **personified** that volcano as a sleeping giant. Underline words in lines 76–80 that show that the village people have personified Popacatépetl.

IDENTIFY

In the paragraph that begins on line 99, what point does Dr. Miller make about the people's refusal to leave the area around Popo? Underline the examples he provides in the next paragraphs to support his opinion.

_____

_____

_____

_____

_____

_____

_____

_____

_____

_____

_____

_____

_____

_____

_____

_____

_____

Location: _____

"It's human nature," said Dan Miller, a research geologist and the chief of the United States Volcano
90 Disaster Assistance Program, which is based in Vancouver, Washington, who has worked in more than a dozen countries, throughout Latin America, Asia, and Africa.

"Wherever we go in the world we have met with the same kind of problem," said Dr. Miller, whose program is run by the United States Office of Foreign Disaster Assistance and the United States Geological Survey.

"People who live in high-risk zones around
100 volcanoes don't expect an eruption to take place, and if it did, they don't expect it to affect them. Government scientists in the U.S. and elsewhere meet with mistrust when they issue proclamations or recommendations. People don't understand or believe their warnings."

The same thing happened at the Mount St. Helens eruption in Washington State 20 years ago. "When Mount St. Helen's woke up after 123 years, a fair number of people refused to be evacuated, and
110 many of the 57 people killed had illegally entered into closed-off and restricted areas," Dr. Miller said.

Late last year in Ecuador, at least 22,000 villagers were evacuated by the government when the 16,475-foot volcano called Tungurahua—"Throat of Fire" in the Quechua Indian language—showed signs that a violent explosion was coming. "Now 15 months have

gone by and the predicted devastating events haven't occurred," Dr. Miller said. "And the people have fought their way through military barricades back

120 home. And they're there now, even though the eruptions continue."

This evening, though some villages were all but deserted, it appeared that roughly 30,000 people— slightly more than half of the 56,000 people the government wanted to protect—had accepted the offer of shelter, said the interior minister, Santiago Creel. Mr. Creel, who like the rest of the government of President Vicente Fox has been in power only 18 days, said he saw the **futility** of forcing the others

130 to leave.

"We don't think there's a clear way for us to remove the whole population," he said.

And Mr. Fox, touring Cholula, the largest town near the smoking cone of Popocatépetl, spoke for many of the villagers when he said the future under the volcano was as clear as the ashen cloud over it.

"We have to wait and see what Mr. Popocatépetl says," Mr. Fox observed. "Because he's the one setting the agenda here. Nobody else can."

VOCABULARY DEVELOPMENT

futility (fyo͞o·til′ə·tē) *n.:* uselessness.

· · · · · · **Notes** · · · · · ·

_____
_____
_____
_____
_____
_____
_____
_____
_____
_____
_____

WORD KNOWLEDGE

What does Mr. Fox mean by saying "the future under the volcano was as clear as the ashen cloud over it" (line 135)? Draw a box around the simile.

_____
_____
_____
_____

OWN THE TEXT

PRACTICING THE STANDARDS

Clarify Text   Summarize the main points made by the writer of this news article. Be sure to refer to the notes you made while reading. Remember to cite the author and title of the article in your summary and to state briefly what you see as its main idea. Filling out the graphic organizer that follows will help you identify the main idea of the article and the supporting details.

_____

_____

_____

_____

_____

_____

_____

_____

_____

_____

_____

_____

_____

KEEPING TRACK

Personal Word List   Add new words from this news article to your Personal Word List.

Personal Reading Log   As you add this news article to your Personal Reading Log, note other news articles about nature you have enjoyed. Then, give yourself 3 points on the Reading Meter.

Checklist for Standards Mastery   Assess how well you have mastered the standards for this chapter. Where did you make the most progress? Where can you improve?

Mexicans Resist Flight from "Friendly" Volcano ▪ *Interactive Reading,* page 202

Interact with an Informational Text

Main-Idea Chart In preparation for writing a summary of this article, fill out the following main-idea chart. Fill in the boxes of details first. When you have your boxes filled in, try out several statements of what you think is the main idea of the article. Your details should support that statement of your main idea.

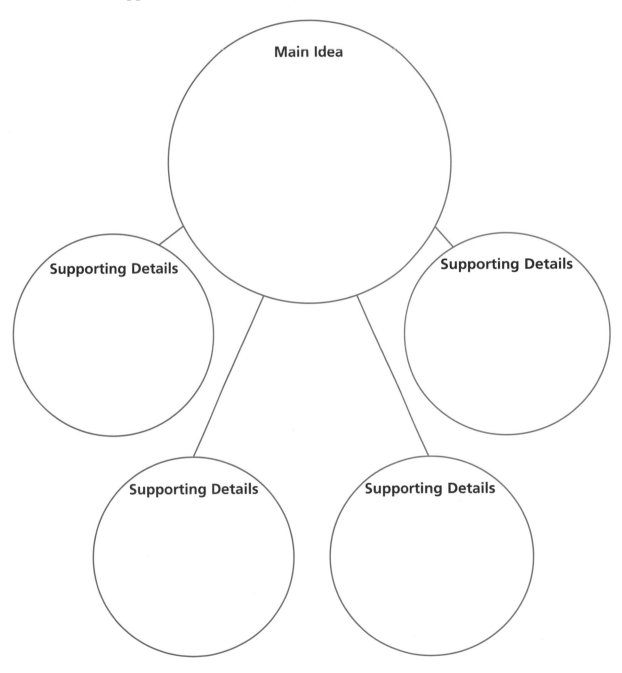

Main Idea

Supporting Details

Supporting Details

Supporting Details

Supporting Details

Literature

BEFORE YOU READ

Myths that explain how natural events began are called **origin myths.** The Native American Nisqually myth "Loo-Wit, the Fire-Keeper" explains how Mount St. Helens and several other nearby mountains came into existence. Like many myths, this one contains several *metamorphoses* (met'ə·môr'fə·sēz), which are marvelous changes from one form into a completely different form.

Here are some facts to know before you read the myth:
- The setting of the myth is in the northwestern United States.
- The Nisqually are one of twenty-eight native peoples known as the Northwest Coast Indians.
- The mountains in the story are part of the beautiful Cascade group. Mount Adams is in Washington State; south of it is Mount St. Helens, also in Washington. Further south is Mount Hood, which is in Oregon.
- The Columbia River is the border between Washington and Oregon.

Reading Standard 3.1
Articulate the expressed purposes and characteristics of different forms of prose (for example, short story, novel, novella, essay).

Loo-Wit, the Fire-Keeper

retold by Joseph Bruchac

When the world was young, the Creator gave everyone all that was needed to be happy.

The weather was always pleasant. There was food for everyone and room for all the people. Despite this, though, two brothers began to quarrel over the land. Each wanted to control it. It reached the point where each brother gathered together a group of men to support his **claim.** Soon it appeared there would be war.

The Creator saw this and was not pleased. He waited
10 until the two brothers were asleep one night and then carried them to a new country. There a beautiful river flowed and tall mountains rose into the clouds. He woke them just as the sun rose, and they looked out from the mountaintop to the land below. They saw what a good place it was. It made their hearts good.

"Now," the Creator said, "this will be your land." Then he gave each of the brothers a bow and a single arrow. "Shoot your arrow into the air," the Creator said. "Where your arrow falls will be the land of your people, and you
20 shall be a great chief there."

The brothers did as they were told. The older brother shot his arrow. It **arched** over the river and landed to the south in the valley of the Willamette River. There is where he and his people went, and they became the Multnomahs. The younger brother shot his arrow. It flew to the north of the great river. He and his people went there and became the Klickitats.

TEXT REFORMULATION

Underline the problem that begins the story. Write a sentence that begins with "Unfortunately, . . ." to follow the statement "Fortunately, the weather was pleasant and there was food and room for everyone."

_____

_____

_____

VOCABULARY DEVELOPMENT

claim (klām) *n.:* demand for something; here, demand for land.

arched (ärcht) *v.:* traveled in an arc, or overhead curve.

TEXT REFORMULATION

Pause at line 20. How is the brothers' problem solved? Begin your answer with "Fortunately."

_____

_____

_____

Pause at line 32. Why is a
bridge a good symbol of
peace between two nations?

_____

_____

_____

_____

_____

_____

_____

_____

_____

_____

_____

_____

_____

_____

_____

_____

_____

TEXT STRUCTURE

Repetition is often used
in myths and fairy tales.
Underline the two quotations
in this paragraph. Here, the
repetition creates a rhythm.
It also stresses the idea that
each group is doing and
saying the same thing.

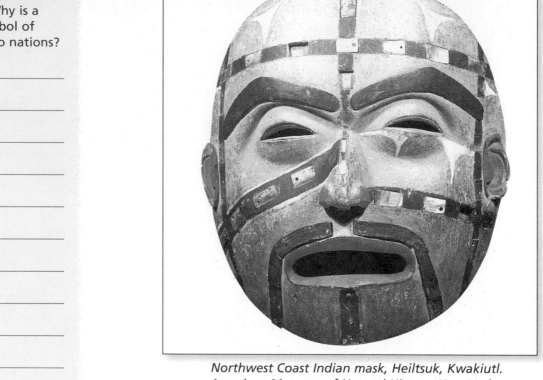

Northwest Coast Indian mask, Heiltsuk, Kwakiutl.
American Museum of Natural History, New York.

Then the Creator made a Great Stone Bridge across the
river. "This bridge," the Creator said, "is a sign of peace. You

30 and your peoples can visit each other by crossing over this
bridge. As long as you remain at peace, as long as your
hearts are good, this bridge will stand."

For many seasons the two peoples remained at peace.
They passed freely back and forth across the Great Stone
Bridge. One day, though, the people to the north looked
south toward the Willamette and said, "Their lands are
better than ours." One day, though, the people to the south
looked north toward the Klickitat and said, "Their lands are
more beautiful than ours." Then, once again, the people

40 began to quarrel.

The Creator saw this and was not pleased.

The people were becoming greedy again. Their hearts were becoming bad. The Creator darkened the skies and took fire away. Now the people grew cold. The rains of autumn began and the people suffered greatly.

"Give us back fire," they begged. "We wish to live again with each other in peace."

Their prayers reached the Creator's heart. There was only one place on Earth where fire still remained. An old woman named Loo-Wit had stayed out of the quarreling and was not greedy. It was in her lodge only that fire still burned. So the Creator went to Loo-Wit.

"If you will share your fire with all the people," the Creator said, "I will give you whatever you wish. Tell me what you want."

"I want to be young and beautiful," Loo-Wit said.

"That is the way it will be," said the Creator. "Now take your fire to the Great Stone Bridge above the river. Let all the people come to you and get fire. You must keep the fire burning there to remind people that their hearts must stay good."

The next morning, the skies grew clear and the people saw the sun rise for the first time in many days. The sun shone on the Great Stone Bridge, and there the people saw a young woman as beautiful as the sunshine itself. Before her, there on the bridge, burned a fire. The people came to the fire and ended their quarrels. Loo-Wit gave each of them fire. Now their homes again became warm and peace was everywhere.

One day, though, the chief of the people to the north came to Loo-Wit's fire. He saw how beautiful she was and wanted her to be his wife. At the same time, the chief of the people to the south also saw Loo-Wit's beauty. He, too,

TEXT REFORMULATION

Pause at line 45. How are the people behaving? What does the Creator do? Describe the events in an "Unfortunately" statement.

_____

_____

_____

_____

TEXT REFORMULATION

According to lines 53–61, why is Loo-Wit rewarded? Answer in a "Fortunately" statement.

_____

_____

_____

_____

_____

_____

FLUENCY

Read the boxed passage aloud, timing yourself. Then read the passage aloud a second time, aiming to improve your speed.

TEXT
REFORMULATION

How does the Creator solve
the brothers' latest quarrel?
Write an "Unfortunately"
statement.

_____

_____

_____

_____

_____

_____

_____

_____

INTERPRET

What is the myth explaining
in the paragraph beginning
on line 77?

_____

_____

_____

_____

_____

_____

_____

_____

_____

_____

_____

_____

wanted to marry her. Loo-Wit could not decide which of
the two she liked better. Then the chiefs began to quarrel.
Their peoples took up the quarrel, and fighting began.

When the Creator saw the fighting, he became angry.
He broke down the Great Stone Bridge. He took each of the
two chiefs and changed them into mountains. The chief of
80   the Klickitats became the mountain we now know as Mount
Adams. The chief of the Multnomahs became the mountain
we now know as Mount Hood. Even as mountains, they
continued to quarrel, throwing flames and stones at each
other. In some places, the stones they threw almost blocked
the river between them. That is why the Columbia River is
so narrow in the place called The Dalles° today.

Northwest Coast Indian mask.
American Museum of Natural History, New York.

___

°   **The Dalles** (dalz): town in Oregon on the steep, rocky banks of the
Columbia River.

Loo-Wit was heartbroken over the pain caused by her beauty. She no longer wanted to be a beautiful young woman. She could no longer find peace as a human being.

90   The Creator took pity on her and changed her into a mountain also, the most beautiful of the mountains. She was placed so that she stood between Mount Adams and Mount Hood, and she was allowed to keep the fire within herself which she had once shared on the Great Stone Bridge. Eventually, she became known as Mount St. Helens, and she slept peacefully.

Though she was asleep, Loo-Wit was still **aware,** the people said. The Creator had placed her between the two quarreling mountains to keep the peace, and it was
100   intended that humans, too, should look at her beauty and remember to keep their hearts good, to share the land and treat it well. If we human beings do not treat the land with respect, the people said, Loo-Wit will wake up and let us know how unhappy she and the Creator have become again. So they said, long before the day in the 1980s when Mount St. Helens woke again.

In the first two paragraphs on this page, we have the *climax* of the story. Based on what you know about Mount St. Helens, what do you think the "fire within herself" stands for?

_____

_____

_____

_____

VOCABULARY DEVELOPMENT

aware (ə·wer′) *adj.*: knowing; conscious.

INFER

What does the teller of this myth suggest is the reason Mount St. Helens exploded in the 1980s?

_____

_____

_____

_____

_____

_____

_____

_____

_____

OWN THE STORY

Purpose of Prose   In a paragraph, explain why this is called an **origin myth.** Use the word *metamorphosis* in your explanation.

_____

_____

_____

_____

_____

From Myth to Article   Complete the outline on the following page. Then, turn "Loo-Wit, the Fire-Keeper" into a news article. Share your finished article with a small group of classmates.

_____

_____

_____

_____

_____

_____

_____

_____

KEEPING TRACK

Personal Word List   Be sure to add the word *metamorphosis* to your Personal Word List, along with other words you learned.

Personal Reading Log   As you add this selection to your Personal Reading Log, write your ideas about the myth form. Do you enjoy myths? Give yourself 2 points on the Reading Meter.

Checklist for Standards Mastery   Use the Checklist for Standards Mastery to see how far you have come in mastering the standards. Identify areas where you can improve.

Loo-Wit, the Fire-Keeper

Interactive Reading, page 211

Interact with a Literary Text

Myth-Reformulation Outline   A newspaper article usually answers six questions: *who, what, when, where, why,* and *how.* To reformulate the myth as a newspaper article, you would have to think about and answer these questions. For example, *who* was in the myth? *What* happened in the myth? *When* and *where* did the myth take place? *Why* did the events in the myth happen? And finally, *how* did the events happen? Fill out the graphic organizer to help you identify and clarify information from the myth form, and turn it into a newspaper article.

Title of Article: _____
WHO? _____ _____ _____
WHAT? _____ _____ _____ _____
WHEN? _____ _____
WHERE? _____ _____
WHY? _____ _____
HOW? _____ _____ _____ _____ _____

Graphic Organizer   **217**

Chapter 6

Where I Stand
Literary Criticism

Chapter Preview   In this chapter you will—

Strategy Launch:
"Shape It Up"

LITERARY FOCUS: LITERARY ELEMENTS

When you, the reader, respond to a story, you are reacting to one or more of its **elements—**its **plot, characters, setting,** and **theme.** Writers of reviews also respond to the elements of a literary work. When you read reviews, be alert to which elements shape the reviewer's response.

A STRATEGY THAT WORKS: "SHAPE IT UP"

The "Shape It Up" strategy is fun and easy to use. Use it when you are reading a review or critique of a literary work. It helps you figure out which literary elements are focused on in the review.

POINTERS FOR USING THE "SHAPE IT UP" STRATEGY

To use the "Shape It Up" strategy, follow these simple steps:

》➡ Identify which literary element or elements are focused on in the response or review. To do this, draw a shape around each type of literary element it mentions. For example, circle the words and phrases that relate to (plot,) underline the words and phrases that relate to character, star the words and phrases that relate to setting,* and put a box around the words and phrases that relate to theme. (Instead of drawing shapes, you may prefer to use color coding.)

》➡ Look over your markings to determine the focus of the reviewer. Ask yourself: In what way did the reviewer's focus affect his or her conclusions?

Reading Standard 1.2 Use knowledge of Greek, Latin, and Anglo-Saxon roots and affixes to understand content-area vocabulary.

Reading Standard 2.6 Assess the adequacy, accuracy, and appropriateness of the author's evidence to support claims and assertions, noting instances of bias and stereotyping.

Reading Standard 3.6 Analyze a range of responses to a literary work, and determine the extent to which the literary elements in the work shaped those responses.

BEFORE YOU READ

The legend of King Arthur and the Knights of the Round Table has been told many times and in many different ways. Why tell it again? Writers and readers find the story hard to resist. The legend includes a romantic medieval setting, a love story, heroic characters, and battles, with jealousy, betrayal, and loss thrown into the mix. Writers enjoy reinventing the plot and presenting the characters as they imagine them.

After you finish the story, read two very different responses to it.

Guinevere and the Round Table

retold by Meish Goldish

IDENTIFY

Star the words that reveal the story's setting. What kind of story does this setting suggest?

_____

_____

_____

_____

VOCABULARY DEVELOPMENT

preoccupied (prē·ăk′yōō·pīd′) *adj.*: lost in thought.

The prefix *pre-* comes from the Latin *prae,* which means "earlier."

One day, on the way to his castle at Camelot, a weary King Arthur stopped to rest at a home near the city of Cameliard. A beautiful young maiden came outside to greet the king and his men. She served them delicious fruits and vegetables, plus a pitcher of cool, sweet water. The hungry king happily ate and drank, so weak and **preoccupied** that he did not talk to the woman.

Later, while continuing on his way, Arthur asked one of his men, "Who was the woman that served us?"

10 The assistant replied, "My lord, she was Princess Guinevere, the daughter of King Leodegrance of Cameliard, who gave your father the beautiful Round Table as a gift."

The king smiled and said, "She is indeed a beautiful and generous princess."

Arthur had little time to think about Guinevere, however. For soon he had reached Camelot, where he

found his court in chaos. The knights were busy arguing
over which of them had displayed the most bravery in war,
and who among them now deserved to sit next to King
20 Arthur at his banquet table. Some knights ordered others
to sit at the ends of the table, far from the king. But even
those knights who were young or inexperienced were
outraged by the order. All the knights argued loudly with
one another, some even threatening to abandon Camelot
and seek another kingdom for themselves.

   With his charming personality and affection, King
Arthur was able to end the bickering and restore calm. But
even Arthur wasn't sure how long that peace might last.

   Just then, Merlin, an old magician and friend of
30 Arthur, approached the king. "My lord," said Merlin, "it is
time for our king to have a queen. Are there any among the
maidens of the land who please you?"

   Immediately, Arthur recalled the kind woman who had
tended to him in Cameliard.

   "Yes, Merlin," the king replied. "There is one particular
maiden who does appeal to me greatly. She is Princess
Guinevere, the daughter of King Leodegrance."

   A look of **concern** fell on Merlin's face. "What is the
matter?" the king asked.

40 "With all due respect, my lord," explained Merlin,
"I would advise you against marrying Guinevere. As you
know, I have powers that allow me to see into the future.
And I foresee that if Guinevere is your queen, she may
bring great harm to your kingdom."

   King Arthur placed his arm in a friendly manner
around Merlin's shoulder. He said, "Thank you for your
honesty, my fair magician. But lest you forget, I, too,
have great powers. For I am Arthur, king of all England.
Therefore shall Guinevere be my bride and queen!"

INFER

Why are the knights
arguing? What does their
arguing tell you about them?

_____

_____

_____

_____

_____

_____

_____

_____

_____

_____

_____

_____

_____

_____

_____

_____

VOCABULARY
DEVELOPMENT

concern (kən·surn′) n.:
worry; anxiety.

Concern is built on the Latin
prefix *com-*, meaning "with,"
and *cernere*, which means
"understand."

VOCABULARY DEVELOPMENT

consent (kən·sent') n.: agreement.

Consent is built on the Latin prefix *com-,* meaning "with," and *sentire,* meaning "feel."

PREDICT

What do you think "strange feeling" in line 70 foreshadows?

_____

_____

_____

_____

_____

_____

_____

INFER

Underline Guinevere's actions in lines 78–81. What do her actions reveal about her?

_____

_____

_____

_____

_____

_____

50   "As you wish," Merlin said, bowing respectfully.

King Arthur thought a moment and then added, "Yet I would never force Guinevere to marry me. I will wed her only if she herself consents. I hope, Merlin, you will aid me with your magic to win her **consent.**"

Merlin nodded and immediately began to form a plan in his mind. Soon after, he had the king ride toward Cameliard, where Arthur left his horse and walked quite a distance to Guinevere's home. Arthur knocked on the door and asked a servant if he might be employed as a
60   gardener's assistant at the princess's home.

The servant did not recognize the visitor as King Arthur, nor did anyone else, for that matter. Merlin had disguised the king with an old, torn black cap. The cap's magic had changed Arthur into a gardening boy.

Merlin had also arranged for the present gardener's assistant to be fired that very day. So an assistant was indeed badly needed, and Arthur was immediately hired.

The following morning, Princess Guinevere took a walk in the garden. She saw the new gardener's assistant
70   busy at work. A strange feeling overcame her. She thought she knew the boy, but could not recall from where.

Princess Guinevere's attendants approached the gardener.

"Young man," one attendant said, "you should respectfully remove your cap in the presence of the princess."

The boy looked shyly toward the ground and replied, "I cannot do that, ma'am. I must wear my cap at all times."

The attendants were about to scold the gardener again when Guinevere stopped them. "Leave the boy alone," she
80   said in a soft tone. "Perhaps he has some blemish on his head that embarrasses him."

Every day, Guinevere continued to walk in her garden and eye the boy curiously. One day, her thoughts were suddenly interrupted by the arrival of a knight on horseback.

"Beware! Beware!" the knight shouted. "King Ryence of North Wales is approaching Cameliard with a large army! He intends to capture King Leodegrance's castle and take Princess Guinevere as his bride!"

The upsetting news spread quickly throughout the
90 kingdom. People grew quite worried, for they knew that good King Leodegrance had grown old and was no longer a strong leader. Over the years, all his boldest knights had either died in combat or left to serve other kings.

"Who will defend us?" the people wondered.

Quietly that evening, Arthur, still disguised as the gardening boy, left the castle.

The next morning, King Ryence's army gathered on a field in Cameliard. One of the king's knights, the duke of Northumberland, came forward on his horse and called to
100 the people of Cameliard, who watched from a distance.

"Who among you is brave enough to joust[1] with me?" the boastful duke cried. There was dead silence. The duke snorted with laughter.

"Is there not even one brave soul in this entire land who is willing to joust?" he sneered. "What cowards you are!"

Just then, from out of nowhere, came an **unidentified** knight astride[2] a snow-white horse. He carried a jeweled sword and rode directly up to the duke.

"I will joust with you," the stranger announced
110 boldly. A murmur went through the crowd. Then the

---

1. **joust** (joust) *v.:* engage in a fight using long spears. The jousters are two knights on horseback.
2. **astride** (ə·strīd′) *prep.:* with a leg on either side.

PREDICT

Pause at line 94. Who do you think will take up the challenge? Why do you think as you do?

VOCABULARY DEVELOPMENT

unidentified (un′ī·den′tə·fīd) *adj.:* unknown; without established identity.

The Anglo-Saxon prefix *un-*, meaning "not," changes the meaning of the base word.

intruder (in·trōōd'ər) *n.:* someone who pushes in.

Intruder is made of the Latin prefix *in-*, meaning "into," and the word *trudere,* meaning "push" or "thrust."

INFER

In lines 135–137, what do you think Guinevere might suspect or not suspect?

_____

_____

_____

_____

_____

_____

_____

_____

_____

_____

_____

_____

_____

_____

_____

stranger trotted on his horse to the castle balcony where Guinevere stood.

"Fair lady," the mysterious knight said, looking up to her. "I ask you to please give me, for good luck, the pearl necklace you are wearing. I promise to return it after I defeat this **intruder,** in your honor."

The princess suddenly felt a strange sensation, similar to the one she had experienced in the garden. She thought she somehow knew this knight, but wasn't sure from where. 120 Guinevere removed her necklace and dropped it from the balcony. The knight caught it on his sword, placed it on his wrist, and then rode directly into battle with the duke.

The two men battled fiercely with each other, horses galloping and lances[3] clanking. Dust flew for hours as the challengers charged at each other. Finally, the knight thrust his lance into the chest of the duke, who fell off his horse into the dust.

A great roar rose from the crowd. The knights of King Leodegrance, who had held back until now, suddenly 130 rushed onto the battlefield. King Ryence's soldiers lost their nerve and turned and fled the field.

The joyous King Leodegrance asked that the victorious knight be brought inside the castle. But, alas, the stranger was nowhere to be found! He had disappeared as mysteriously as he had arrived! Everyone was puzzled, including Guinevere, although she thought she might have some idea of what was happening.

That night, King Leodegrance warned his daughter, "We may yet have more trouble from King Ryence, my 140 dear. He does not give up so easily. But with our brave knight now gone, who will fight for us when Ryence returns?"

---

3. **lances** (lan'səz) *n.:* weapons for thrusting, made of long wooden shafts with sharp metal spearheads.

The next morning, the army of King Ryence indeed did reappear. King Ryence himself rode to the front of the line and shouted to the citizens of Cameliard, "Where is your brave knight today?" His knights stood behind him, prepared to attack.

Suddenly, a second army of knights appeared far in the distance. Everyone stood frozen in surprise as the army grew nearer. Soon the new knights were on the battlefield, 150 led by the mysterious knight from the day before.

All at once, a violent battle erupted between the two groups of knights. Swords clashed with swords, and bodies fell from horses. The knights fought fiercely, and blood drenched the battlefield.

After hours of battle, a blinding mist settled over the bloody field. Merlin the magician had brought the mist himself. When it lifted, all fighting had stopped. Many of King Ryence's knights were dead. Those still alive staggered off the battlefield and returned home.

160 That evening, King Leodegrance hosted a special banquet in honor of his men's rousing victory. The day's hero, the unidentified knight, entered the banquet hall with Princess Guinevere's pearl necklace still clasped to his wrist. On his other wrist was tied the old, torn black cap of the gardening boy. The knight walked directly to the princess, who sat with her father.

"Now I am sure!" Guinevere cried. "You are the gardening boy, and you are also King Arthur!"

King Leodegrance was puzzled. "What do you mean, 170 my dear?" he asked.

Guinevere explained to her father how she had served King Arthur during his initial visit to their home. "I remember his face," the princess exclaimed.

EVALUATE

Pause at line 159. Circle the passage that describes Merlin's actions. Is this plot event expected?

_____

_____

_____

_____

_____

_____

_____

_____

_____

_____

_____

PREDICT

Pause at line 166. What do you predict will be revealed in this story's climax?

_____

_____

_____

_____

_____

_____

_____

_____

_____

_____

_____

_____

INTERPRET

What does this story have to say about life? Is the story really about honor? love? tables?

_____

_____

_____

_____

_____

_____

_____

SHAPE IT UP

Now re-read the story, putting shapes around the literary elements you found particularly important or effective. Underline passages that tell about the story's characters; star passages about setting; put a circle around story events; put a box around passages that contribute to the story's theme.

"And I remember yours," King Arthur smiled. "And it is too pretty a face to be lost to King Ryence. That is why I am now asking you, with your father's permission, to marry me."

A huge smile broke out on Guinevere's face. "Gladly would I be your wife and queen," the princess declared.

180   "And glad am I to have the noble and brave King Arthur as my son-in-law," King Leodegrance announced.

A great cheer went up from the guests in the banquet hall.

King Leodegrance continued. "And for this perfect royal marriage, I have the perfect royal gift. It is the Round Table, Arthur, that I had Merlin make for your father many years ago. It is a magnificent table that seats one hundred and fifty people."

King Arthur was led to another room to view the

190   Round Table, a remarkable piece of work made of marble and ebony.

King Arthur smiled and said, "It is my hope that this grand Round Table will bring true harmony to my knightly court. For each knight will now have an equal seat. Since the table is round, no one can feel insulted being at the far end, for there is no far end!"

A roar of laughter arose from the knights. King Arthur instructed them to stand around the table and raise their swords.

200   "May our swords work together as a single blade," King Arthur exclaimed. "May we use our power to protect the weak and innocent and to stamp out tyranny wherever it may arise. May good will and brotherhood inspire us, so we can bring honor to everyone."

*Now read two very different responses to
"Guinevere and the Round Table."*

What's Love Got to Do with It?

by Buzby King for *Schoolhouse News*

The story of King Arthur and Queen Guinevere is considered one of the world's greatest love stories. However, based on "Guinevere and the Round Table," I don't think it is. If Arthur's love for Guinevere is a theme in this story, I couldn't find it. For example, King Arthur never declares that he loves Guinevere.

Let's look at reality. In the first paragraph, Arthur is "so weak and preoccupied" that he does not talk to Guinevere when she serves him food and refreshment. Weak from what and preoccupied about what, the writer does not tell us. Later Arthur simply asks, "Who was the woman that served us?" When one of his men tells him who she is, Arthur only remarks that she is beautiful and that she was a "generous princess," which is to repeat that she gave him food. Are these the comments of someone deeply in love? I think not!

When Merlin asks Arthur if he has considered anyone to marry, Arthur says he'd like to marry Guinevere. Arthur wants to marry a woman whom he hasn't spoken to because she is good-looking and served him a snack? Merlin advises against the marriage, as he foresees harm coming to Arthur's kingdom as a result. Heaping absurdity

10

20

SHAPE IT UP

Re-read the first paragraph. What is the reviewer focusing on? Put a box around the word that reveals the focus.

SHAPE IT UP

Put a box around the words that tell about the theme of love. What does this reviewer think of the story's theme? Explain why the reviewer feels as he does, using an example from the review.

_____
_____
_____
_____
_____
_____
_____
_____

Underline the words on this page that comment on Arthur's character. What is the reviewer's attitude toward Arthur?

_____

_____

_____

_____

_____

_____

Circle the plot events that the reviewer discusses. What is the reviewer's response to these events?

_____

_____

Put a box around the details that comment on the story's theme. What is the reviewer's reaction to these story details? (See also page 229.)

_____

_____

_____

_____

_____

_____

_____

on his ridiculous declaration, Arthur then tells Merlin, "I, too, have great powers. For I am Arthur, king of all England. Therefore shall Guinevere be my bride and queen!" What an ego this Arthur character has. Arthur must think he's going to do the honorable thing by Guinevere when he continues and says, "Yet I would never force Guinevere to marry me. I will wed her only if she

30 herself consents." How big of him. So far, he's said nothing about being in love with Guinevere, and even if he did, how could he be? He's only seen her once, and he hasn't even spoken to her, not even so much as a thank you for the snack she served him.

Next Arthur's yes-man, Merlin, concocts a plan to disguise Arthur as a gardening boy to work in the princess's garden. How this is supposed to win Guinevere's heart is unclear. What it says about the characters of Merlin and Arthur is that they are sneaky.

40 When King Ryence comes to King Leodegrance's kingdom of Cameliard, the reader is told that "He [King Ryence] intends to capture King Leodegrance's castle and take Princess Guinevere as his bride!" Disguised as a knight, Arthur asks Guinevere for her necklace to show that he is defending her father's kingdom in her honor. Arthur defeats King Ryence's knight, but does not reveal his true identity. Why Arthur keeps his identity a secret when the goal is to win Guinevere's consent in marriage is unclear.

The next morning, King Ryence appears again, as well
50 as the mysterious knight, and a battle royal follows. Merlin clouds the battlefield with mist, and when the mist clears, King Ryence and his men lay dead.

Arthur reveals himself and asks Guinevere to marry him. She says yes and Arthur exclaims, "May good will and brotherhood inspire us, so we can bring honor to everyone."

In the setting of sword and sorcery, it appears that he with the strongest sword is the most honorable. What's love got to do with it?

INTERPRET

Review the markings you made as you read. To what literary element did the reviewer respond most strongly?

_____

_____

_____

The Adventures of the King

by A. J. Durr for *Schoolhouse News*

There are many different stories about King Arthur, the great Briton king, who legend has it, fended off the invading Saxons until his own family caused his downfall. "Guinevere and the Round Table" is one of the best of those stories; it is full of fun, magic, and excitement.

In this story, King Arthur first sees his future queen, Guinevere, near the city of Cameliard. Arthur is on his way back to Camelot, probably from some quest. Guinevere serves Arthur and his soldiers food and drink, and Arthur

10 is immediately attracted to her. His men tell him that she is the daughter of King Leodegrance.

When Arthur returns to Camelot, his knights argue over their status at court, and they compete to sit next to Arthur at his banquet table. Arthur settles the disputes and then turns to his magician, Merlin, to learn more about

IDENTIFY

What opinions about the story does the reviewer reveal right away?

_____

_____

_____

_____

WORD KNOWLEDGE

A *quest* (line 8), a journey in pursuit of a noble goal, is built on the Latin *quaerere*, meaning "ask."

SHAPE IT UP

Re-read lines 16–37. Draw a circle around each main event of the story's plot.

· · · · · · Notes · · · · · ·

_____

_____

_____

_____

_____

_____

_____

_____

_____

_____

_____

IDENTIFY

What words does the reviewer use to describe his reaction to the story? (See also page 231.)

_____

_____

_____

_____

_____

Guinevere. Merlin, who can foresee the future, warns Arthur that marriage to Guinevere will mean trouble for his kingdom.

20 Arthur does not heed Merlin's advice. Merlin then gives Arthur a magic cap that turns him into a boy and tells him to seek employment in Guinevere's garden. Guinevere notices this new boy and is curious about him. Then King Ryence of North Wales comes to Cameliard with his army to take Guinevere as his bride. Arthur appears disguised before Ryence's army and asks to wear Guinevere's pearl necklace for good luck. He defeats Ryence in an extended battle. Ryence's army flees in terror.

The next day, Ryence returns with his army, and Arthur, once again disguised, appears with his army and 30 defeats Ryence, with help from Merlin, who provides a blinding fog. Guinevere now recognizes the mysterious knight as her garden boy and King Arthur. Arthur asks Guinevere to marry him, and King Leodegrance presents them with the Round Table, which Merlin had made for Arthur's father years ago. The Round Table will solve Arthur's problem of which knight sits where, because each knight will have an equal seat.

This story is a charming one. The idea of the great King Arthur taking a lowly position at King Leodegrance's 40 castle to serve Guinevere is very much in keeping with the other stories about courtly love. Arthur's willingness to disguise himself as a gardener helps to make the legend more humane in the eyes of readers. Guinevere's fascination with the disguised Arthur helps convey to readers that her love for Arthur is real, even though the romance moves quickly.

In fact, everything moves fast in this story. I would
have been happier had Arthur had more encounters with
Ryence, rather than two. That would have made the story
50   even more exciting for me.

Still, the story is really worth reading. It has magic,
excitement, and love all rolled into one. That's about all
one could ask for and all one could want from a legend.

SHAPE IT UP

The reviewer thinks that
the plot moved too quickly.
Circle the solution the
reviewer suggests to slow
the plot down. Do you agree
or disagree? Explain why.

_____

_____

OWN THE SELECTIONS

PRACTICING THE STANDARDS

Literary Elements   Fill out the chart on the following page to
identify the focus of each review of "Guinevere and the Round
Table." Then, write a short analysis of how each reviewer's focus
contributed to his opinion of the original work.

_____

_____

_____

_____

KEEPING TRACK

Personal Word List   Record the new words you learned from this
story in your Personal Word List. Star your favorite words, and
underline words you think you will use in your writing.

Personal Reading Log   Record this series of selections in your Personal
Reading Log, and give yourself 6 points on the Reading Meter.

Checklist for Standards Mastery   Review the Checklist for Standards
Mastery. Indicate which standards you have practiced while completing this selection.

Reviews of Guinevere and the Round Table ■ *Interactive Reading, page 220*

Interact with Informational Texts

"Literary Element" Chart   What literary elements in "Guinevere and the Round Table" did each reviewer focus on? Fill in the chart below to find out.

Review	Comments on Character	Comments on Setting	Comments on Plot	Comments on Theme
"What's Love Got to Do with It?"				
"The Adventures of the King"				

King Arthur:
The Sword in the Stone

LITERARY
ELEMENTS

Interact with a Literary Text

Chain of Events   **Legends** are stories that are based on a real person or event. Complete the chain-of-events chart below. Then, indicate whether each event is likely to be based on actual, historic events or on the writer's imagination. To do this, place a check mark under events you think are based on real events.

Event	Event	Event	Event

Event	Event	Event	Event

Event	Event	Event	Event

Three Responses to Literature

for use with
Holt Literature and Language Arts,
page 433

Interact with Informational Texts

Ratings Chart   You can analyze how well each writer responded to the essay question by using a ratings chart. The standards for a good essay on this topic are cited in the chart below. Giving a 0 means that the writer didn't discuss the standard at all. A 4 means that the writer fulfilled the standard completely. Fill in the ratings chart after you read each essay.

Does the essay—	(Give a score: 0 1 2 3 4)		
	Essay 1	**Essay 2**	**Essay 3**
1. focus on Arthur's character—his actions, words, and deeds?			
2. use direct quotes from Arthur or about Arthur to support claims?			
3. define the qualities necessary for greatness?			
4. state the main ideas clearly?			
5. support the main ideas with specific examples from the text?			
6. answer the question directly?			
7. use convincing evidence to answer the question?			
Totals:	_____	_____	_____

Merlin and the Dragons

Interact with a Literary Text

"Most Important Word" Map   In some stories, a word can stand out so much that it is hard to ignore it. For example, in "Merlin and the Dragons," it would be hard to pick a word more important than the word *dreams*. Use details from the story to complete the graphic organizer below.

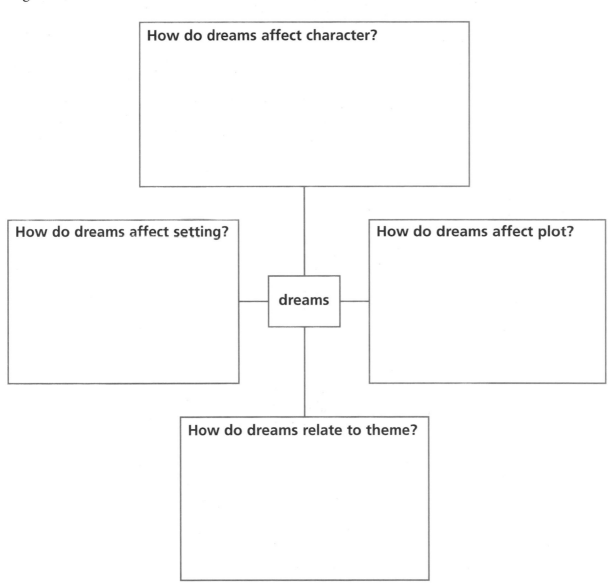

How do dreams affect character?

How do dreams affect setting?

dreams

How do dreams affect plot?

How do dreams relate to theme?

Sir Gawain and the Loathly Lady

for use with
Holt Literature and Language Arts,
page 452

Interact with a Literary Text

Comparison Chart   You compare two characters to see how they are alike, and you contrast them to find out how they are different. Completing a comparison chart can help you see how characters change in the course of a story.

Fill in the comparison chart. What is significant about how Dame Ragnell changed?

How Dame Ragnell Changed

Dame Ragnell before she was married	Dame Ragnell both before and after she married	Dame Ragnell after she was married

Conclusion: _____
_____
_____
_____

He's No King

Interact with an Informational Text

Word Chart   *Bias* refers to an inclination to think a certain way in spite of the facts. A *stereotype* is a fixed notion about all members of a group of people. When people think in terms of stereotypes, they do not allow for any individuality.

Complete the chart below by writing examples from the text that express a bias or stereotype. Then, explain what the bias or stereotype is. An example is done for you.

Words or Phrase	The words show . . .
"We may as well have a girl ruler for all he is worth."	bias against girls being rulers

Letter to the Editor

for use with
Holt Literature and Language Arts,
page 469

Interact with an Informational Text

Reasoning Organizer   Assessing a writer's evidence means looking for facts and opinions and then deciding if the evidence given to support a claim is accurate, adequate, and appropriate. Complete the chart below. Under "Evidence," cite three statements the writer makes to support her position. Under "Assess," write your assessment of the evidence.

Position Statement
Playing video games does not necessarily cause violent behavior in children but may isolate them from others.

Evidence:

Assess:

Evidence:

Assess:

Evidence:

Assess:

Conclusion:

Assess:

Literature

SHORT STORY

ARTHURIAN LITERATURE STUDY

The legendary King Arthur has inspired stories, poems, songs, and even movies. Stories about King Arthur are most probably based on a real person who led the Britons against the invading Saxons in about A.D. 500. The tales of heroism and sorrow that developed around King Arthur, Queen Guinevere, Camelot, Merlin, and the Knights of the Round Table have been passed from generation to generation all over the world.

BEFORE YOU READ

In "The Changing of the Shrew" we meet the future King Arthur as a ten-year-old boy. His teacher is Merlin, a magician, who has his hands full trying to teach such a curious boy. Read this story to find out what it might be like to have a teacher who has magical powers!

Here's what you should know before you read the story:
- A shrew is a tiny animal that has a long pointed snout and is related to a mole. Some types of shrews are poisonous.
- Boys who were destined to be knights learned the rules of chivalry, which included skill in arms, loyalty, generosity, courtesy, and obedience to God.

First, read the story. Then, read the review that follows it.

Reading Standard 3.6
Analyze a range of responses to a literary work, and determine the extent to which the literary elements in the work shaped those responses.

The Changing of the Shrew

Kathleen Kudlinski

VOCABULARY DEVELOPMENT

progression (prō·gresh'ən) *n.:* sequence; order of events or things.

IDENTIFY

Pause at line 13. Who are the story's main characters? Underline them.

WORD KNOWLEDGE

The term "fenny snakes" (line 10) refers to "snakes from the fens." A *fen* is a bog or wetland.

INTERPRET

Underline the words in italics. The writer uses italics to show Merlin's inner thoughts, which Arthur doesn't hear. How does this technique help readers understand Merlin?

_____

_____

_____

_____

_____

"We will study planetary **progression** today, Arthur, because *that* is the lesson I have prepared." Merlin pushed a damp lock of gray hair off his forehead.

"But it's spring!" Arthur stood with his arms spread to catch the sunshine as it poured over the cold stone windowsill. "Can't we just study spring, instead?"

The wizard looked over Arthur's shoulder at the first soft green on the far hillside pasture. "If you know the heavens well," he tried to tell the boy, "you'll know the
10 seasons." Merlin wondered if the first fenny snakes were out basking in that warm sunshine. Curing a rash of winter fevers in the drafty castle had burned up nearly all of his snake tongues.

"Please, Merlin. For once can't we do something that isn't planned?"

"I suppose you'd rather play games," he said harshly. *But, Jove! It did sound good. This truly must be spring.* "How about a race to the far hilltop?"

The boy's eyes reflected disbelief, then surprise, joy,
20 then anger. "No fair. You'll fly!"

And that is what the wizard did. Spreading his arms wide, he placed the tips of his thumbs against the second joints of his third fingers. Humming a perfect A-flat, he stepped out through the window and drifted toward the kitchens below.

He flattered the cook into packing a hearty lunch for them, wheedled the dairy maid into giving up two crocks of buttermilk, and, floating on a lovely breeze up the hillside, charmed a dozen snakes into parting with their

30 tongues. *A good morning's work,* he thought, shaking the cool spring air out from under his robes. But it had scarcely given him time to plan a lesson for a future king. *What to do with the boy?*

"Well, what shall we study?" Arthur panted as he finally crested the hill.

"Precisely." Merlin nodded sagely. "I thought we'd discuss it over lunch." He patted the cloth spread beside him, hoping the boy would sit quietly and let him think.

"Oh, Merlin. It's too early to eat. What can you show

40 me about spring? Couldn't we do something magic?"

Why couldn't Arthur be in a growth spurt this spring, Merlin wondered, *instead of an intellectual stage?* He toyed with the idea of casting a growth spell, but decided against it. Cook hadn't packed enough food for that.

"Well?"

"All right, Arthur." Merlin was thinking on his feet, which was hard, for he was seated on the grass and quite winded from his flight. *Spring fancies were for younger men,* he reminded himself. *Or should be.* "Perhaps I'll try

50 something with you that I hadn't intended to do for several more years."

"I'm ready." Arthur plopped down beside the wizard.

"I'm not so sure you are. There may be some danger." As he heard his own words, Merlin could have kicked himself. A threat of danger never discouraged any ten-year-old.

Arthur jumped back to his feet, shouting, "On with it, then!"

"Very well," Merlin said, though he knew that was not the case at all. "Listen closely, for I shall not be with you

COMPARE & CONTRAST

Re-read lines 21–30. Circle the actions of Merlin that seem ordinary or human. Then, put a box around the actions that come from his use of magic.

· · · · · · Notes · · · · · ·

_____

_____

_____

_____

_____

_____

_____

INTERPRET

What does Merlin mean when he says he was "thinking on his feet" (line 46)?

_____

_____

_____

_____

_____

_____

_____

Why do you think Merlin says that magic *should* frighten Arthur?

_____

_____

_____

_____

_____

_____

_____

_____

_____

What might Arthur learn from being changed into a mouse?

_____

_____

_____

_____

_____

_____

_____

_____

_____

_____

60 after I cast the spell." Arthur quieted down as Merlin knew he would. He'd not used magic on the boy as yet, and it had frightened him. *As it should.*

"I am going to cast you into an animal's body. While you are there you must fend for yourself, for I cannot go with you."

Arthur clapped and shouted, "Oh, make me an eagle! Perhaps a lion? Or a stallion? . . ."

Merlin knew now he'd made an error. The boy was clearly too young, but it was too late to change courses.

70 *What to do?*

"How about a griffon?[1] Oh, could I be a dragon? Or maybe a . . ."

They both glanced down as a tiny animal scampered across the picnic cloth toward the cook's basket.

"A mouse!" Merlin roared, considerably relieved.

Arthur stopped in the middle of his heroic list. "You're going to make me into a mouse?"

"Yes. Do you have any questions?"

"Couldn't it be something more, well, grand?"

80 Merlin shook his head, hoping the boy would decide to skip the whole lesson.

Arthur sat silently for a moment. "Will I be able to read the mouse's mind while I'm inside his body?"

"No. *His* mind will be in *your* body, beside me here on the picnic cloth." Merlin was beginning to regret the whole idea.

"So you get to talk to a giant mouse?" Arthur laughed aloud.

Merlin looked at the sky and began chanting.

90 As he finished the spell, Merlin watched the boy closely. Although Arthur looked the same to him, from

---

1. griffon: mythical animal that is part eagle and part lion.

his tangled brown hair to his worn leather boots, Merlin knew that a mouse's mind was taking over the strong young body. Soon the boy's muscles began to tremble. His eyes jerked wide open, and he jumped to his feet.

"Oh, my!" the mouse-in-Arthur whimpered as he tried to hide Arthur's body behind the lunch basket.

"Easy, easy," Merlin said gently. "I won't hurt you."

"But you are so big!" said the boy-shaped mouse, wringing his hands.

"Look at yourself, mouse. You, too, are big now." Moving slowly so he wouldn't frighten the timid animal, Merlin pointed toward Arthur's body. "I've played somewhat of a trick on you. You will be a boy for a few moments while I use your body for some magic."

The mouse-in-Arthur's eyes widened. When he opened his mouth, Merlin expected a yowl of terror. Instead, the giant mouse squeaked, and ran to hide behind a small tree.

"Really, now, old fellow," Merlin called to him. "There is nothing to worry about." The boy's shoulders stuck out on both sides of the sapling, but he did not move. "I'll protect you," Merlin promised.

Now Arthur's nose was **visible** on one side of the tree trunk. It was wiggling.

"I have some cheese in the basket," Merlin coaxed. "Come closer and I'll show you."

The mouse-in-a-boy hurried back, glancing over his shoulder as he came.

At the distant scream of a hawk, he grabbed the edge of the cloth and dove under it, upsetting the cheese, the sausage pasties,[2] the wine, and the wizard.

---

2. **sausage pasties:** sausage pies.

WORD KNOWLEDGE

Underline "mouse-in-Arthur" and "boy-shaped mouse." The writer uses these terms to emphasize to readers that Arthur is still under Merlin's spell.

· · · · · · Notes · · · · · · ·

_____

_____

_____

_____

_____

_____

_____

_____

_____

VOCABULARY DEVELOPMENT

visible (viz′ə·bəl) *adj.:* able to be seen.

Visible contains the Latin word *videre*, meaning "see," and the Latin suffix *-ible*, meaning "capable of being."

Re-read lines 132–153. Circle the word *danger* each time it appears. What effect does this repetition have on your reading experience? Explain.

_____

_____

_____

_____

_____

_____

_____

_____

_____

_____

_____

_____

_____

_____

_____

_____

_____

Merlin sighed deeply and dusted off his robes. As he began picking up the scattered dinner, a whisper came through the cloth. "Do you have food?"

"Yes. Will you come out and share a bite?"

A moment passed and Merlin repeated his offer. "Did you hear me?" he asked the quivering cloth.

"Yes," the boy-shaped mouse whispered. "You mustn't speak so loudly. They'll find us."

130   "Who?" Merlin found himself whispering back.

"Don't jest about the Deaths," came the offended reply.

"Someone wants to kill you?" Merlin knew that Arthur's mind was somewhere near, planted in this mouse's tiny body. If that body died, so would Arthur. "Just how much danger is there for you?" he prodded.

The boy-mouse picked up the edge of the cloth and waved Merlin in. The old wizard looked around the field before he, too, climbed under the picnic cloth.

"The sky is full of danger," the mouse whispered in a

140 sing-song voice. "Hawks and herons by day and owls by night. The grass crawls with danger: snakes and lizards and spiders." Merlin felt himself crouching further as he listened. "Danger pads on quiet paws: ferrets and weasels, badgers and foxes, cats and . . ." the mouse's whisper dropped to a hiss, ". . . shrews."

A cow mooed and the mouse-in-Arthur's-body stopped breathing.

"Are you all right?" Merlin whispered quickly.

The boy-mouse looked at him angrily and put his

150 hand over Merlin's mouth.

When a few moments of silence had passed, the mouse continued, "The water swims with danger: bullfrogs and bass, turtles . . ."

"Don't mice think of anything besides being eaten?" Merlin wondered aloud.

"No," the mouse answered. "What else is there?"

"Enough!" Merlin shouted, throwing the cloth off their heads. He had to get the real Arthur back before he was eaten by one of these **predators.** As the mouse-in-Arthur's-body cowered in the grass at his feet, Merlin chanted the spell of undoing.

With the last words, the boy's body trembled. "Not now!" he whispered angrily. "I had almost reached the cheese in safety!"

Merlin looked at their picnic, once again spilled about on the grass.

"Oh, do get up," the wizard said. "We don't need to learn any more about mice."

"But I liked being small," Arthur answered. "I could hide anywhere."

"You kept yourself hidden?"

Arthur nodded **emphatically.** "It was so exciting to know there could be enemies everywhere. I still can feel that thrill."

Merlin wondered if he hadn't acted too quickly. Knowing how to hold a keen edge of caution could certainly help the future king in his court.

"Please make me a mouse again," Arthur begged. "I'll be perfectly safe." Merlin's eyebrows rose. "Well, I will be very careful. And I learned so much."

Merlin nodded, stroking his chin. They both had. "You want to be small again?"

Arthur nodded.

"But what shall you be? We must choose something safer than a mouse."

predators (pred′ə·tərz) *n.*: those who capture and feed upon other animals.

emphatically (em·fat′ik·lē) *adv.*: forcefully; insistently.

· · · · · · Notes · · · · · ·

_____

_____

_____

_____

IDENTIFY

Why does Arthur say he liked being small (line 169)? Underline his explanation.

· · · · · · Notes · · · · · ·

_____

_____

_____

_____

_____

_____

_____

_____

_____

_____

_____

_____

_____

_____

_____

_____

_____

_____

_____

_____

_____

INTERPRET

Re-read lines 209–215. What does this paragraph tell you about the extent of Merlin's powers?

_____

_____

_____

_____

_____

_____

_____

_____

"Could I be a cat, Merlin? How about a falcon?"

"Hush, child, let me think." Which was the most dreaded animal on the mouse's list? Quiet and frightened, the mouse's voice came back to him: *"Badgers and foxes,*

190   *cats and SHREWS."* That was it. "Would you like to learn about shrews?" he asked, though he already knew the answer.

"What a wonderful idea! They are bloody good fighters, Merlin. And they even have a poison bite. Can I start right off?"

Merlin again began the chant. Again there was no change to be seen in Arthur's body as the shrew's mind took over. As before, the eyes were the first clue that the change was complete. This time, they opened clear and

200   alert. When they found Merlin, the shrew-in-Arthur's eyes narrowed.

"Oh, dear," muttered the wizard, backing off the cloth.

The boy-sized shrew sprang at him, caught his hand and sunk his teeth into Merlin's finger.

"Oh, do stop," Merlin cried. "This is all wrong." He tried to pull the boy's head away from his throbbing finger. The boy-sized shrew just ground his teeth in more deeply and watched Merlin's distress with obvious glee.

"Freeze!" Merlin shouted, and every living thing

210   stopped. Bird song was stilled. The cows froze in place. Butterflies stopped flapping and fell to the soft grass. It was the only spell Merlin could think of on such short notice, and it hadn't quite solved the problem. He looked at the shrew-in-Arthur locked to his finger with astonishingly sharp teeth.

"Listen, shrew. You are, like it or not, a boy for a while. I am going to lift the spell and you will try to behave like a boy."

220 Merlin cast a release over the meadow. Bird and insect song filled the air. A rainbow's worth of butterflies flew up from the grasses. The cows again chewed their cud. And the shrew-in-Arthur gave one last crunch to the wizard's finger before he released his bite.

"Let's just sit here quietly, shrew, shall we? And wait for it all to be over." Merlin still didn't like the look in those wild eyes, but he was relieved to see the boy's body settling at the far corner of the picnic cloth.

"I am simply starving," said the shrew. "And you will provide my lunch."

230 "No, I think not," said Merlin. "Cook packed just enough for Arthur and me."

"You mistake me," said the shrew. "You've had your turn to hold me still. Now it is my turn." He pointed to Merlin's bloody finger. "My bite is poisonous. In moments you won't be able to move. It doesn't hurt to be eaten that way. At least none of my other victims have complained."

Merlin just smiled and waited.

The shrew-in-Arthur hummed tunelessly for a moment. "I am simply starving. Can you still move?" He 240 looked hopefully at Merlin.

The magician raised his hand and waved at him.

"You know, if I don't eat every four hours, I shall die. I am quite truly starving. That is how we shrews are." He shrugged and looked hungrily at the cows grazing, then back at the wizard. "I say, aren't you feeling the least bit stiff yet?"

WORD
KNOWLEDGE

Release (line 219) comes from the Latin *relaxare*, meaning "relax" or "set free." In this context, *release* is used as a noun meaning "act of freeing."

· · · · · · Notes · · · · · ·

FLUENCY

Read the boxed passage expressively, showing the difference in the characters' ages and the humor in their words.

Circle the word *eating* (line
258). How would you com-
pare what it was like being
a shrew with what it was
like being a mouse? What
do you think the author is
trying to say?

_____

_____

_____

_____

_____

_____

_____

Re-read lines 265–269. What
word would you choose that
tells what Merlin fears in the
story's climax? Why? Put a
box around the word.

_____

_____

_____

_____

_____

_____

_____

Merlin simply waved and grinned. "It is as I said. You are no more a shrew than I am. You are a boy."

The shrew-in-Arthur blinked once. "What do these

250   boys eat?"

"For one thing, boys do not eat wizards." The idea left Merlin chuckling until he noticed the look on the shrew's face. He added firmly, "Never."

The wizard hoped this lesson was going more smoothly for his student. He had a sudden rush of affection for Arthur, a boy with such a quick, open mind and loving heart.

"Don't you ever think of anything besides eating?" he asked the shrew.

260   "No," the shrew answered. "What else is there?"

In the uneasy silence that followed, Merlin saw a tiny furry body in the grass beside the cloth. Before he could move he saw the shrew-in-Arthur grab the little animal and bite its head off.

Merlin yelped in surprise. Then he froze, staring at the small, headless body in horror. *What if the shrew-in-Arthur had just eaten Arthur-in-the-shrew? Was the real Arthur dead? What would become of Britain with this brutal creature as its king?*

270   "Mouse," the shrew-in-Arthur said, offering the limp, headless body to Merlin. "Care to try a bite?"

Merlin gagged and shook his head no. He watched, horrified, as the shrew-in-Arthur finished the morsel and picked his teeth. Finally he had to ask, "Are you sure that was a mouse?"

"Yes, quite. Meadow mouse, by the taste of it. Deer mice are sweeter. I'll catch that one over by the basket, if you'd like to try it."

280 "No!" cried Merlin. "Lessons are quite over for the morning." He raced through the spell of undoing.

At the last word, Arthur's glance darted quickly left, then right. "Where is that mouse!" he said. "I almost had him."

"Arthur," Merlin said gently. "We do not eat mice." He watched the boy's eyes cloud with confusion, then clear.

"I would actually have eaten a mouse?"

"Yes. Raw."

Arthur's face twisted and he swallowed hard. "I don't think I want to study any more today."

290 Merlin reached across the cloth and hugged the boy fiercely. Then they unpacked the cheeses, pasties, and buttermilk.

Arthur grabbed a morsel, crying, "I am simply starving!"

Merlin looked at him sharply. The boy grinned. "No, I guess I'm not *that* starving. But I'll never forget how real hunger feels." He appeared to be lost in thought. "Having a poison bite made everything different. It felt so powerful to know that if I could just make the first move, I would be in

300 control of things. I wonder if that works with people, too?" His grin faded as he noticed the bloody tooth marks in Merlin's finger.

"The shrew, or rather, *I* did that to you?" he asked, in a tiny voice. And in a tinier voice still, "I would actually have eaten you?"

"Yes. Raw." Merlin magicked away the wound and smiled kindly at the future king. "But you didn't."

Arthur was quiet a moment. "I guess that getting in the first move isn't a good idea until you're sure you're not

310 hurting a friend."

INTERPRET

What did Arthur learn when he became a shrew? Circle the words that told you.

Think about what Arthur
learned in the story. How
does what he learned
reveal the story's theme,
or message about life?

Merlin nodded, then asked, "Would you mind if I don't plan this sort of lesson again for some time?"

"Fine." Arthur grinned at him. "Only, Merlin, when we do study this way, shouldn't we hold the lessons *after* lunch?" Without waiting for an answer, he bit into the cheese.

A Review

Magical Merlin

by Linda Rodriguez for *Schoolhouse News*

SHAPE IT UP

Read the review carefully.
As you read, circle the words
and phrases that relate to
plot, underline those that
refer to character, star those
that relate to setting, and
box the words and phrases
that relate to theme.

· · · · · · Notes · · · · · ·

No story about King Arthur would be complete without a mention of Merlin, Arthur's tutor and friend. In "The Changing of the Shrew," the relationship between Arthur and Merlin is vividly brought to life. Through this story you understand just why Merlin is such a memorable literary character.

The first thing you notice about Merlin in "The Changing of the Shrew" is his humanity. Although he possesses great magical powers and the wisdom of years,
10 Merlin never loses touch with his human side. For example, he lets Arthur talk him into abandoning the day's lesson in favor of exploring the beauty of a spring day.

What is also striking about Merlin in this story is his concern for Arthur and his well-being. Merlin, while anxious to enrich Arthur's life, is also concerned about going too far too fast: "He'd not used magic on the boy as yet, and it had frightened him." Merlin's relationship with Arthur seems to be that of teacher, father, and friend all rolled into one. For example, when Arthur is "mouse-in-

20 Arthur," Merlin calms him and gently guides him. But when the situation turns potentially dangerous, Merlin overrides mouse-in-Arthur's objections and reverses the spell.

Because Merlin is so likable, readers can sometimes forget that he has great magical powers. When Arthur is a shrew, he repeatedly bites Merlin, paying no attention to Merlin's cries to stop. When he can stand no more, Merlin cries "Freeze!" and everything in the world stops— a testimony to his abilities.

Besides being magical and wise, Merlin also displays
30 a wonderfully warm sense of humor. In the following passage, Merlin displays a wry sense of humor as he talks with Arthur, who had been turned into an always-hungry shrew:

> "For one thing, boys do not eat wizards." The idea left Merlin chuckling until he noticed the look on the shrew's face. He added firmly, "Never."

Above all, however, Merlin has the ability to love. He "had a sudden rush of affection for Arthur, a boy with such a quick, open mind and loving heart." It is this aspect of the
40 Arthur-Merlin relationship that lingers in my mind after reading this story. It is not every day that you meet some-one as interesting, wise, powerful, understanding, and loving as Merlin, the magician of Camelot.

SHAPE IT UP

Review the shapes you drew as you marked up this review. What literary element is focused on in this essay?

EVALUATE

Do you agree with the reviewer's assessment of Merlin's character? Explain why or why not.

OWN THE STORY

Literary Elements   Write a short review of "The Changing of the Shrew." In your review, focus on one or two literary elements. Then, exchange reviews with a partner. Have your partner identify the literary elements you responded to.

_____

_____

_____

_____

_____

_____

_____

Allusions and Titles   William Shakespeare wrote a comedy about the battle between the sexes, called _The Taming of the Shrew._ In Shakespeare's title the word _shrew_ refers to a bad-tempered woman. What does the title "The Changing of the Shrew" mean?

_____

_____

KEEPING TRACK

Personal Word List   List the vocabulary words for this story in order of difficulty in your Personal Word List.

Personal Reading Log   What parts of the story did you have trouble understanding? Jot down your responses to the story in your Personal Reading Log. Then, give yourself 6 points on the Reading Meter.

Checklist for Standards Mastery   Use the Checklist for Standards Mastery to see how well you have done mastering the standards and where you can improve.

The Changing of the Shrew

■ *Interactive Reading,* page 240

LITERARY ELEMENTS

Interact with a Literary Text

"Your Reaction" Chain   In folk tales and fairy tales, characters are often changed into animals. In "The Changing of the Shrew," Merlin puts spells on Arthur, turning Arthur's mind first into a mouse's and then into a shrew's. The world looks different from the point of view of each of those animals.

Complete the graphic organizer below. After completing Part A, write how you responded to each character in Part B.

	Arthur-as-a-Mouse	Arthur-as-a-Shrew
A Arthur's character traits		
Arthur's attitude toward life		
Food Arthur eats		
B My reaction		

BEFORE YOU READ

This article will tell you more about the historical background of the legendary King Arthur. The photographs will help you visualize the information. As you read, evaluate the evidence the writer provides to support her claim that the legend of King Arthur may have been based on a real person and real places that existed in the sixth century.

Reading Standard 2.6 Assess the adequacy, accuracy, and appropriateness of the author's evidence to support claims and assertions, noting instances of bias and stereotyping.

In Search of King Arthur

Mara Rockliff

IDENTIFY

Pause at the end of the first paragraph. Underline the question that this article will try to answer.

VOCABULARY DEVELOPMENT

resistance (ri′zis·təns) *n.:* movement to oppose governing power.

ruthless (rōōth′lis) *adj.:* pitiless; cruel.

The suffix *-less* comes from Anglo-Saxon and means "without." *Ruth* comes from the Anglo-Saxon *rewthe* or *ruthe* and means "pity" or "sorrow for others."

Stories tell us that King Arthur ruled with strength and wisdom from his court at Camelot. Stories also say that Arthur was badly wounded in battle and sailed to the Isle of Avalon to be healed. But who was this mysterious man, whose legend grew while written record of his reign vanished from the face of the earth?

Historical Evidence

Some historians believe that the real Arthur lived in the sixth century A.D. He seems to have been a great Celtic
10 warrior who drove the Saxon invaders back at the Battle of Badon Hill (possibly at the present-day Liddington Castle). This warrior won his people forty years of peace before their part of the country finally gave up its **resistance** to the **ruthless** Anglo-Saxons. This Celtic warrior is mentioned by a sixth-century writer named Gildas and by a ninth-century monk named Nennius. Both say that this

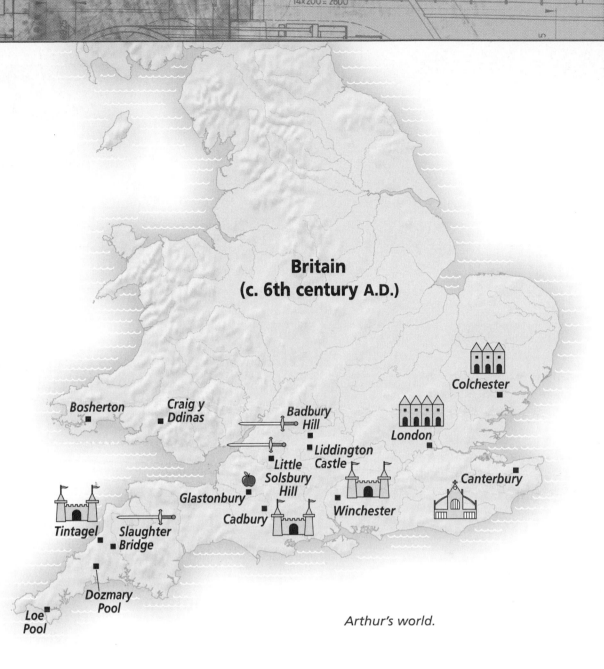

Britain
(c. 6th century A.D.)

Colchester

Bosherton
Craig y Ddinas
Badbury Hill
London
Liddington Castle
Little Solsbury Hill
Glastonbury
Canterbury
Cadbury
Winchester
Tintagel
Slaughter Bridge
Dozmary Pool
Loe Pool

Arthur's world.

leader halted the Anglo-Saxons and won twelve battles for the Britons. Gildas calls the warrior Ambrosius Aurelianus. Nennius calls him Artorius (Latin for "Arthur").

20 ## Archaeological Evidence

Archaeologists have searched for solid evidence of Arthur's existence. In 1998, it seemed they might have found it. At

IDENTIFY

Pause at the end of the section called Historical Evidence. Underline the historical evidence that supports the existence of a real Arthur.

Is this Arthur's tomb?

---

excavations (ek′skə·vā′shənz) *n.:* things or places unearthed by exploratory digging.

The Latin prefix *ex-* means "out of." The Latin word *cavare* means "to make hollow."

IDENTIFY

Underline two facts that could support the claim that Arthur lived at Tintagel.

IDENTIFY

Underline the facts that prove that the Round Table at Winchester is not King Arthur's Round Table.

Tintagel Castle, long believed by locals to be Arthur's birthplace, **excavations** made by archaeologists produced a piece of slate dating back to the sixth century. Inscribed on it in Latin is the name Artognou, pronounced *Arthnou*.

Something else was dug up at the site: massive quantities of expensive sixth-century pottery imported from the Mediterranean. This find shows that during Arthur's time 30 *someone* very rich and powerful lived at Tintagel.

Where Was Camelot?

Sir Thomas Malory placed Camelot in Winchester, in his famous book *Le Morte d'Arthur* (*The Death of Arthur*), published in 1485. The proof hung in the Great Hall of Winchester Castle: the Round Table itself.

As it turns out, though, this could not be *the* Round Table. Measuring eighteen feet across and weighing 2,400 pounds, the round table at Winchester certainly is impressive. And it's old. But not that old. In 1976, tree-ring and carbon dating, 40 along with research into medieval carpentry, revealed that the table was built around 1270—perhaps for King Edward I, who was a huge fan of the Arthur legend.

So where was the real Camelot? Some say it was Colchester, an ancient British city whose Roman name could hint at a connection: Camulodunum. A more likely bet is Cadbury Castle. It's not what most people think of as a castle. Actually it's a hill—a high, steep hill—flat on top, but ringed by giant mounds that hide the hilltop from below. In Arthur's time, say archaeologists, it was a fortress.

50 They've dug up evidence: ruined fortifications, signs of a cobbled road that led through a wooden gatehouse, even the remains of a great timber hall for feasts. South Cadbury is near a village called Queen Camel—another possible source for the name Camelot.

Where Is Arthur Buried?

The Welsh say that Arthur sleeps in Wales, beneath a giant rock called Craig y Ddinas. In 1191, however, the monks of Glastonbury Abbey claimed to have unearthed Arthur's grave. They dug up a cross of lead inscribed in Latin "Here

60 lies buried the renowned King Arthur with Guinevere, his second wife, in the Isle of Avalon." Digging deeper, they found a hollow tree trunk. Inside lay two skeletons, of a woman and a man.

Unfortunately even the cross has disappeared, and many experts now believe the finding was a fake. It might have been cooked up to lure pilgrims to the abbey, which needed funds following a disastrous fire.

Still, Glastonbury could be Avalon. It's not an island—in fact, it's miles from water—but towering above the abbey

70 is the rocky peak of Glastonbury Tor. Today farmland surrounds it; in Arthur's time, it was a soggy marsh. Rising

IDENTIFY

Underline the archaeological evidence that supports the claim that Camelot was at Cadbury Castle.

· · · · · · Notes · · · · · ·

_____

_____

_____

_____

_____

_____

_____

_____

_____

_____

_____

IDENTIFY

Underline the evidence that shows that the claim that Arthur is buried at Glastonbury might not be true.

from the mist, the tor may very well have seemed an enchanted isle. Long ago the tor was known as Inis Avalon, the apple-bearing island.

Will archaeologists ever find proof that Arthur did exist? No one knows. (It would certainly be hard to prove he didn't!) But man or myth, one thing is certain: In the hearts of those who cherish his heroic ideals, King Arthur lives— and will live forever.

OWN THE TEXT

PRACTICING THE STANDARDS

Author's Evidence Does the writer give enough evidence to support the idea that there may have been a real Arthur? Why or why not? Share your ideas with another student, and score the persuasiveness of your theories, with 4 the highest score and 1 the lowest. The more details you use from the text to support your opinion, the higher your score!

KEEPING TRACK

Personal Word List Add to your Personal Word List the words you learned in this selection. Keep an eye out for these words in books and articles about history or geography.

Personal Reading Log As you note this selection in your Personal Reading Log, tell what you liked or disliked about the structure of the article. Give yourself 2 points on the Reading Meter.

Checklist for Standards Mastery Use the Checklist for Standards Mastery to see how far you have come in mastering the standards.

In Search of King Arthur ▪ *Interactive Reading,* page 254

Go Beyond an Informational Text

"More About Arthur" List   You can search for King Arthur yourself. Read more stories about the legend of Arthur. Dig deep into the history of England for other historical evidence that indicates the existence of Arthur.

Use the library or the Internet to make a list of books, tapes, or Internet sources about Arthur.

For a book, list these details: Author or editor. Title. Publisher. Year.

For a Web site, list the name and address of the site.

A sample of each type of entry is already done for you.

Books: Barron, T. A. The Mirror of Merlin. Book Four of The Lost Years of Merlin. Philomel Books, 1999.

_____

_____

_____

_____

_____

_____

_____

Web Sites: Historical King Arthur Web site.
http://www.freespace.virgin.net/david.ford2/arthur.html

_____

_____

_____

Audio Books: King Arthur and His Knights. Award-Winning Storyteller Jim Weiss, narrator. CD, Homeworks, Inc.

_____

_____

_____

BEFORE YOU READ

Alan Jay Lerner wrote the lyrics, or words, for the songs in the musical *Camelot.* The musical uses dialogue and song to tell a story about King Arthur and his kingdom of Camelot. In the song titled "Camelot," King Arthur explains to Guinevere, his soon-to-be wife, what a wonderful place Camelot is.

First, read the song lyrics. Then, write your own lyrics to a song about Arthur.

Camelot

words by **Alan Jay Lerner**

INTERPRET

What might "a distant moon ago" mean?

_____

_____

VOCABULARY DEVELOPMENT

legal (lē′gəl) *adj.:* according to the law.

Legal comes from the Latin *legalis,* meaning "law."

lingers (liŋ′gərz) *v.:* delays leaving.

Lingers comes from the Old English *lengen,* meaning "delay."

conditions (kən·dish′ənz) *n.:* the way things are.

A law was made a distant moon ago here
July and August cannot be too hot;
And there's a **legal** limit to the snow here
In Camelot.

5 The winter is forbidden till December
And exits March the second on the dot.
By order summer **lingers** through September
In Camelot.

Camelot! Camelot!
10 I know it sounds a bit bizarre.
But in Camelot! Camelot!
That how **conditions** are.

The rain may never fall till after sundown.

By eight the morning fog must disappear.

15 In short, there's simply not a more **congenial** spot

For happ'ly ever-aftering than here in Camelot!

Camelot! Camelot!

I know it gives a person pause,

But in Camelot! Camelot!

20 Those are the legal laws.

The snow may never slush upon the hillside.

By nine P.M. the moonlight must appear.

In short, there's simply not a more congenial spot

For happ'ly ever-aftering than here in Camelot!

VOCABULARY
DEVELOPMENT

congenial (kən·jēn'yəl) *adj.*:
agreeable; suited to one's
needs.

Congenial contains the Latin
prefix *com-*, meaning "with"
or "together," plus the Latin
word *genius,* meaning
"natural inclination."

RHYME

Circle the rhyming words in
this song. Look for internal
rhymes (within the lines) as
well as end rhymes.

WORD
KNOWLEDGE

The phrase "happ'ly ever-
aftering" is a poetic way
of saying "living one's life
happily ever after."

TEXT STRUCTURE

A stanza or group of lines
that is repeated in a song is
called a *refrain.* A refrain
usually contains the song's
most important idea. Underline the most important idea
in this refrain.

· · · · · · Notes · · · · · ·

PRACTICING THE STANDARDS

Literary Elements   When you read this song, what stands out for you? Do you think the song has a strong rhythm or rhyme? Do you think the lyrics present strong images, similes, or metaphors? Discuss your responses with a partner, and work together to identify features of the song that you think are outstanding.

_____

_____

_____

_____

Fluency   Read the lyrics aloud to a partner. As you read, vary your tone and speed to best convey the song's message. Ask for feedback from your partner. Then, switch roles.

KEEPING TRACK

Personal Word List   Record the new words you learned in your Personal Word List. Also add rhyming words that you think you might be able to use in a song or a poem.

Personal Reading Log   Add this selection to your Personal Reading Log. Tell whether you thought it was easy or hard to read. Give yourself 2 points on the Reading Meter.

Checklist for Standards Mastery   Use the Checklist for Standards Mastery to see how much you have learned. Review the standards that you plan to work on to improve your understanding.

Camelot ▪ *Interactive Reading,* page 260

PROJECT

Go Beyond a Literary Text

Song Lyrics   Re-read the lyrics to the song "Camelot." Then, write your own lyrics to a song sung by Arthur that could be included in your version of a musical about King Arthur and his times. Will your purpose be to tell a story or to appeal to the emotions of your listeners? Will your song be serious or humorous?

Write the lyrics to your song below. In your song, experiment with imagery, rhythm, and rhyme. Write two different verses and the chorus.

Song title: _____

Verse: _____
_____
_____
_____

Chorus: _____
_____
_____
_____

Verse: _____
_____
_____
_____

Chorus: _____
_____
_____
_____

Chapter 7 Reading for Life

Chapter Preview   In this chapter you will—

Strategy Launch:
"Close Reading"

READING FOCUS: INFORMATIONAL WRITING

We learn about the world around us by gathering information. Staying informed makes everyday living easier. Documents containing information about policies and procedures help us on the job and at school. Newspapers and public documents inform us about current events and civic issues. Directions and how-to guides tell us how to get from here to there or how to assemble things, and contracts and warranties spell out our rights as consumers.

Because informational texts are meant to help you, they may be closely packed with facts, details, explanations, and directions. One way to make sure that you absorb the information in such documents is to use the "Close Reading" strategy.

A STRATEGY THAT WORKS: "CLOSE READING"

Most people do not read public documents, workplace documents, or technical directions for pleasure: They read informational materials to learn something. To achieve this goal, you should read carefully and slowly—find and take in what the text has to say. This type of reading strategy is called "Close Reading."

POINTERS FOR USING THE "CLOSE READING" STRATEGY:

- Identify your purpose for reading. For instance, are you reading to find out when an event will occur, how to make something, or what to do in an emergency?

- Skim the informational text. Take note of heads, lists, and special features.

- Read carefully to make sure you fully understand the text. Refer to diagrams and illustrations for guidance. If a glossary or footnotes have been provided, use them.

- Re-read to clarify any information that is complex or that you find confusing.

Reading Standard 2.2
Locate information by using a variety of consumer, workplace, and public documents.

Reading Standard 2.5
Understand and explain the use of a simple mechanical device by following technical directions.

Sometimes you have to read informational texts to gain the information you need to have fun. In the following series of informational documents, trace the journey of one boy from reading a public announcement in the newspaper to embarking on a summer adventure.

The Information Trail

Mara Rockliff

Skim the series of documents in this section. Then identify each type of document.

_____

_____

_____

_____

_____

_____

_____

_____

_____

_____

expedition (eks′pə·dish′ən) *n.:* journey; voyage; march.

★ Public Announcement ★

Attention Trailblazing Teens!

Nothing to do this summer? How about saving the earth?

Come join the Junior Conservation Corps, a three-week summer trail-building **expedition** run by the Pine Ridge Mountain Club. It's open to kids ages 12–14 who live in Wellnough County.

- Blaze new trails, fix old trails.
- Develop basic, outdoor survival skills.
- Learn the "whys" as well as the "hows" of conservation.
- Make a real difference!

For further information, contact Marsha Jones at (000) 333-2222 or kidcrew@brmc.org.

10

From: taylor3168@searchme.com
To: kidcrew@brmc.org
Subject: JCC summer program

Ms. Jones:

20   I am a seventh-grader at Jefferson Middle School in Urban, Virginia. I love the outdoors and I am very concerned about the environment. Could you please send me more information about the Junior Conservation Corps and an application? Thanks very much. Here's my address:

Taylor Wyant
000 Broad St.
Urban, VA 00000

Junior Conservation Corps Application

Name _____ Date of Birth _____ Gender: ❏ M ❏ F

30   Street Address _____

City _____ State _____ Zip _____

Phone (___) _____

I would prefer to work in

     ❏ Shenandoah National Park

     ❏ George Washington National Forest

     ❏ no preference

Have you ever been camping before?   ❏ YES   ❏ NO

Do you own (or can you buy or borrow) a tent?   ❏ YES   ❏ NO

If yes, are you willing to share your tent with

40   another JCC volunteer?   ❏ YES   ❏ NO

Please describe any outdoor skills and experience: _____

_____

What do you feel you can contribute to the Junior Conservation

     Corps? _____

_____

Your signature _____ Date _____

Parent or guardian signature _____ Date _____

---

mail to: JCC, c/o Pine Ridge Mountain Club, P.O. Box 00,
       Whitewood, VA 00000

CLOSE READING

What kind of information is given in this e-mail?

_____

_____

_____

_____

_____

_____

_____

CLOSE READING

What type of information is this application intended to gather? Why would this information be important to reviewers?

_____

_____

_____

_____

_____

_____

_____

_____

_____

_____

Skim each paragraph in the letter, and tell what instruction is given in each.

_____

_____

_____

_____

_____

_____

_____

_____

_____

_____

_____

_____

_____

_____

INFER

Why might signing a document such as this be a requirement for campers?

_____

_____

_____

_____

_____

_____

_____

50

Pine Ridge Mountain Club
P.O. Box 00
Whitewood, VA 00000

Taylor Wyant
000 Broad St.
Urban, VA 00000

Dear Taylor:

Congratulations! I am pleased to inform you that you have been accepted into this summer's Junior Conservation Corps program. Please sign and return the JCC volunteer conduct agreement. It's a

60 requirement for admission.

Your tentmate will be: Jamie Shifflett
                         Hamilton, VA
                         (000) 555-6666

I strongly encourage you to practice your tent-making skills before you arrive. It's a skill that will come in very handy, especially on the first night out on the trail!

I also suggest getting in touch with your tentmate before joining us. Not only will you feel more comfortable when you meet on the trail, but you may be able to trim your shopping list and lighten your

70 backpack!

Don't hesitate to call or e-mail me if you have any questions. I am looking forward to meeting you in July!

Marsha Jones
Program Director

Junior Conservation Corps
Code of Conduct

- I will respect nature.
- I will respect others.
- I will listen and learn.

80
- I will work with others as a team.
- I will work hard to conserve the environment.

Your signature: _____

Tough Tent 2J6

COMPONENT LIST

- Tent Body (1)
- Tent Fly (1)
- Frame Members (2)
- Carry Bag (1)
- Pole Bag (1)
- Stake Bag (1)
- Stakes (8)
- Seam Sealer (1)

ASSEMBLY

1. Begin by laying the tent body out on the ground. In windy conditions, the windward corner of the tent should be staked down. Take all of the poles out of the carry bag and assemble them to their full lengths.

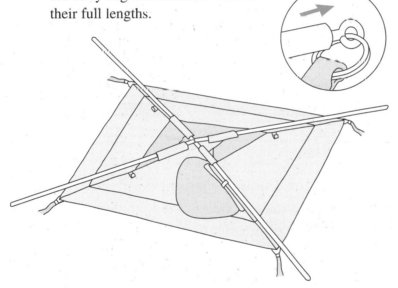

2. Insert the two long poles through the rod sleeves in the tent body. They should run from corner to corner, crossing in the center.

3. Once both of the poles are inserted, place a corner pin inside of the end of one of the poles. From the opposite corner, take the pole in one hand and the ring in the other, and slowly feed the pole up, making sure that it is bending evenly along its length. Make sure that the ferrules don't get caught inside the rod sleeves. Place the pin into the end of the pole to maintain tension.

Repeat with the other pole.

Attach all clips to the frame members.

90

100

110

VOCABULARY DEVELOPMENT

component (kəm·pō′nənt) *n.:* one of the main parts.

DECODING TIP

Draw a line between the two parts that make up the word *windward* (line 95). Then, look at surrounding context clues. What might this word mean?

_____

_____

_____

_____

INFER

How would you go about identifying what *ferrules*, in line 106, are?

_____

_____

_____

_____

_____

_____

_____

_____

_____

_____

VOCABULARY DEVELOPMENT

substantial (səb·stan′shəl)
adj.: strong; solid; firm.

• • • • • • **Notes** • • • • • •

_____

_____

_____

_____

_____

4. The tent can now be staked out through the corner rings. Work by staking opposite corners while applying tension to remove wrinkles from the floor.

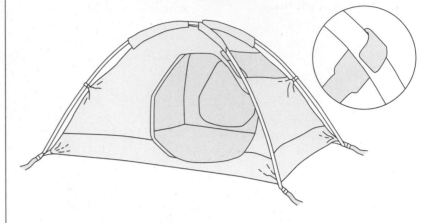

While general purpose stakes have been included, sand or snow conditions may require a more **substantial** stake. These can be purchased at your local camping store.

OWN THE TEXT

PRACTICING THE STANDARDS

Locating Information   Fill out the graphic organizer on the following page as you re-read "The Information Trail." Then, analyze your completed chart to see what kinds of information you found in each document.

KEEPING TRACK

Personal Word List   Add to your Personal Word List the words you learned. Which words had you never seen or heard before? Which words were a bit more familiar but unclear?

Personal Reading Log   Give yourself 2 points on the Reading Meter.

Checklist for Standards Mastery   Use the Checklist for Standards Mastery to see how far you have come in mastering the informational standards. Note areas where you do best and where you can improve.

The Information Trail ■ *Interactive Reading,* page 266

LOCATING INFORMATION

Interact with Informational Texts

"Close Reading" Chart   Close reading enables you to find and understand key information in various kinds of documents. Fill out the chart below with the key information you found in each document in "The Information Trail."

	Public Document: Advertisement/ Notice	**Workplace Document: Letters and e-mails**	**Consumer Document: How-to Instructions**
Key Information			
Key Information			
Key Information			
Key Information			
Key Information			

Public Documents

for use with
Holt Literature and Language Arts,
page 484

Interact with Informational Texts

Information-Locator Wheel   Write the number of each item from the Information Bank in the area that shows the kind of document where the information can be found.

Information Bank

1. age of character Sam might play

2. age at which you can work in entertainment in California

3. how the actor playing the part should look

4. title of the book that StreetWheelie Productions is making into a movie

5. name of a main character in the movie

6. types of people who must declare that Sam can work in the entertainment industry

7. requirements for trying out for a part in the movie

8. Sam's birth date

9. time and place of audition

10. the city where the movie will be set

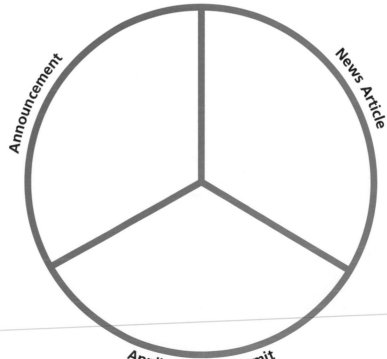

Workplace Documents

Interact with Informational Texts

"Where to Find It" Chart   Sam is such a thorough person that she actually makes up a chart to remind herself which documents to look at for which types of information. Unfortunately, she had to go to dance class before finishing her chart. Please fill in all the remaining spaces for her. Remember, the types of documents are **business letter, workplace instructions, e-mail memo,** and **e-mail directory.**

To Find Out . . .	Look in This Document
latest shooting schedule	
what to do when I arrive on location	
how to do my hair	
schedule change for 8/8/02	
	business letter
	workplace instructions
	e-mail directory

Consumer Documents

for use with
Holt Literature and Language Arts,
page 496

Interact with Informational Texts

Information Booth   Suppose you are in charge of an information booth for the Bay Area Rapid Transit Company. In your booth you have four kinds of documents: a **BART system map,** a **Bikes on BART** handout sheet, a **ticket guide,** and a **train schedule.** Each type of document is stacked in its own separate cubbyhole. When a person comes to you with a question, you must decide which document to give the person. Since you're always thinking ahead, you'll prepare by filling in this organizer.

For each type of document, write two questions that the document might answer. Write the question in the proper cubbyhole. Then, write the answer to the question. A sample question and answer have been written for you.

BART System Map	Bikes on BART
Q: What's the nearest stop to 18th St. and Mission?	**Q:**
A: 16th St. and Mission	**A:**
Q:	**Q:**
A:	**A:**

Ticket Guide	Train Schedule
Q:	**Q:**
A:	**A:**
Q:	**Q:**
A:	**A:**

How to Change a Flat Tire

Interact with an Informational Text

Checklist for Tire Repair   The following checklist tells you the major pieces of information given in "How to Change a Flat Tire." Unfortunately, the items are out of order. In the boxes, number the items in the correct order. (Some of the ten items listed in the article have been divided into two items on this checklist.)

	Get the spare tire and tire-changing tools from the trunk.
	Lower car, and remove the jack.
	Finish unscrewing lug nuts, and store in wheel cover.
	Position the jack on the car on a solid, flat surface.
	Park the car off the road.
	Put on spare tire.
	Remove the wheel cover from the tire.
	Raise the car 2–3 inches off the ground with the jack.
	Loosen the lug nuts partway.
	Put the tools and the flat tire in the trunk.
	Finish tightening lug nuts.
	Tighten the lug nuts by hand.
	Remove flat tire.

Bonus Item: What should you do next?

_____

Information

BEFORE YOU READ

There are all kinds of ways kids can make money: by baby-sitting, doing chores, holding a yard sale, or using a special talent, such as music or design. Once kids have the money, though, what do they do with it? Lots of young people spend their earnings as fast as they can. Others set some aside to save.

The following article may open your mind to a whole new way of handling money: investing it so that it grows.

from Boys' Life, October 2000
Make Your Money Grow

Kristin Baird Rattini

CLOSE READING

Skim this article, and circle the headings you find. Then, set a purpose for reading. What is your purpose?

_____

_____

_____

_____

_____

_____

VOCABULARY DEVELOPMENT

prudent (prōo′dənt) *adj.:* wise; cautious.

Dave Pfitzner, 19, of Kent, Washington, near Seattle, recently conducted an experiment. Dave put half of his money into a savings account and bought stock with the other half. For six months, he watched his two investments grow.

"I made a couple of hundred dollars on my stock," Dave says, "but just a couple of dollars in the bank accounts."

Dave discovered a
10   basic investment lesson: While it's always **prudent** to be a saver, you also must master the essentials of investing if you want your money to really grow.

Does money grow on trees?

How It Works

Investing is different from saving.

With a piggy bank, for example, you accumulate only as much
money as you push through the
slot. Worse, *inflation*, the rising
cost of products and services, can
actually shrink the buying power
of piggy bank savings.

Let's say there's a bike you
really want. It costs $100, and you
save all year for it. But when you finally go to the bike shop
with a crisp Ben Franklin—your hot wheels now cost $105.
That five bucks is inflation at work.

Money does grow in a savings account; it earns
interest, what the bank pays you to use your cash. If,
however, the interest rate is low (as it has been recently),
you earn only a few pennies a year on each dollar you
deposit. That's slow growth.

Getting Started as an Investor

Ginger Milam, manager of Youth Event Services for the
Stock Market Institute of Learning and a main instructor
for the Youth Wall Street Workshop, teaches teenagers
strategies for investing.

Among her lessons:

- Practice by making lots of pretend trades before
  your first real one.
- Invest in companies you know and like.
- **Don't buy on the buzz.** Thoroughly research any
  company before investing in it.

20

30

40

Line 46 contains the idiom
"put all your eggs in one
basket." What does the
idiom mean?

_____

_____

_____

_____

_____

_____

_____

_____

_____

_____

_____

_____

_____

_____

**VOCABULARY
DEVELOPMENT**

privilege (priv′ə·lij) *n.:* special
right.

resources (rē′sôrs′əz) *n.:*
sources of support; things
available to help.

- Don't put all your eggs in one basket. Diversify your investments.
- Keep a journal of every trade so you can see how your investment strategy is working.
50 • Never invest money you cannot afford to lose.
- Dedicate yourself to continuing education.

For more information or to start a simulated investment club in your school (free starter packs available): Youth Event Services, Stock Market Institute of Learning, 14675 Interurban Avenue South, Seattle, WA 98168-4664; 800-872-7411.

Investment Options

By contrast, when you make an investment, your money works harder for you. Although you can invest in anything
60 from land to lima beans, we'll focus here on two common types of investment, *bonds* and *stocks.*

A bond is a loan you make to the government or to a company, which pays you interest for the **privilege** of using your money for a fixed time.

You also can become part owner of a company when you buy its stock, or shares. Your investment often is used to pay for new equipment or other production **resources.** If all turns out well, the investment leads to greater sales, more profit, and a higher stock value.
70 However, nothing is guaranteed.

Investing Lessons

Until recently, almost everyone relied on brokers to recommend stocks and to make their investments for them. Today, many people save money by doing their own

WORD
KNOWLEDGE

Savvy (line 76) is a slang term meaning "know-how" or "knowledge."

VOCABULARY
DEVELOPMENT

secure (si·kyoor') *adj.*: solid; safe; sure.

· · · · · Notes · · · · · ·

research, buying and selling on the Internet. That's where computer savvy kids come in.

"When my dad came home from work, he'd go online and check his stocks," says 11-year-old Jonathan Spital of Miami, Fla. "I started asking him a bunch of questions."

80   Pretty soon, Jonathan himself was investing in a restaurant chain. (Minors cannot own stocks directly; Jonathan's parents set up what's called a *custodial* investment account for him and helped him manage it.)

Taking Chances

Risk and reward are both part of investing. In general, the greater the risk you take, the greater your chance of making, or losing, money.

Some investors play it safe. They stick with risk-free savings accounts or very **secure** government bonds.

90   Others reduce their overall risk by *diversifying;* that is, investing in a variety of companies. That way, if one stock investment does not perform well, the others help balance out that loss.

TEXT STRUCTURE

Why do lines 95–97 appear in boldface type?

_____

_____

_____

_____

_____

_____

_____

_____

_____

_____

_____

_____

CLOSE READING

Which parts of the text should you re-read to be sure you understand them?

_____

_____

_____

_____

_____

_____

_____

This type of investor often purchases *mutual funds,* which offer stock in a mix of companies. **It's like a box of crayons. Each color is an individual company's stock. The whole box is the fund.**

100 Jonathan Spital invests in a mutual fund that owns shares in companies familiar to kids, such as a toymaker and an entertainment business that creates kid movies, theme parks, and more.

Doing Your Homework

The important thing is to learn as much as possible about a company before investing your money.

Last year, Chris Stallman, 16, of Bradley, Ill., asked his dad to buy him a hot new Internet stock. After some research Mr. Stallman had concerns about the company and decided against the investment. Good thing. The per share price of the stock soon fell from $27 to $9.

110 Chris learned his lesson. He now looks for companies with a proven money-earning record. He also satisfies himself that their stocks are not overpriced.

"I have realized that it takes research to find a good, stable company with an opportunity for growth," he says.

Chris also believes more kids should become serious investors.

"People shouldn't be scared about investing," he says. "If you do the research you likely will have a positive return."

Rule of 7: The Fast Road to Riches

It sounds a little like a new video game, but the Rule of Seven is a lot more amazing. If you save for seven years and then stop, you'll accumulate nearly as much as a person who delays saving during those seven years, but then continues for 45 years!

See for yourself:

If you save $50 a month from birth to age 7, then stop, that money, based on 12 percent compounded annually, grows thusly.

At 18, you'll have	$22,955
At 45	$488,508
At 52	$1,082,145

Likewise, if you start saving $50 a month from age 7 to 52:

At 18, you'll have	$13,730
At 45	$455,837
At 52	$1,083,462

So, when are you going to start saving . . . and start building serious wealth?

120

130

INTERPRET

Restate in your own words the "rule of 7."

OWN THE TEXT

Locating Information   Suppose you keep this article in your files for future reference. Six months later, you become interested in investing, and you get out the article. Which text structures in the article will help you locate information? What specific information will they help you locate?

_____

_____

_____

_____

_____

_____

_____

_____

_____

_____

_____

_____

KEEPING TRACK

Personal Word List   The words you learned in this article don't just have to do with investing money. Write these words in your Personal Word List.

Personal Reading Log   What have you learned from this article that might someday help you in life? Jot down a memo to yourself about it in your Personal Reading Log. Give yourself 2 points on the Reading Meter.

Checklist for Standards Mastery   Find the standard in the Checklist for Standards Mastery that relates to what you have just learned. If you've mastered that standard, mark it on the checklist.

Make Your Money Grow ■ *Interactive Reading,* page 276

PROJECT

Go Beyond an Informational Text

Follow and Chart Stocks   It's easy to practice investing. Just follow some stocks in the newspaper.

- Work on your own or with one or more partners. Each person should pick at least one stock to follow. Most major newspapers include stock-exchange listings in their business sections. The stocks might be on the New York Stock Exchange or the NASDAQ list. The first thing you'll notice is that stocks are listed by abbreviations, in alphabetical order. Get help, if necessary, in finding the abbreviations of companies you are interested in.

- Follow your stocks for at least one week. (The longer, the better.) Check the stocks' prices every day. Make a line graph showing the changes in your stocks' prices, day by day. Plot each stock as a separate line on the same graph.

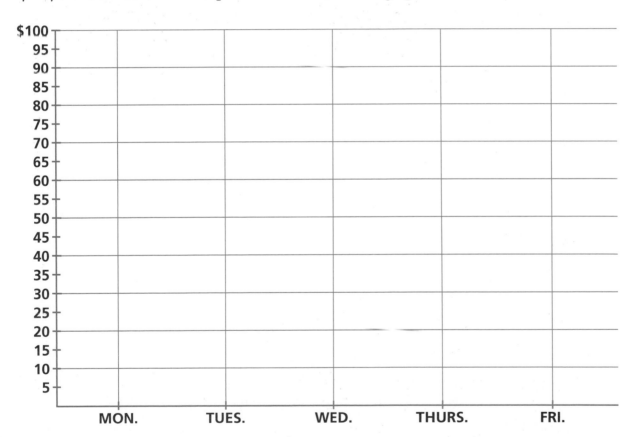

- Suppose you invested one thousand dollars in each of your stocks on the first day. How much money would you have made or lost by the final day?

_____

Information

INVENTOR'S HANDBOOK

BEFORE YOU READ

Why would someone starting a business want to write out a formal plan in advance? There are two main reasons. First, it helps the business owner stay on track. Second, it convinces others, such as banks or investors, that the business is likely to succeed.

Reading Standard 2.2 Locate information by using a variety of consumer, workplace, and public documents.

A SAMPLE BUSINESS PLAN

Steven Caney

VOCABULARY DEVELOPMENT

adjustable (ə·just'ə·bəl) *adj.:* able to have changes made to it, so that it fits or works better.

CLOSE READING

Underline the subheads of this business plan. Why do you think the objective is noted first?

_____

_____

_____

_____

_____

_____

_____

_____

An **adjustable** bicycle kickstand for sloping, rocky, or soft ground.

Objective: To invent an adjustable kickstand that will securely keep a bicycle standing on sloping, uneven, rocky, or soft ground. I will build and improve models through to a final prototype and then try to sell the invention to a bicycle accessories manufacturer for royalty payments.

Competition: Nothing is presently available like my idea,

10   although the manager of one bicycle shop claims some older English bikes do have a kickstand length adjustment. My idea for an adjustable kickstand is different, with a length adjustment plus an adjustable foot for greater stability on soft or rocky ground.

Product development: Most of my experiments will be modifications of existing kickstands. The length of my kickstand will be easily adjustable from long to short to accommodate uneven and sloping ground surfaces, and the foot of the kickstand will easily adjust from a

284   Chapter 7   **Reading for Life**

20 single point for hard and rocky ground to a flat foot for soft surfaces. When not in use, the kickstand will **conveniently** fold back out of the way (in the conventional manner) and not interfere with the rider's movements.

Market research: The need for an adjustable and stable bicycle kickstand is **obvious** to anyone who has tried to stand a bike on sloping, rocky, or soft ground. I have talked with two local bicycle shop managers and they presently do not sell and have never heard of a kick-

30 stand like the invention I propose. Both managers think it is a good idea. The store managers also claim that most new bikes do not come with a kickstand; it is usually purchased as an **accessory** when the bike is new.

The first manager I spoke with claims to sell about 200 kickstands a year; the other manager estimates 250 to 300 kickstands sold per year. My kickstand will probably be more expensive than the $4 to $12 models now being sold. Both managers think that my invention could represent 10 to 20 percent of their kickstand

40 sales if the retail price is under $20.

VOCABULARY DEVELOPMENT

demonstrate (dem′ən·strāt′)
v.: show how something
works or what it is.

CLOSE READING

Go back and review all the
subheads in this business
plan. Put a check next to
each heading word or
phrase you feel you understand. Then, go back to
the ones without checks
on them. Look the words
up in a dictionary. Ask a
classmate or your teacher
for clarification if necessary.

INFER

What is that extra 20 percent
for (line 70)?

_____

_____

_____

_____

_____

_____

_____

_____

_____

_____

_____

_____

Marketing: When the final prototype is complete, I plan to take several photographs of the kickstand in use, to **demonstrate** its features and benefits. I will also write a specifications sheet listing these features and benefits along with a detailed drawing showing dimensions and other specifications.

Both bicycle store managers I spoke with have agreed to show these materials to representatives from the bicycle accessories companies they do business

50 with. I can also send these materials (plus a cover letter explaining that I want to sell the invention for a royalty) to bicycle accessory manufacturers. I will get these company names and addresses from the boxes of accessories I see in bicycle shops and by researching bicycle accessory manufacturers in the *Thomas Register* (a comprehensive listing of manufacturers in America) and other catalog listings at the public library.

If a manufacturer shows interest, I will try to negotiate a royalty sale agreement. My older cousin is

60 a lawyer and he has agreed to help me negotiate for a fair royalty.

Financing: To complete a final prototype and produce marketing photographs, my only costs will be for materials. I have the tools necessary to do the experimenting and to build the prototype. Here is my estimated budget:

Buy new and used kickstands to modify, plus miscellaneous hardware:	$35.00
Film and processing:	9.00
	44.00

70 | | |
|---|---:|
| 20 percent contingency for unexpected expenses, such as long-distance phone calls, postage, and bus fare: | 8.80 |
| Total | $52.80 |

NOTE: I plan to use money from my savings account, and I will not need financing from someone else unless my expenses exceed $75.00. If I do need additional money, I will then decide whether I should borrow it from my parents or figure out an investment plan to trade a part of the ownership in my invention for the money I need
80   to finish development.

OWN THE TEXT

PRACTICING THE STANDARDS

Sources of Information   How might this business plan be a source of different kinds of information to (1) a banker and (2) a fellow student of the planner's?

_____

_____

_____

KEEPING TRACK

Personal Word List   This brief selection contained many words used in the world of business. On your Personal Word List, write down the five vocabulary words and any others that you want to learn at this time.

Personal Reading Log   If you were the parent of the student who made this business plan, how would you respond to it? Write a response in your Personal Reading Log. Give yourself 2 points on the Reading Meter for this reading experience.

Checklist for Standards Mastery   Use the Checklist for Standards Mastery to see how far you have come in mastering the standards.

A Sample Business Plan

Interactive Reading, page 284

Go Beyond an Informational Text

Create a Business Plan   Think of a business idea of your own that will set the world on fire. Use this format as a template for your own business plan. In the space below each heading, write a brief description of your business idea.

Objective: What you aim to produce, make, or sell
Competition: What other products or services already exist that might take away from your business
Product Development: How you will design and make the product or create the service
Market Research: What your product or service will cost and how much money it will make
Marketing: How you will advertise
Financing: How much money you will need to start work

TECHNICAL DIRECTIONS

A constellation is a cluster of stars that appear close to one another in the night sky. Ancient astronomers named the constellations according to their shapes in order to classify and memorize them.

Following is a Web site that gives directions for finding the seven bright stars in the night sky that make up the constellation of Ursa Major, also known as the Big Bear or the Big Dipper. You'll also learn how to identify the fainter stars that make up Ursa Minor, also known as the Little Bear or the Little Dipper.

Here are some pointers about locating the Big and Little Dippers:

- You can locate the Big Dipper low in the evening sky during autumn.
- If you live above the 40th parallel, you'll see the Big Dipper at all times of the year. It will be low in the sky, near the northern horizon, at 10:00 P.M. from September through November. The 40th parallel runs through New Jersey, Pennsylvania, Ohio, Indiana, Illinois, Missouri, the Kansas-Nebraska border, and the route taken by the transcontinental railway through northern Colorado, Utah, Nevada, and California.

Reading Standard 2.5
Understand and explain the use of a simple mechanical device by following technical directions.

VOCABULARY DEVELOPMENT

hemisphere (hem′i·sfir′) *n.:* area that lies within a specific half-section of Earth.

CLOSE READING

Circle the list of things you'll need before you can follow the step-by-step directions.

INFER

Why do you think you need to be in a dark place to see the stars in the sky?

_____

_____

_____

_____

_____

_____

_____

_____

_____

_____

_____

_____

Back Forward Reload Home Search

Location: _____

from eHow: How to Do Just About Everything

How to Locate the Big and Little Dippers

Bill Kramer

The constellations called the Big Dipper and the Little Dipper are in the northern sky, near the pole. You must be located in the northern **hemisphere** to see them both clearly. These constellations are also known as Ursa Major and Ursa Minor, the Great Bear and the Little Bear. Because it has seven bright stars, the Big Dipper is easy to find in the night sky. The Little Dipper is harder to see because it's made up of fainter stars.

10 **The Things You'll Need:**

sky chart	binoculars
telescope flashlight	lawn chair
telescope	blanket

Steps:

1. Look for the Big Dipper from a dark site. You'll be able to find it if you're in the suburbs of a city with no bright lights shining nearby. You'll need to have very dark sky conditions (away from city lights) to see the Little Dipper.

20 2. Look for the shape of a soup ladle. Three of the Big Dipper's stars form the curved handle

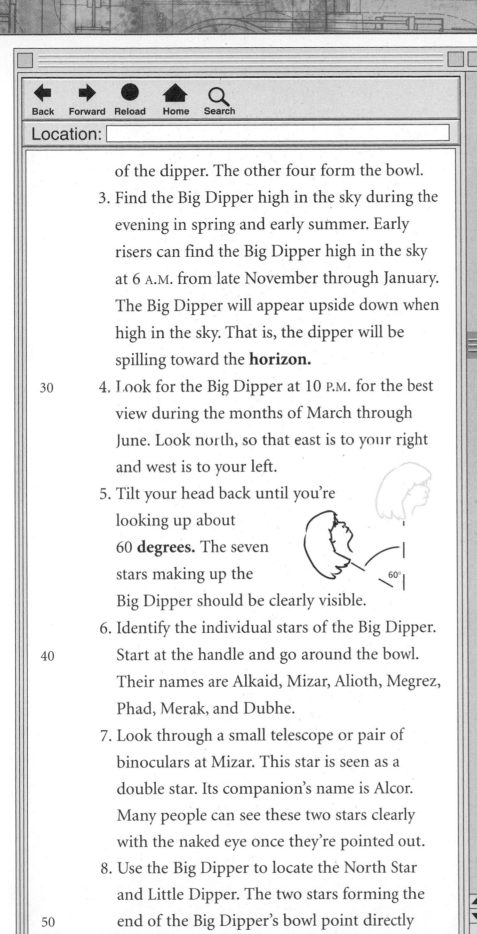

of the dipper. The other four form the bowl.

3. Find the Big Dipper high in the sky during the evening in spring and early summer. Early risers can find the Big Dipper high in the sky at 6 A.M. from late November through January. The Big Dipper will appear upside down when high in the sky. That is, the dipper will be spilling toward the **horizon.**

30   4. Look for the Big Dipper at 10 P.M. for the best view during the months of March through June. Look north, so that east is to your right and west is to your left.

5. Tilt your head back until you're looking up about 60 **degrees.** The seven stars making up the Big Dipper should be clearly visible.

6. Identify the individual stars of the Big Dipper.
40   Start at the handle and go around the bowl. Their names are Alkaid, Mizar, Alioth, Megrez, Phad, Merak, and Dubhe.

7. Look through a small telescope or pair of binoculars at Mizar. This star is seen as a double star. Its companion's name is Alcor. Many people can see these two stars clearly with the naked eye once they're pointed out.

8. Use the Big Dipper to locate the North Star and Little Dipper. The two stars forming the
50   end of the Big Dipper's bowl point directly

60°

VOCABULARY DEVELOPMENT

horizon (hə·rī′zən) *n.:* line where the sky seems to meet the earth.

degree(s) (di·grēz′) *n.:* A degree is one 360th part of the circumference of a circle.

INFER

What do you think the stars are named after (lines 41–42)?

_____

_____

_____

_____

_____

_____

_____

_____

_____

_____

_____

_____

_____

_____

_____

_____

_____

_____

_____

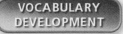

VOCABULARY DEVELOPMENT

essentially (ə·sen'shə·lē) *adv.*: basically.

INFER

Why do you think sailors use Polaris to navigate?

_____

_____

_____

_____

_____

_____

_____

_____

_____

_____

_____

_____

_____

_____

_____

_____

_____

_____

_____

_____

_____

Back   Forward   Reload   Home   Search

Location:

at the North Star. The Little Dipper has **essentially** the same shape as the Big Dipper, but its handle is curved the other way.

9. Identify the North Star, which is also known as Polaris and is the end of the handle of the Little Dipper. When you find the North Star, you'll know what direction true north is from your current location. The North Star is about the same brightness as the seven major stars of the Big Dipper.

60

Tips:

- Use an easy-to-read star map.
- Read with a red-coated flashlight.
- Binoculars and a telescope are optional.
- Get comfortable. Use a lounge chair or put a blanket on the ground. Wear warm clothing and insect repellent when needed.

Paraphrasing Instructions   Paraphrasing the instruction in this article, tell a classmate how to find the Big Dipper. When you are finished, compare your paraphrase with that of a classmate. Take note of similarities and differences in the words you chose.

_____

_____

_____

_____

_____

_____

_____

_____

_____

_____

_____

_____

Personal Word List   Add this selection's vocabulary words to your Personal Word List. Some of them will leap out at you from the pages of science textbooks. Which ones have more general uses?

Personal Reading Log   Respond to this selection in your Personal Reading Log, and give yourself 2 points on the Reading Meter.

Checklist for Standards Mastery   Reading technical instructions is rarely easy. Even professionals often have trouble reading instructions in their special fields. You've got some good practice in this selection, though. Use the Checklist for Standards Mastery to check your improvement.

How to Locate the Big and Little Dippers ▪ *Interactive Reading,* page 290

Go Beyond an Informational Text

Write and Illustrate Instructions   Think of something you know how to build, make, or do. It should be something simple enough to explain on one or two pages but complex enough to require several separate steps. It may be something common, such as how to ride a bicycle, or something unusual, such as how to tie a specific kind of knot.

Write a set of numbered instructions, and illustrate steps that need it. Your illustrations don't have to be great art! They do need to be clear enough to help a reader understand the instructions.

How-to Title: _____

1. _____
   _____

2. _____
   _____

3. _____
   _____

4. _____
   _____

5. _____
   _____

6. _____
   _____

7. _____
   _____

8. _____
   _____

PUBLIC DOCUMENT

State parks are run by individual states but open to all visitors. With millions of visitors per year, how do these parks stay so beautiful and safe? A code of rules and regulations is one solution to the problem. These rules are made and enforced so that all visitors to state parks can enjoy the beauties of nature.

You're about to read a summary of the rules and regulations for California state parks. This information is made available to the public online as well as through the state government's Office of Communications.

Reading Standard 2.2
Locate information by using a variety of consumer, workplace, and public documents.

California State Parks: Rules and Regulations

California State Parks Commission

Rules and regulations protect California State Parks for the enjoyment of future generations as well as for the convenience and safety of the park visitors. To ensure your visit is a pleasant one, please
10 observe the following:

CLOSE READING

Who created this page of rules and regulations? How can you tell?

_____

_____

_____

_____

_____

_____

_____

_____

_____

_____

_____

_____

_____

_____

_____

_____

_____

_____

_____

_____

designated (dez′ig·nāt′əd) v.: specially marked for a purpose.

hazard (haz′ərd) n.: dangerous condition.

facilities (fə·sil′ə·tēz) n.: places equipped for specific uses.

NATURAL SCENERY, PLANTS, AND ANIMAL LIFE are the principal attractions of most state parks. They are integral parts of the ecosystem and natural community. As such they are protected by Federal, State, and Park laws. Disturbance or destruction of these resources is strictly forbidden.

LOADED FIREARMS AND HUNTING are not allowed in units of the State Parks System. Possession of loaded firearms or air rifles is prohibited. Exceptions are for hunting in recreation areas that have been **designated** by the State

20 Park and Recreation Commission.

DEAD AND DOWN WOOD is part of the natural condition. Decayed vegetation forms humus and assists the growth of trees and other plants. For this reason the gathering of down wood is prohibited. Fuel is sold in the parks for your convenience. (When considered a **hazard,** down wood is removed by park personnel.)

FIRES are permitted only in **facilities** provided for this purpose. This is necessary to prevent disas-

30 trous fires. Portable stoves may be used in designated areas. It is the responsibility of every visitor to use extreme caution with any burning materials, including tobacco. All fireworks are prohibited.

ANIMALS, including cats, may not be turned loose in park units. All animals, other than grazing animals, must be under immediate physical control. Dogs must be on a tended leash no more than 6 feet or confined in an

40 enclosed vehicle, tent, or pen. Unless posted to the contrary, dogs, other than those that assist the permanently disabled, are prohibited on trails, beaches, and wherever

posted. Visitors with vicious, dangerous, noisy, or disturbing animals will be **ejected** from park units.

NOISE—ENGINE DRIVEN ELECTRIC GENERATORS which can disturb others, may be operated only between the hours 10:00 A.M. and 8:00 P.M. Loud disturbing noise is prohibited at all times, as is disturbing those asleep between 10:00 P.M. and 6:00 A.M.

50 **ALL VEHICLE TRAVEL** must be confined to designated roads or areas. The speed for all vehicles is 15 miles per hour in camp, picnic, utility, or headquarters areas and areas of general assemblage. Parking is permitted only in designated areas. Blocking parking spaces is prohibited.

CAMPSITE USE must be paid for in advance. To hold a campsite, it must be reserved or **occupied.** To prevent encroachment on others the limits of each campsite may be regulated by the District Superintendent. Checkout time is **12:00 NOON.** In order to provide

60 for the greatest number of visitors possible the **CAMPING LIMIT** in any one campground is 30 days per calendar year.

REFUSE, including garbage, cigarettes, paper boxes, bottles, ashes, and other rubbish, shall be placed only in designated receptacles. Your pleasure and pride in your parks will be enhanced when they are kept clean.

PLEASE clean up after yourself so that others may enjoy the beauty of these parks.

LEAVE ONLY FOOTPRINTS—

70 **TAKE ONLY MEMORIES**

OWN THE TEXT

Locating Information   With a partner, take turns asking each other specific informational questions that can be answered in these state-park rules. Make the questions hard but not impossible or tricky. You get 1 point if you can find the answer in ten seconds or less. Play till you each get 5 points.

_____

_____

_____

_____

_____

KEEPING TRACK

Personal Word List   Add the words you learned to your Personal Word List. Put a star next to words you might use in everyday speech.

Personal Reading Log   Did this selection make you want to spend more time visiting California's state parks? Respond in your Personal Reading Log. You get 2 points on the Reading Meter.

Checklist for Standards Mastery   This selection is intended to help you master Reading Standard 2.2. Check the Checklist for Standards Mastery to see how much you've benefited.

California State Parks: Rules and Regulations *Interactive Reading,* page 295

Go Beyond an Informational Text

Create a Code of Regulations Here's your chance to tell the world how it ought to behave. Make up a code of regulations of your own. Think of a specific topic—for example, regulations on how to behave in your room. Write your code of regulations below.

Code of Regulations for _____

1.
2.
3.
4.
5.

Personal Word List

Keep track of all the new words you have added to your vocabulary by filling out the following chart. Review these words from time to time to make sure they become part of your permanent vocabulary.

WORD

DEFINITION: _____

_____

_____

WORD

DEFINITION: _____

_____

_____

WORD

DEFINITION: _____

_____

_____

WORD

DEFINITION: _____

_____

_____

WORD

DEFINITION: _____

_____

_____

WORD

DEFINITION: _____

_____

_____

WORD

DEFINITION: _____

_____

_____

WORD

DEFINITION: _____

_____

_____

WORD

DEFINITION: _____

_____

_____

WORD

DEFINITION: _____

_____

_____

WORD

DEFINITION: _____

_____

_____

WORD

DEFINITION: _____

_____

_____

WORD

DEFINITION: _____

_____

_____

WORD

DEFINITION: _____

_____

_____

WORD

DEFINITION: _____

_____

_____

WORD

DEFINITION: _____

_____

_____

WORD

DEFINITION: _____

_____

_____

WORD

DEFINITION: _____

_____

_____

WORD

DEFINITION: _____

_____

_____

WORD

DEFINITION: _____

_____

_____

WORD

DEFINITION: _____

_____

_____

WORD

DEFINITION: _____

_____

_____

WORD

DEFINITION: _____

_____

_____

WORD

DEFINITION: _____

_____

_____

WORD

DEFINITION: _____

_____

_____

WORD

DEFINITION: _____

_____

_____

WORD

DEFINITION: _____

_____

_____

WORD

DEFINITION: _____

_____

_____

WORD

DEFINITION: _____

_____

_____

WORD

DEFINITION: _____

_____

_____

WORD

DEFINITION: _____

_____

_____

WORD

DEFINITION: _____

_____

_____

WORD

DEFINITION: _____

_____

_____

WORD

DEFINITION: _____

_____

_____

WORD

DEFINITION: _____

_____

_____

WORD

DEFINITION: _____

_____

_____

WORD

DEFINITION: _____

_____

_____

WORD

DEFINITION: _____

_____

_____

WORD

DEFINITION: _____

_____

_____

WORD

DEFINITION: _____

_____

_____

WORD

DEFINITION: _____

_____

_____

WORD

DEFINITION: _____

_____

_____

WORD

DEFINITION: _____

_____

_____

WORD

DEFINITION: _____

_____

_____

WORD

DEFINITION: _____

_____

_____

WORD

DEFINITION: _____

_____

_____

WORD

DEFINITION: _____
_____
_____

WORD

DEFINITION: _____
_____
_____

WORD

DEFINITION: _____
_____
_____

WORD

DEFINITION: _____
_____
_____

WORD

DEFINITION: _____
_____
_____

WORD

DEFINITION: _____
_____
_____

WORD

DEFINITION: _____
_____
_____

WORD

DEFINITION: _____
_____
_____

WORD

DEFINITION: _____
_____
_____

WORD

DEFINITION: _____
_____
_____

WORD

DEFINITION: _____
_____
_____

WORD

DEFINITION: _____
_____
_____

WORD

DEFINITION: _____

_____

_____

WORD

DEFINITION: _____

_____

_____

WORD

DEFINITION: _____

_____

_____

WORD

DEFINITION: _____

_____

_____

WORD

DEFINITION: _____

_____

_____

WORD

DEFINITION: _____

_____

_____

WORD

DEFINITION: _____

_____

_____

WORD

DEFINITION: _____

_____

_____

WORD

DEFINITION: _____

_____

_____

WORD

DEFINITION: _____

_____

_____

WORD

DEFINITION: _____

_____

_____

WORD

DEFINITION: _____

_____

_____

WORD

DEFINITION: _____

_____

_____

WORD

DEFINITION: _____

_____

_____

WORD

DEFINITION: _____

_____

_____

WORD

DEFINITION: _____

_____

_____

WORD

DEFINITION: _____

_____

_____

WORD

DEFINITION: _____

_____

_____

WORD

DEFINITION: _____

_____

_____

WORD

DEFINITION: _____

_____

_____

WORD

DEFINITION: _____

_____

_____

WORD

DEFINITION: _____

_____

_____

WORD

DEFINITION: _____

_____

_____

WORD

DEFINITION: _____

_____

_____

WORD

DEFINITION: _____

_____

_____

WORD

DEFINITION: _____

_____

_____

WORD

DEFINITION: _____

_____

_____

WORD

DEFINITION: _____

_____

_____

WORD

DEFINITION: _____

_____

_____

WORD

DEFINITION: _____

_____

_____

WORD

DEFINITION: _____

_____

_____

WORD

DEFINITION: _____

_____

_____

WORD

DEFINITION: _____

_____

_____

WORD

DEFINITION: _____

_____

_____

WORD

DEFINITION: _____

_____

_____

WORD

DEFINITION: _____

_____

_____

WORD

DEFINITION: _____
_____
_____

WORD

DEFINITION: _____
_____
_____

WORD

DEFINITION: _____
_____
_____

WORD

DEFINITION: _____
_____
_____

WORD

DEFINITION: _____
_____
_____

WORD

DEFINITION: _____
_____
_____

WORD

DEFINITION: _____
_____
_____

WORD

DEFINITION: _____
_____
_____

WORD

DEFINITION: _____
_____
_____

WORD

DEFINITION: _____
_____
_____

WORD

DEFINITION: _____
_____
_____

WORD

DEFINITION: _____
_____
_____

WORD

DEFINITION: _____

_____

_____

WORD

DEFINITION: _____

_____

_____

WORD

DEFINITION: _____

_____

_____

WORD

DEFINITION: _____

_____

_____

WORD

DEFINITION: _____

_____

_____

WORD

DEFINITION: _____

_____

_____

WORD

DEFINITION: _____

_____

_____

WORD

DEFINITION: _____

_____

_____

WORD

DEFINITION: _____

_____

_____

WORD

DEFINITION: _____

_____

_____

WORD

DEFINITION: _____

_____

_____

WORD

DEFINITION: _____

_____

_____

WORD

DEFINITION: _____

_____

_____

WORD

DEFINITION: _____

_____

_____

WORD

DEFINITION: _____

_____

_____

WORD

DEFINITION: _____

_____

_____

WORD

DEFINITION: _____

_____

_____

WORD

DEFINITION: _____

_____

_____

WORD

DEFINITION: _____

_____

_____

WORD

DEFINITION: _____

_____

_____

WORD

DEFINITION: _____

_____

_____

WORD

DEFINITION: _____

_____

_____

WORD

DEFINITION: _____

_____

_____

WORD

DEFINITION: _____

_____

_____

WORD

DEFINITION: _____

_____

_____

WORD

DEFINITION: _____

_____

_____

WORD

DEFINITION: _____

_____

_____

WORD

DEFINITION: _____

_____

_____

WORD

DEFINITION: _____

_____

_____

WORD

DEFINITION: _____

_____

_____

WORD

DEFINITION: _____

_____

_____

WORD

DEFINITION: _____

_____

_____

WORD

DEFINITION: _____

_____

_____

WORD

DEFINITION: _____

_____

_____

WORD

DEFINITION: _____

_____

_____

WORD

DEFINITION: _____

_____

_____

WORD

DEFINITION: _____
_____
_____

WORD

DEFINITION: _____
_____
_____

WORD

DEFINITION: _____
_____
_____

WORD

DEFINITION: _____
_____
_____

WORD

DEFINITION: _____
_____
_____

WORD

DEFINITION: _____
_____
_____

WORD

DEFINITION: _____
_____
_____

WORD

DEFINITION: _____
_____
_____

WORD

DEFINITION: _____
_____
_____

WORD

DEFINITION: _____
_____
_____

WORD

DEFINITION: _____
_____
_____

WORD

DEFINITION: _____
_____
_____

WORD

DEFINITION: _____

_____

_____

WORD

DEFINITION: _____

_____

_____

WORD

DEFINITION: _____

_____

_____

WORD

DEFINITION: _____

_____

_____

WORD

DEFINITION: _____

_____

_____

WORD

DEFINITION: _____

_____

_____

WORD

DEFINITION: _____

_____

_____

WORD

DEFINITION: _____

_____

_____

WORD

DEFINITION: _____

_____

_____

WORD

DEFINITION: _____

_____

_____

WORD

DEFINITION: _____

_____

_____

WORD

DEFINITION: _____

_____

_____

WORD

DEFINITION: _____

_____

_____

WORD

DEFINITION: _____

_____

_____

WORD

DEFINITION: _____

_____

_____

WORD

DEFINITION: _____

_____

_____

WORD

DEFINITION: _____

_____

_____

WORD

DEFINITION: _____

_____

_____

WORD

DEFINITION: _____

_____

_____

WORD

DEFINITION: _____

_____

_____

WORD

DEFINITION: _____

_____

_____

WORD

DEFINITION: _____

_____

_____

WORD

DEFINITION: _____

_____

_____

WORD

DEFINITION: _____

_____

_____

Personal Reading Log

Each time you complete a selection in *Interactive Reading,*
you will have moved closer to meeting California's goal for students
completing middle school—the goal of having the ability to read
one million words on your own.

Reading Meter

If you read all the interactive selections in this book, you will have
read close to 45,000 words, and you will have achieved 100 points.
Fill in the Reading Meter to show how far you've come.

Number of Words in Selection	Points
About 500 words	1 point
About 1,000 words	2 points
About 1,500 words	3 points
About 2,000 words	4 points
About 2,500 words	5 points
Over 5,000 words	10 points
Bonus for reading every selection	10 points

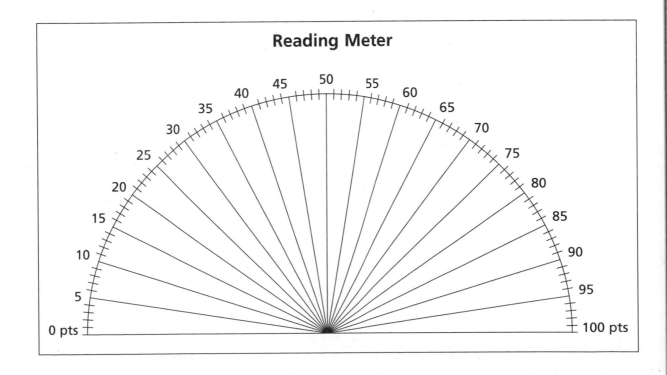

Reading Meter

DATE _____ Selection/Author: _____

Summary: _____

_____

_____

_____

_____

Comments and Evaluation: _____

_____

_____

_____

	READING METER

DATE _____ Selection/Author: _____

Summary: _____

_____

_____

_____

_____

Comments and Evaluation: _____

_____

_____

_____

	READING METER

DATE _____ Selection/Author: _____

Summary: _____

_____

_____

_____

_____

_____

Comments and Evaluation: _____

_____

_____

_____

_____| READING METER |

_____

DATE _____ Selection/Author: _____

Summary: _____

_____

_____

_____

_____

_____

Comments and Evaluation: _____

_____

_____

_____

_____| READING METER |

_____

DATE _____ Selection/Author: _____

Summary: _____

_____

_____

_____

_____

_____

Comments and Evaluation: _____

_____

_____

_____

_____

	READING METER

DATE _____ Selection/Author: _____

Summary: _____

_____

_____

_____

_____

_____

Comments and Evaluation: _____

_____

_____

_____

_____

	READING METER

DATE _____ Selection/Author: _____

Summary: _____
_____
_____
_____
_____
_____

Comments and Evaluation: _____
_____
_____
_____

	READING METER

DATE _____ Selection/Author: _____

Summary: _____
_____
_____
_____
_____
_____

Comments and Evaluation: _____
_____
_____
_____

	READING METER

DATE _____ Selection/Author: _____

Summary: _____

_____

_____

_____

_____

_____

Comments and Evaluation: _____

_____

_____

_____

_____

READING METER

DATE _____ Selection/Author: _____

Summary: _____

_____

_____

_____

_____

_____

Comments and Evaluation: _____

_____

_____

_____

_____

READING METER

DATE _____   Selection/Author: _____

Summary: _____

_____

_____

_____

_____

Comments and Evaluation: _____

_____

_____

_____

	READING METER

DATE _____   Selection/Author: _____

Summary: _____

_____

_____

_____

_____

Comments and Evaluation: _____

_____

_____

_____

	READING METER

DATE _____ Selection/Author: _____

Summary: _____

_____

_____

_____

_____

_____

Comments and Evaluation: _____

_____

_____

_____

_____

| READING |
| METER |

DATE _____ Selection/Author: _____

Summary: _____

_____

_____

_____

_____

_____

Comments and Evaluation: _____

_____

_____

_____

_____

| READING |
| METER |

DATE _____ Selection/Author: _____

Summary: _____

_____

_____

_____

_____

Comments and Evaluation: _____

_____

_____

_____

_____

	READING METER

DATE _____ Selection/Author: _____

Summary: _____

_____

_____

_____

_____

Comments and Evaluation: _____

_____

_____

_____

_____

	READING METER

DATE _____   Selection/Author: _____

Summary: _____

_____

_____

_____

_____

_____

Comments and Evaluation: _____

_____

_____

_____

_____

	READING METER

DATE _____   Selection/Author: _____

Summary: _____

_____

_____

_____

_____

_____

Comments and Evaluation: _____

_____

_____

_____

_____

	READING METER

DATE _____ Selection/Author: _____

Summary: _____

_____

_____

_____

_____

_____

Comments and Evaluation: _____

_____

_____

_____

_____

	READING
	METER

DATE _____ Selection/Author: _____

Summary: _____

_____

_____

_____

_____

_____

Comments and Evaluation: _____

_____

_____

_____

_____

	READING
	METER

DATE _____ Selection/Author: _____

Summary: _____

_____

_____

_____

_____

_____

Comments and Evaluation: _____

_____

_____

_____

_____

	READING METER

DATE _____ Selection/Author: _____

Summary: _____

_____

_____

_____

_____

_____

Comments and Evaluation: _____

_____

_____

_____

_____

	READING METER

DATE _____ Selection/Author: _____

Summary: _____

_____

_____

_____

_____

_____

Comments and Evaluation: _____

_____

_____

_____

_____

| READING |
| METER |

DATE _____ Selection/Author: _____

Summary: _____

_____

_____

_____

_____

_____

Comments and Evaluation: _____

_____

_____

_____

_____

| READING |
| METER |

Checklist for Standards Mastery

Each time you read, you learn something new. Track your growth as a reader and your progress toward success by checking off skills you have acquired. You may want to use this checklist before you read a selection, to set a purpose for reading.

✓	California Reading Standard (Review)	Selection/Author
☐	**2.2 (Grade 6)** Analyze text that uses the compare-and-contrast organizational pattern.	
☐	**2.4 (Grade 6)** Clarify an understanding of texts by creating outlines, logical notes, summaries, or reports.	

	California Grade 7 Reading Standard	Selection/Author
☐	**1.0 Word Analysis, Fluency, and Systematic Vocabulary Development:** Students use their knowledge of word origins and word relationships, as well as historical and literary context clues, to determine the meaning of specialized vocabulary and to understand the precise meaning of grade-level-appropriate words.	
☐	**1.1** Identify idioms, analogies, metaphors, and similes in prose and poetry.	
☐	**1.2** Use knowledge of Greek, Latin, and Anglo-Saxon roots and affixes to understand content-area vocabulary.	
☐	**1.3** Clarify word meanings through the use of definition, example, restatement, or contrast.	

✓	California Grade 7 Reading Standard	Selection/Author
☐	**2.0 Reading Comprehension:** Students read and understand grade-level-appropriate material. They describe and connect the essential ideas, arguments, and perspectives of the text by using their knowledge of text structure, organization, and purpose.	
☐	**2.1** Understand and analyze the differences in structure and purpose between various categories of informational materials (for example, textbooks, newspapers, instructional manuals, signs).	
☐	**2.2** Locate information by using a variety of consumer, workplace, and public documents.	
☐	**2.3** Analyze text that uses the cause-and-effect organizational pattern.	
☐	**2.4** Identify and trace the development of an author's argument, point of view, or perspective in text.	
☐	**2.5** Understand and explain the use of a simple mechanical device by following technical directions.	
☐	**2.6** Assess the adequacy, accuracy, and appropriateness of the author's evidence to support claims and assertions, noting instances of bias and stereotyping.	
☐	**3.0 Literary Response and Analysis:** Students read and respond to historically or culturally significant works of literature that reflect and enhance their studies of history and social science. They clarify the ideas and connect them to other literary works.	

✓	California Grade 7 Reading Standard	Selection/Author
☐	**3.1** Articulate the expressed purposes and characteristics of different forms of prose (for example, short story, novel, novella, essay).	
☐	**3.2** Identify events that advance the plot, and determine how each event explains past or present action(s) or foreshadows future action(s).	
☐	**3.3** Analyze characterization as delineated through a character's thoughts, words, speech patterns, and actions; the narrator's description; and the thoughts, words, and actions of other characters.	
☐	**3.4** Identify and analyze recurring themes across works (for example, the value of bravery, loyalty, and friendship; the effects of loneliness).	
☐	**3.5** Contrast points of view (for example, first and third person, limited and omniscient, subjective and objective) in narrative text, and explain how they affect the overall theme of the work.	
☐	**3.6** Analyze a range of responses to a literary work, and determine the extent to which the literary elements in the work shaped those responses.	

Index of Authors and Titles

Vocabulary Development

Pronunciation guides, in parentheses, are provided for the vocabulary words in this book. The following key will help you use those pronunciation guides.

As a practice in using a pronunciation guide, sound out the words used as examples in the list that follows. See if you can hear the way the same vowel might be sounded in different words. For example, say "at" and "ate" aloud. Can you hear the difference in the way "a" sounds?

The symbol ə is called a **schwa.** A schwa is used by many dictionaries to indicate a sort of weak sound like the "a" in "ago." Some people say the schwa sounds like "eh." A vowel sounded like a schwa is never accented.

The vocabulary words in this book are also provided with a part of speech. The parts of speech are *n.* (noun), *v.* (verb), *pro.* (pronoun), *adj.* (adjective), *adv.* (adverb), *prep.* (preposition), *conj.* (conjunction), and *interj.* (interjection). To learn about the parts of speech, consult the *Holt Handbook.*

To learn more about the vocabulary words, consult your dictionary. You will find that many of the words defined here have several other meanings.

---

at, āte, cär; ten, ēve; is, īce; gō, hôrn, look, to͞ol; oil, out; up, fur; ə *for unstressed vowels, as* a *in ago,* u *in* focus; ' *as in* Latin (lat'ʼn); chin; she; zh *as in* azure (azh'ər); thin, *the*; ŋ *as in* ring (riŋ)

Picture Credits